CONSUMER-CENTRIC
CATEGORY
MANAGEMENT

CONSUMER-CENTRIC CATEGORY MANAGEMENT

How to Increase Profits by Managing Categories Based on Consumer Needs

ACNielsen

with

John Karolefski and Al Heller

WILEY

JOHN WILEY & SONS, INC.

Published by John Wiley & Sons, Inc., Hoboken, New Jersey.
Published simultaneously in Canada.

For general information on our other products and services or for technical support, please contact our Customer Care Department within the United States at (800) 762-2974, outside the United States at (317) 572-3993 or fax (317) 572-4002.

Wiley also publishes its books in a variety of electronic formats. Some content that appears in print may not be available in electronic books. For more information about Wiley products, visit our web site at www.wiley.com.

Library of Congress Cataloging-in-Publication Data:

ACNielsen Company.
   Consumer-centric category management : how to increase profits by managing categories based on consumer needs / ACNielsen, with John Karolefski and Al Heller.
      p. cm.
  ISBN-13: 978-0-471-70359-4 (cloth)
  ISBN-10: 0-471-70359-1 (cloth)
  1. Retail trade—Management.   2. Consumers' preferences.   I. Karolefski, John. II. Heller, Al. III.
  HF5429.K296 2005
  658.7′8—dc22

                                                200521556

Printed in the United States of America.
10 9 8 7 6 5 4 3 2 1

FOREWORD

Reports of category management's death have been greatly exaggerated. Consultants offering their new twists and titles are all too happy to declare the practice dead—so much the better to promote their own offerings. But the reality is that category management is very much alive and, well, continuing to evolve.

In some parts of the world, especially in developing markets, category management today remains a stretch goal—a new idea full of untapped potential. In other areas, the eight-step process detailed by The Partnering Group in the early 1990s forms the foundation of many companies' approach to category management. In still others, particularly in developed countries like the United States, the United Kingdom, and others, refinements are being made—most of them designed to place consumer understanding front and center.

New ideas are emerging—from "trip management" to "aisle management" to "customer management." Some will blossom into full-fledged business processes; some will be plugged into existing processes as improvements on specific steps; others will be cast aside as ineffective or too expensive.

Whether a new descriptor emerges to replace "category management" is yet to be seen. Even if that does happen, what won't change is the overall objective—to help retailers and their manufacturer partners succeed by offering the right selection of products that are marketed and merchandised based on a complete understanding of the consumers they are committed to serving.

At its core, category management is a business fundamental. The complexity of its execution varies from company to company and market to market largely based on the amount and quality of information available to decision makers. Some have highly sophisticated systems at their fingertips that quickly integrate extremely granular and disparate data streams and then create electronic "smart alerts" that help them monitor key performance indicators. Others, especially in developing markets where modern retail stores still drive less than half of all food sales, sometimes have a difficult time just measuring their market share.

This book is for those with a vested interest in category management all along the sophistication spectrum. It can serve such a broad audience because category management is about bringing a structured process to how executives *think* and *make decisions* about their businesses, no matter what information and information technology they have access to.

With this book, we are exploring both the state of and the state-of-the-art in category management. For those who are new to the concept, the first part of the book provides a solid understanding of the core process. It's essential to know where we've come from if we are to make changes for the better. For those who are further along, the case studies and essays about the future of category management should shed new light on how to get more from the process.

Our intention with this book is to facilitate a conversation about category management. Where is the practice today, where is it going, and how can we continue to make improvements? What are the essential steps, how can each step be executed most effectively, and how can consumer understanding increasingly become the centerpiece of the process?

By definition, a book must have a beginning and an end. However, we ask you to view this book differently—to see it as the continuation of an ongoing conversation about a vitally important business practice that will continue to evolve.

Steven M. Schmidt
President and Chief Executive Officer, ACNielsen

CONTENTS

PART III
CATEGORY MANAGEMENT SUCCESS STORIES

PART IV
THE WAY FORWARD

Introduction—Why Category Management Is More Important Than Ever

Bell's Family Markets was facing tough times. The local trading area was very competitive with too many food stores serving a shifting shopper base that was increasingly diverse and demanding. Wal-Mart was planning a supercenter near Bell's flagship store, while shoppers were checking out some new formats that opened in the past year: a limited assortment store, a warehouse club, two extreme value stores, and a Hispanic-oriented grocer. As if that weren't enough, a trendy Italian restaurant chain began promoting gourmet take-out meals at reasonable prices for customers coming home from work and looking for alternatives to cooking dinner from scratch.

As a conventional grocer, family-operated for three generations, Bell's suddenly seemed out of step with the new marketplace. Sales were declining as the new competitors enticed some traditional customers for their shopping needs.

Sound familiar? Such scenarios have been taking place in the United States—and in many markets around the world—for several years. The outcomes are different because retailers deal with adversity in different ways. Some do nothing.

Fortunately, Bell's was proactive. Management first reviewed its go-to-market strategy. Was the corporate strategy still viable? Who was the target customer group? What shopping occasions did Bell's want to own? To support the overall strategy, the retailer worked with key trading partners to implement a consumer-centric category management program that gradually rebuilt the business.

It's a Mad, Mad, Mad, Mad Marketplace!

Although Bell's Family Markets is a fictitious corporation, the pressures described are all too real for retailers today. Many cities are overstored with big-box grocers that look alike and carry the same products. That has opened the door for niche retail formats to chip away at sales. Consumers want more service and better products at lower prices—and not just at the grocery store, but at the bookstore, the electronics store, and everywhere else people shop.

And then there is Wal-Mart. The biggest retailer in the world has rattled the U.S. marketplace ever since it expanded beyond discount stores into new formats that sell grocery products. The Bentonville, Arkansas-based retailer has a toehold outside the United States and the eyes of the retail world wait to see how international expansion eventually plays out.

The success of Wal-Mart is largely due to low prices. Other factors that contribute include assortments, customer service, and efficient distribution. But low prices are the DNA of the retail brand, as well as the primary tactic to attract shoppers, unnerve competitors, and galvanize a marketplace.

Wal-Mart's most powerful format is the cavernous supercenter. These stores, which combine a supermarket with a traditional Wal-Mart discount store, measure some 187,000 square feet. Their stunning success has put smaller retailers out of business and prompted larger ones into decreasing prices, increasing promotions, improving customer service, and all sorts of retail gyrations to hold back the inevitable. Wal-Mart has become the largest grocer in the United States.

The arrival and rise of Wal-Mart into the grocery marketplace caught many traditional supermarket retailers off guard. Many didn't figure that a discount store operator could master grocery retailing so effortlessly. But those retailers that have done well with a supercenter in their backyard are the ones with imagination, merchandising savvy, and a solid strategy in place. They maintained or reestablished a connection with shoppers, and that has made all the difference.

ACNielsen recently conducted a study on how shopping behavior varies in states where Wal-Mart has a high share of business compared to states where they are just starting to develop their business. In the South, Wal-Mart has a 97 percent penetration of the shopping base with an average of 44 trips per household per year and with spending levels of about $55 per trip. On the West Coast and in the Northeast, Wal-Mart has a penetration level of about 65 percent of households, and that's mostly from discount stores, with an average frequency of about 18 trips per year. Wal-Mart will eventually leverage its supercenters to try and drive more frequent shopping trips in these areas.

Meanwhile, consumers today are no longer the classic family with mother, father, and two children. The populace is more splintered than ever into narrow groups: singles, seniors, various ethic segments, and the "sandwich" generation where the middle-aged consumer looks after teenaged children and aging parents at the same time.

These consumers have different wants and needs. At the same time, they are demanding and mobile enough to switch stores easily if dissatisfied with their shopping experience. Serving them well enough to prevent shopper erosion is challenging for every retailer.

At the same time that consumers have been changing, two other trends have developed that are related to the new demographics. One is the rise of competitive distribution channels, and the other is *channel blurring*. This means that many stores in different channels are blurred in the mind of consumers because they can buy the same products seemingly everywhere. That's especially the case with food.

Over the past decade, the growth of conventional supermarkets has trailed the growth of formats and channels that offer value, such as supercenters, warehouse clubs, limited assortment stores, and extreme value stores. These retailers are adding more stores and increasing the frequency of shopping visits—all at the expense of traditional retailers. In addition to Wal-Mart supercenters, some of these banners include Aldi and Save-a-Lot (limited assortment); Costco and BJ's (warehouse club); and Dollar General, Family Dollar, and Dollar Tree (dollar). What all of these formats and retailers have in common are low prices and the perception of value by consumers.

Many also offer one thing that Wal-Mart doesn't: convenience. That's because getting in and out of an extreme value or limited assortment store is easier than doing so in a supercenter because it is so big or a warehouse club because they don't have as convenient locations as supermarkets. These formats tend to draw the same type of shopper: a low- to middle-income consumer. But they also draw the more affluent. In other words, poor people need low prices, rich people love low prices.

The increasing popularity and store count of these formats has led to the phenomenon of channel blurring: Because new brands of food and beverage are promoted so heavily today, some consumers are tempted to buy products no matter where they are if they see something that meets their needs.

Certainly, drugstores are selling more and more food. Office supply stores sell candy, gum, mints, and snacks. Sports drinks are available in sporting good outlets.

Given the incredible number of new product introductions each year, it's not surprising that there are so many new distribution points nowadays. According to Datamonitor's Productscan Online database of new products, marketers launched some 33,185 new food, beverage, health and beauty, household, and pet products in the United States and Canada in 2004. That total was 1.5 percent less than the record of 33,678 new products in 2003.

New trends in food and health fueled many of these new products. For example, the popularity of "low-carb" diets led to 3,375 new low- and no-carbohydrate product launches in the United States in 2004.

These new products are part of the quest for growth on the part of retailers and manufacturers. The overall population in the United States is growing at just 1 or 2 percent per year. So marketers are focusing on consumers such as seniors, ethnic groups, and other consumer segments of the population because they are going to grow significantly.

How does that translate into new product offerings? The older population is looking for healthier food, and manufacturers are looking to make their products more nutritious. There are already "functional foods" such as orange juice with calcium and vitamin-fortified pasta. Expect manufacturers to develop more. In addition, traditional food makers will continue to launch lines of food products from a multitude of countries as the globe shrinks and people of all backgrounds become exposed to new cuisines.

Against this backdrop of a mad, mad, mad, mad marketplace, retailers and manufacturers of fast-moving consumer goods have been consolidating. The big are getting bigger, while the small are either merging, being acquired, or going out of business.

Marketing Basics and Category Management

The way out of the madness starts with a solid strategic foundation built on the basics of marketing. Who are the customers? What do they want? Even in this era of new competitors, channel blurring, and product proliferation, business success—and indeed survival—is still all about having the right product at the right price with the right promotional support and in the right place.

Category management emerged in the early 1990s as a method of turning marketing basics into an organized process. Its eight-step process is the foundation of every category management program today and is widely used outside the United States in its original form. Many U.S. companies have streamlined and customized the eight-step process to better suit their needs, objectives, and circumstances. But the traditional process remains as a starting point and a framework for deploying a retail strategy.

Category management builds on the marketing basics to help retailers and manufacturers reach consumers. Clearly, understanding how to manage categories for these groups is critical. Trading partners need to leverage the power of categories to drive higher shopper penetration, increase shopping frequency, and encourage larger basket size. Shoppers go to the store to buy products. Retailers must figure out what categories will drive desirable behavior in the store.

For example, if there is a category with high penetration and high frequency, retailers must focus on having those products in the right location because consumers want them. Retailers have to be concerned about pricing and promotion. The more often a category is purchased, the more familiar consumers are with price, and the more they expect to get some promotion to drive their buying. So, how a category is purchased by consumers can be leveraged by retailers in terms of how they go to market in their stores. Manufacturers can help them in that regard.

Category management is all about finding out what shoppers want and providing it better than the competition can. In that way, the process solves the key problem of shopper erosion. If retailers select the right products for target customers and then price and merchandise them appropriately, the result should be a satisfied consumer who remains loyal to a store.

Shopper loyalty is critical today because of consumer mobility. People are willing to shop at different stores to fill shopping needs. In addition, they are willing to drive out of their way to shop in a format that caters to their special interests.

This trend has led to the notion of *trip management* as the next level of category management. In other words, the process has to be more than managing categories. It has to be also managing the types of trips that consumers make to the stores and how well retailers capture various trips compared to the competition. These trips include the standard weekly shopping trip, fill in, stock up, special occasion, and many others.

At a glance, it may seem that category management is addressing yesterday's problems that are still with us: intense competition, demanding shoppers, and product proliferation. While that's true in general, there are specific differences. Today's retail competition is coming from new channels of distribution. Demanding shoppers are now divided into narrow segments, and product proliferation is indeed at an all-time high. After all, how many brands of olive oil does a grocery store need to stock? Isn't there a lesson in the fact that limited assortment stores and warehouse clubs are very successful with a fraction of the number of SKUs that a typical supermarket carries?

The bottom line: Category management is needed more today than ever before.

What Is the Purpose of This Book?

In 1992, ACNielsen published a book on category management. It outlined a process that was relatively new to retailers and manufacturers. The book sought to position organizations to win in the marketplace.

Many changes have taken place since then. Many organizations—and certainly the marketplace—are not the same. The traditional process of category management focused on categories managed as business units. While that is still true today, category management now elevates the importance of the consumer. For leading practitioners, the process has evolved into *consumer-centric* category management. The new focus: using categories to target the "right" consumer segments to ensure the long-term health of the shopper base, while supporting the retail position and strategy. Consumer understanding—demographics, attitudes, interests, shopping occasions, and much more—is at the center of it all.

The industry needs an update and that is the main purpose of this book. Its aim is also to educate. Readers will learn how to reach more customers more profitably. What could be more important today?

Part I is a brief overview. Part II looks closely at each of the original eight steps of category management. Veterans of the process and its current practitioners will benefit from this detailed refresher course. Newcomers will learn about the roots of category management and connect the dots to the customized processes of today.

In Part III, a portfolio of case studies provides real examples of category management in action. Readers will see how trading partners have creatively applied the process to suit their needs and solve their problems. These best practices are shining examples of the power of the process.

The book ends with a look back and a look ahead. First, there is a summary of the lessons learned between the two covers, including conclusions reached about the state of the art of category management. Finally, a group of experts peers into the future to predict how the process will evolve.

Who Should Read This Book?

Every retail executive in every trade channel, plus their trading partners and representatives, should read this book closely. It makes no difference if the organization is large or small. The principles apply to everyone who works with the process.

While category management began in the United States for supermarket retailing, the process has spread beyond grocery to other channels of distribution. In addition, it has spread to other retail industries such as electronics, books, home centers, and many others.

Executives in those sectors will learn from the principles outlined in this book.

Others will benefit as well—vendors, consultants, academics, students, and more.

The business of fast-moving consumer goods has morphed into a restless, cluttered industry full of demands and compressed deadlines. To succeed today, executives in every corner of the world seek a clear path forward. Consumer-centric category management will provide the map. The chapters that follow are the directions.

IN THE BEGINNING—THE PURPOSE OF CATEGORY MANAGEMENT

Category management began as a process that enabled retailers to manage product categories as individual business units. The original version had eight steps, beginning with category definition and ending with a review. Along the way, a category plan was created and deployed.

The process has evolved over the years into various customized versions with fewer steps. However, the traditional process remains the starting point for many companies and its original intent and spirit remain.

Today, category management is more than a way to manage a category as a business. It is essential to operating a successful retail operation. Moreover, the process can give retailers a powerful competitive advantage if executed properly. The winners in the marketplace will be those companies that satisfy consumer needs by knowing how to blend data, insights, and merchandising savvy.

CHAPTER

1

The Evolution of Category Management and the New State of the Art

In the early 1990s, grocery retailers in the United States were ready for a better way to run their business. Margins of about 1 percent at that time were unacceptable. New products were proliferating, while consumers were becoming more diverse and demanding. Other classes of trade such as warehouse clubs were emerging. Wal-Mart was getting ready to roll out its supercenter format that combined the retailer's traditional general merchandise store with a full-line grocery store under one roof.

Clearly, a dramatic change was needed. Retailers sought a way to improve margins and compete more effectively. They wanted to reconnect with consumers and satisfy their needs, or face the prospect of an eroding shopper base. Given the endless variety of new products pouring into the marketplace, retailers wanted to ensure that their shelves were stocked with products that consumers wanted to buy. Mainly, they wanted to stay in business.

Birth of the Eight-Step Process

Many progressive retailers and manufacturers realized that there was gold in the reams of data available from retail point-of-sale (POS) systems. Was it possible to figure out which products to stock in a certain store? Could analysis of the data tell retailers how to customize the shelf sets in all the stores of a chain according to what shoppers were buying and wanted to buy? Could they attract and retain specific niches of high-value shoppers?

The answer was yes. The way to do it was a process called category management that was developed in the early 1990s by The Partnering Group (TPG), a consulting firm. A few of the larger retailers began testing the process. Soon the manufacturers jumped on board with advice and support. They then started to help other retailers adopt the principles as well. In no time, category management was promoted enthusiastically and became a must-have process for retailers and manufacturers.

TPG's process, which is now considered the traditional form of category management, consists of eight steps:

1. Category definition
2. Category role
3. Category assessment
4. Category scorecard
5. Category strategies
6. Category tactics

7. Plan implementation
8. Category review

Early Practitioners

The retailers that pioneered category management are among the largest chains in the United States. Safeway was one of the original practitioners. Others included Kroger, Albertson's, and Publix. SUPERVALU, the first wholesaler to practice category management, brought the process to small independent retailers.

On the manufacturer side, Phillip Morris and the Coca-Cola Company were early supporters of category management. The latter developed a training program about the process that is still distributed to retailers. It helps them understand what category management is all about and what Coca-Cola's role in the process is.

Some of the early practitioners saw nearly immediate benefits through reduced inventories and increased sales. For others, it took more time. But word soon spread about the potential of this new process.

Evolution of Category Management

The original version of category management started a revolution in the way retailers operated their businesses. More and more retailers built their businesses around its principles through the 1990s.

Eventually, however, the process proved to be too complicated for many retailers to adhere to. There were too many details and variables. It was too cumbersome and unwieldy. Too much coordination was needed from too many departments such as logistics and finance.

Problems even developed on the manufacturer's side when salespeople were asked to learn the intricacies of category management. Their primary job was developing relationships, moving products, and building the top line. They weren't analysts. As a result, many manufacturers created category management departments staffed with analysts to support the salespeople. But even then, training somebody to be capable with the entire category management process remained a daunting task.

Meanwhile, some larger manufacturers came up with their own way to simplify matters.

They restricted their proprietary category management to the larger retailers; that is, they invested most of their time and effort on full-time account teams for their largest customers. Smaller chains received less interest and support.

Role of Technology

The development of technology and its steady growth spurred the use of the process. But the journey from the beginning to today was full of obstacles.

In the early days, the software applications for category management required too much number crunching. Instead of talking to customers, salespeople were sitting behind a personal computer pulling data, putting it on Excel sheets, and then creating PowerPoint slides for a presentation. The process was tedious and time consuming.

The problem of data overload and the time spent crunching numbers led to a major change in category management. Companies were forced to streamline their approach to data analysis and develop appropriate applications for the job. Proprietary systems emerged that simplified and quickened the process for many practitioners. Training focused on working with user-friendly template-based customized software as opposed to a process of pulling data and learning to manipulate it.

Category Management Today

Many retailers and manufacturers refined the process of category management over the years. They still began with the traditional eight steps, but developed processes with fewer steps while keeping to the objectives of the original version. The resulting processes are shorter, tighter, and easier to absorb and act on. Some processes have five steps, others have six. The "standard" eight-step process has become less of a standard and more of a starting point.

In addition, in some organizations the sequence of steps has been rearranged compared to the original eight. For example, financial targets were originally done after the assessment step. Now some companies are starting off with their financial targets, saying, "Here's what we want to achieve. Let's do an assessment of where we are versus those targets. Let's look at the gaps and then figure out what are the strategies and tactics that we are going to use to meet those targets."

Many executives start off with the retailer's goal and financial objectives. "What are we trying to achieve? What margin do we want to hit? What's our growth rate? What are our shopper goals? How many more shoppers do we want to bring into our stores?" They believe that such variations make a lot more sense than starting off by defining the category and its role. Trading partners already know that information and skip over these preliminary steps.

Others have dropped the scorecard down in the sequence, arguing that financial targets cannot be set accurately until the other steps are completed.

Today, major manufacturers have a whole suite of applications that any executive can use effectively. Armed with sophisticated tools, salespeople find the process user friendly and easy to implement.

Consumer-Centric Process

In the early 1990s, everyone involved in category management focused on the data and what the numbers revealed about product movement and the category. Surprisingly, they forgot that the consumer drives what happens in the category. While always part of the process on paper, the consumer got lost amid the accumulation of data.

The biggest change in category management over the years has been more of a focus on the consumer. By the late 1990s, manufacturers were giving retailers data that was more consumer oriented. For example, there was consumer data collected from a panel of households. Analysts could work with data on an account-by-account basis, which was not possible in the early days. Other new sources were demographic/psychographic data.

A new chapter in category management was unfolding. It included components designed to make the process less product-centric and more consumer-centric:

- Segmenting and targeting consumers to get the right products in front of the right shoppers in the right stores
- Clustering stores based on the sales potential of brands or categories
- Demand gapping, or determining the difference between existing sales and potential sales in a category
- Developing a marketing plan for each significant customer group

Retailers also jumped on board with the focus on consumers and started looking to incorporate shopper data collected by a store's loyalty card program. While its use is still relatively new, this creates another whole new dimension in terms for category management.

These new sources of information contribute to embedding the consumer as the centerpiece of category management. Today, executives understand that consumer behavior changes the categories. The new mind-set: If we're not getting a fair share of the category, chances are we're not doing a good job of understanding consumers and satisfying their needs.

Beyond Supermarkets

Category management began as a process for supermarket retailers. Before long, it was clear that its benefits were applicable to other classes of trade. Wal-Mart was using the process before expanding from general merchandise into grocery via its supercenters. Drugstore chains adopted the practice, as well. Even Peapod, the online grocer, uses category management.

Today, the practice has expanded well beyond consumer packaged goods. Retailers as diverse as Home Depot (home improvement) and Borders (books) employ category management.

Role of the Retailer

If the consumer is at the center of category management today, the retailer is the linchpin. The retailer sets the overall tone in terms of the objectives, strategy, tactics, and financial goals. What is the retailer trying to accomplish in the marketplace? Does the retailer want to be perceived as a low-price leader, as an upscale purveyor of goods and services, or as something in between? The decision has implications for assortments, category role, strategy, and tactics.

The retailer's role has a number of key components that we discuss in the next sections.

Sets Strategy

The retailer must communicate corporate goals and category strategy to the vendor partners. Without such communication, trading partners may go in different directions rather than effectively working together. A mutual understanding lays a solid foundation for category management.

Determines Process

What version of category management should be followed? How many steps to the process? Retailers proficient in category management typically take the lead and inform suppliers. However, some retailers defer to their trading partners and their expertise.

Gathers Data

The retailer gathers relevant data for category management applications. This includes POS data, financial data, and perhaps shopper data gathered from their own loyalty card programs and household panels run by marketing information companies like ACNielsen. From manufacturers, the retailer obtains additional information. In some cases, the manufacturer plays the lead role in gathering data. Mining this data yields significant insights about consumers and their buying preferences.

One of the most underrated measures is called *Buyer Conversion*. Using consumer panel data at the account level, Buyer Conversion says, "Okay, Mr. Retailer, you've got 100 shoppers coming into your store every day. Of those 100 shoppers, we know that 80 of them buy soft drinks. And of the 80 who buy soft drinks, 40 buy soft drinks in your store. So that means the other 40 are buying soft drinks somewhere else. But they're still shopping in your store."

What a powerful consumer insight! The retailer has category shoppers in the store, but they're not buying soft drinks there for some reason. They're buying elsewhere. So the strategy is figuring out how to get those 40 category shoppers to buy the category in the store. This is a targeted strategy because the shoppers are already in the store. The retailer must convince them that buying soft drinks there is a better value for them versus cherry picking elsewhere.

Ensures Retail Compliance

Who is responsible for the execution of the plan in the store? The answer varies according to the retailer. Among those getting involved to ensure retail compliance are a manufacturer's direct salesforce, sales agencies representing the manufacturer, merchandising service organizations (MSOs) hired by either the manufacturer or the retailer, and even the store's clerks.

Regardless of who is responsible, here's the bottom line: Category shelf sets are often not maintained in the store, and substandard retail compliance undermines the best-laid category plans across the industry. This problem concerns trading partners, and finding a solution remains a priority.

Ultimate Decision Maker

For category management to be effective, the retailer must make a commitment. Managing categories as independent business units is only part of the process. What does the data reveal? Does it match up with the retailer's goal in the marketplace? If not, what happens?

Retailers determine the destination categories, if any, to promote; that is, those categories that will draw shoppers specifically to the store. Manufacturers can suggest which categories should be destination categories, depending on the number and characteristics of the shoppers in the trading area. But the final decision is the retailer's.

Actually, the retailer ultimately makes all the decisions—or at least should take responsibility for decisions made jointly with a trading partner.

Role of the Manufacturer

Category management gives the retailer a creative and comprehensive way to run a business. The manufacturer can be a valuable business partner by providing support.

How much? That depends on the retailer and the level of expertise in category management.

Retailers with a solid category management process and clear vision for deployment are probably the top volume customers for most manufacturers. They will lead the category reviews and set strategies while manufacturers play a subordinate role, even though they are represented by a full category management account team. For example, grocery chains such as Kroger and Safeway have their own structured category management process. Manufacturers contribute, but they are role players.

Other retailers have a less defined process. They look to the manufacturer, their wholesaler, or a sales agency to take the lead by making recommendations, providing consumer insights, and even actual templates.

For example, among the questions these retailers may have:

- How many people should be covering categories?
- How many categories should there be?
- Are the product mix and the actual category set adequate?
- Are there enough facings to avoid stock outs?
- Should the pack size be increased?

If retailers are not well versed in category management, there is temptation for manufacturers to push their own agenda for the category they're in. A flurry of data will present a convincing case.

What is a 20-store operator to say when dealing with a representative of a strong national brand? Strong-arm tactics should be avoided. Such actions give category management a bad name. Done correctly, the process is about the category, with individual brands supporting the achievement of category objectives.

Regardless of the nature, quality, and amount of support, all manufacturers should come to the table equipped to do the following:

- *Understand the retailer's strategy.* Every retailer has an objective in the marketplace. It may set out to be the low-price leader (Wal-Mart) or an upscale operator with outstanding customer service (Lunds and Byerly's in Minneapolis). The retailer may want to be known for meat (Stater Bros. in southern California), for a full and diverse assortment of products (ShopRite in New York and New Jersey), for ethnic products (Caputo's in Chicago), for organics and healthful fare (Whole Foods), or simply for fun (Stew Leonard's in Connecticut).

The manufacturer needs to understand what the retailer is trying to accomplish and what strategy is used to reach that objective. Such an understanding is the starting point and foundation of category management.

- *Support retail strategy.* The manufacturer presents all of the programs and promotions for the year for evaluation by the retailer. Is there a fit that benefits both parties? Plans that benefit only the brand and not the category and store will be obvious. They should not be considered if the manufacturer wants to remain a valuable partner. The rule is: category first and brand second.

Let's say the retailer wants to increase shopper traffic by leveraging the store as a marketing medium. A manufacturer's promotions should focus on creating in-store excitement while building the retail image. If a promotion deals with, say, *Cinco de Mayo*, the trading partners can both benefit. An elaborate presentation with product samplings and strolling mariachi players—preceded by considerable advance publicity—will create a festive mood, increase traffic, and satisfy shoppers. There will be sales lift in the overall Mexican foods category and the brands in it.

• *Share their own strategy.* Manufacturers should share their corporate strategy with retail customers. They don't always do so. More important, they should determine if their strategy meshes with that of the retailer. Sometimes it doesn't and that can lead to conflict and a breakdown of the trading partnership for category management.

If a salesperson is trying to drive brand volume and a retailer is trying to drive shopper traffic, they have to figure out how to do both together. They should strive for common ground. It may not be ideal, but there must be mutual understanding and shared goals.

In a perfect world, the manufacturer walks into the retailer's office and says, "We understand where you're going. We want to share our strategy and objectives with you. We can work together."

Category Captain

When category management first started in the early 1990s, a retailer would have four or five manufacturers in the same category rushing in with their programs. Each presentation had a different context, rationale, and recommendation. The retailer rightly wondered, "Who's right and who's wrong?" In many cases, the rationale for the plan seemed solid, but in others it didn't.

Retailers eventually selected one manufacturer as a trusted partner that could be relied on. It was a company they believed had the resources, wherewithal, and commitment to grow the category. That company came to be called the *category captain*.

That didn't mean that the other three or four manufacturers competing in the same category were excluded from the process. They became category advisors or validators. They cross-checked the category captain's recommendation. If the captain was doing a good job, the advisor merely provided a little twist or added something that perhaps was missed.

The use of category captains and advisors has increased over the years. Today, most companies use them. The larger retailers typically appoint trusted partners and call them a captain, advisor, valuator, consultant—and sometimes nothing at all. The retailer still has one partner to rely on for advice about the category. Large manufacturers have teams assigned to an account to offer category advice and actually develop planograms, the diagrams that show how and where products should be placed on retail shelves for optimal sales. They sometimes operate out of permanent offices at the retail headquarters.

The largest manufacturer with the largest brands is often chosen to be the category captain, but that's not always the case. A smaller supplier may bring more resources to the table and earn the title—especially if it is enthusiastic and clearly has the best interests of the retailer in mind.

The choice of this trusted partner should take into account the following:

- *Ability to think strategically:* Retailers should work closely with manufacturers who think strategically. And that goes beyond thinking about the category. It means thinking about the implications for the department, the store, and the retailer's shopper base.

- *Ability to be unbiased:* Manufacturers must be unbiased. Instead of pushing its brands, a category captain must focus on the category. That can be very challenging, especially if the vice president of sales insists on meeting quotas for the month. Under those circumstances, it is difficult to talk strategically about competitive brands. It is more difficult for category captains to delist their own brands for the greater good of the category.

- *Ability to access relevant information:* Captains must bring the retailer relevant information. The kinds of data can include consumer panels, RFID, consumer focus groups, and other research. Their recommendations must be based on solid, supported facts.

To be effective in meeting the needs of retail category managers, the top characteristics of an effective supplier are accuracy, timeliness of the information, responsiveness, and creativity. The best suppliers have an intense focus on supporting the initiatives of their own company while working within the retailer's strategic framework to drive sales and profit dollars in the stores. Suppliers must bring a category perspective and not solely a brand outlook.

Supporting Players

Using the principles of category management to operate a business is not confined to retail chains and consumer packaged goods (CPG) manufacturers. There is a host of other players contributing to the design of category plans and their implementation in the store. Here is a look at their roles and importance.

Wholesalers

The primary business of grocery wholesalers is to warehouse products and deliver them to independent retailers. They also supply advertising and marketing support and marketing advice.

In addition, wholesalers can provide a full menu of category management services to the independents. Manufacturers conduct category reviews with wholesalers on behalf of the small retail customers. The wholesalers send shelf sets to the retailers who modify them, perhaps adding products they receive from secondary suppliers or certain items that their top shoppers request. The retailer receives the manpower to reset shelves from the wholesaler, manufacturer, a third-party service company—or sometimes a combination of the three.

These services are neither mandatory nor free. Independents must sign up and pay a weekly fee for them. Given the complexity of category management and the limited resources of independents, it's hard to imagine deploying the process without this help.

The task calls for dealing with several different formats, retail strategies, and even markets. Because of the number of different retailers served, a wholesaler must have enough room in the distribution center to carry all of the products that different category management plans call for.

Perhaps the biggest challenge for wholesalers is communication. They are always looking to improve and speed up the way information is delivered to their customers. Shelf sets are usually available online, along with any changes that need to be made or suggested.

"We look for input from retailers on a regular basis about how they want to run their operation," says Michael Terpkosh, director of category management development for SUPERVALU, the country's largest grocery wholesaler. "We have people in the field calling on them on a regular basis to talk about what's happening in the store with resets and the category management program. It provides them with the opportunity to give us feedback."

Sales Agencies

Sales agencies work for CPG manufacturers largely by representing them to retail customers. Sales agencies provide outsourced sales, merchandising, marketing, and promotional services. In other words, they do the work of a manufacturer's direct salesforce and represent the brand to the retailer.

They also provide a full slate of category management services just like a manufacturer would. But there is a difference. Since they represent many manufacturers, sales agencies are positioned to advise retailers on department or aisle management in which the principles or disciplines of category management are applied to a group of categories, such as dairy. In addition, since they can represent manufacturers in related categories, such as mustard, charcoal, and relish brands, sales agencies can help retailers put together creative merchandising themes for seasonal promotions.

"On an everyday standpoint, we manage our business under basic category management disciplines," says Michael Bernatchez, senior vice president of corporate marketing for Acosta Sales and Marketing Company. "Whenever we go in with a business proposition for a retailer, we try to take category management principles into that dialogue."

Merchandising Service Organizations

Called the arms and legs of manufacturers, they specialize in retail detail. They are merchandising service organizations (MSOs) employed by manufacturers and sometimes retailers to work in the aisles of stores. They reset shelves according to a new schematic, cut in new products, set up displays, and perform related tasks in the store.

MSOs are perhaps the most critical player in the execution of category management. They carry out the category plan in the aisles and maintain the integrity of the shelf. That is where the plan often falls apart—usually because an MSO is not patrolling the aisles.

In fact, their role is probably underutilized in terms of what they can contribute to the category management process. They see things live and in real time that executives at headquarters rarely see. The MSO is a valuable resource with potential that has yet to be fully developed.

Research and Data Providers

Effective analysis of categories, markets, and consumers is made possible by providers of research, demographic/psychographic data, and syndicated data. In fact, they potentially could play a bigger role in category management by working closer with manufactures to prepare presentations for retailers.

When manufacturers are defining what the category hierarchy is, a data company can provide a perspective organized by category, subcategory, and brand. They can give manufacturers a more in-depth look via examples of the hierarchy. They also provide input about the day-to-day job of category managers. What should they be looking at? When should they consider changing the product assortment? How often should they change the planogram?

With proper information from research and data providers, trading partners gain a unique view of the market. Then, it's a matter if interpreting what the market is saying and reacting to that analysis.

The Promise of Category Management

Category management does more than contribute to the success of a retail operation. It is an essential component. In fact, it is difficult to imagine a retailer winning in the marketplace without relying on the direction that this valuable process provides.

Product categories are the building blocks of the store. Category management leverages them to enable retailers to operate effectively. Some categories may be larger than others and some may contribute more to the bottom line. But all of them must work well individually and must come together to present a cohesive whole to discriminating shoppers.

Expertise in category management is certainly a competitive advantage. It empowers retailers to make better business decisions that help them achieve financial objectives. Well-managed categories will enable retailers to keep their present shoppers and attract new ones. The nature of the business today demands nothing less.

So, what's next?

A toothpaste manufacturer may be able to help a retailer analyze the category, determine shelf space, and eventually contribute to an increase in sales—for that category. Meanwhile, the two or three categories nearby—say, cold remedies, shaving cream, and analgesics—could be in terrible shape. But the toothpaste manufacturer doesn't know it and doesn't have data to analyze why.

Welcome to the world of aisle management and department management. Helping retailers manage an aisle or department is the next major step forward in category management. Some large manufacturers are already offering these services to retailers. However, it is largely an emerging practice.

The use of shopper data from loyalty card programs and data from RFID systems are also emerging. The former is already being used by such chains as Kroger and Big Y. Both sources of data will contribute to the enrichment of category management as the process continues to evolve.

The industry may have taken its eye off the consumer in the early days of data overload and number crunching, but that time has past. Today, the best practitioners are focused on consumer-centric category management. The consumer now stands at the center of the process and drives all decisions about the category today and its direction tomorrow.

Retailers and manufacturers need to pay attention.

CHAPTER 2

Category Management Begins with the Retailer's Strategy

The most successful retailers today are those with a strong strategy. They are profitable because their stores satisfy the needs of diverse and demanding shoppers. A bond exists between merchants and consumers who buy into the promise of the retail brand.

What exactly is a strategy? It's a compass that points the way to success. It distinguishes companies in a crowded, chaotic, and competitive marketplace. It helps determine which opportunities to pursue and which ones to walk away from.

All retailers—from grocery chains and electronics stores to bookstores and pet supply stores—have some sort of strategy in place. But the execution of that strategy separates the winners from the also-rans. Is the strategy consistent over time? Does it change if the marketplace changes? Does change make sense to shoppers?

Once a company decides what kind of retailer it wants to be, everything—from customer service to assortments to the quality of private label goods—has to support that strategy. Consistency is king.

Some retailers can use the same strategy no matter where they are located. Wal-Mart offers low prices everywhere. Whole Foods sells wholesome food in every store regardless of location. But chains that operate stores in upscale and downscale parts of town, or in urban as well as rural areas, need to do one of two things: (1) either localize their corporate strategy or (2) make it broad enough to cover all locations.

When carried out, a strategy positions the retailer to be meaningful to consumers. This is easier said than done. Take a fairly large grocery retailer in a congested trading area. What message should be given to convince shoppers to fill 80 percent of their shopping needs in the store? That's a tough proposition.

If the message is low prices, that opens up the door to competing with Wal-Mart, dollar stores, and extreme value retailers. If it is promoting a wide variety of products, that creates a space problem in the store because of the large number of products needed, which is probably going to increase the likelihood of top-selling items being out of stock.

Why should retailers have a strategy in the first place? Because it gives them a means to measure their performance against their objectives. If they want to offer everyday low prices, they can measure themselves against that strategy. If they want to be more of a premium player that differentiates on service and upscale assortments, they can develop a process that measures them against those key performance objectives.

Category management provides a way to evaluate the success or failure of the tactics of a strategy. At the same time, manufacturers shouldn't practice category management without knowing what the retailer's strategy is. Without such knowledge, the manufacturers' efforts could be a waste of time and effort.

Components of a Good Strategy

Most retailers know a good strategy when they see one, but it's very difficult to maintain it over time. The components of a good strategy are:

- *Know who you are.* The retailer must be aware of the store's position in the market. It comes down to knowing how to price and set up assortments, as well as deciding on the ambiance of the store and the level of employee/customer interaction. Retailers can communicate with customers using signage, in-store circulars, e-mails, and regular mail. Communication can be direct or indirect, including sponsoring in-store and out-of-store events.

- *Know your consumers.* The retailer needs to know who the shoppers are, what their perceptions of the store are, and what they want in a store. If shoppers are blue-collar families, a low-price format seems desirable. If they are largely a professional, white-collar crowd, high-end merchandise and high-touch customer service are effective. If many shoppers are Hispanic, a culturally appropriate format might be in order, or at least an increased number of Hispanic products. The mix of store employees should also reflect the target shopper base.

- *Be able to execute.* Suppose a retailer learns about the shoppers and what they want. That may call for some changes in approach that requires buy-in from operations executives and store associates. They need to know the new strategy and why things are changing. And they have to accept it for the good of the store. In other words, the retailer will be able to carry out the strategy more easily if everyone from the executive suite to store level understands the strategy and works to execute it.

For example, Whole Foods Market relies on one of the most complete and thoughtful strategies to secure and maintain its position in the market. An abridged version of The Whole Philosophy that is presented on www.wholefoodsmarket.com follows:

- *Declaration of interdependence:* "Our ability to instill a clear sense of interdependence among our various stakeholders (the people who are interested and benefit from the success of our company) is contingent upon our efforts to communicate more often, more openly, and more compassionately. Better communication equals better understanding and more trust."
- *Our core values:* They include "selling the highest quality natural and organic products available, satisfying and delighting customers, team member happiness and excellence, creating wealth through profits and growth, and caring about communities and the environment."
- *Our quality standards:* "We carry natural and organic products because we believe that food in its purest state—unadulterated by artificial additives, sweeteners, colorings, and preservatives—is the best tasting and most nutritious food available."
- *Sustainability and our future:* Whole Foods Market's vision of a sustainable future means that "our children and grandchildren will be living in a world that values human creativity, diversity, and individual choice. . . . We are starting to implement this new vision of the future by changing the way we think about the relationships between our food supply, the environment, and our bodies."

How Do You Develop a Strategy?

Developing a strategy begins with Marketing 101: Who are the shoppers and what do they want? Every retailer should ask these questions when building a store, remodeling, or planning a new format.

It makes sense to study the local community. Whole Foods and Wild Oats know they are serving consumers interested in health and wellness and therefore stock foods that make sense for those shoppers. SUPERVALU's Save-a-Lot chain is a low-price, low-service format that fills a niche in many states.

Most retailers have a heritage they adhere to. It is based on principles that may have remained unchanged over time. These principles form the basis of a retail strategy that may be constant over the years, as well. A "clean-floor" policy, meaning a lack of promotional displays and other in-store promotional "clutter," may be working well in a community, so why change?

Other retailers are more inclined to adapt to the changing times. If time-pressed shoppers welcome more services, then adding banks and hot meals to go makes sense. Many supermarkets have added such services over the years.

Sometimes a format needs a radical overhaul to remain competitive. Kash n' Karry, a 104-store supermarket chain based in Florida, is completely reinventing itself. After researching the competition and the consumers, the retailer decided there was a market for a store that celebrates food with vibrancy, flair, and a bit of an ethnic flavor. The former price-oriented format is now morphing into an elastic, lifestyle brand called Sweetbay Supermarkets. Remodeling all the stores will take a few years, but the new focus should rejuvenate its shopper base for years to come.

Should the development of a strategy be based on solid research, intuition, or a combination of the two? That depends. Some retailers have a knack of knowing just the right approach in their marketplace. They know their customer base and if it's changing. Others need a more formalized process to obtain the same information.

Examples of Strategies

There are several kinds of retail strategies. Some are successful and many are not. But if the retailers know who they are, know their shoppers, and deliver on their brand promise, they will survive and prosper even in today's hotly competitive environment.

What does the neighborhood need and want from a grocery store? Here are some approaches:

- *Traditional:* The neighborhood grocery store carries all of the essentials for families, as well as offering them an array of specialty departments. Operators of these modern conventional supermarkets have been around for decades. For example, Pittsburgh-based Giant Eagle dominates its markets with an extensive selection of fresh, high-quality food items as well as several convenience-oriented departments. The depth and quality of the products and services is the manifestation of the corporate strategy. Another part of the strategy is pricing, which has changed to provide better value to shoppers. Giant Eagle reduced prices on thousands of items storewide, while continuing its existing approach to promotions in the form of aggressive weekly specials and double coupons, seasonal and holiday offers, promotions through a loyalty card, and discounts on fuel for buying certain groceries.

- *Variety:* Stores that have a wide variety in their assortments earn a reputation among shoppers. Consumers know they can always find a product there, and the store is always the first to stock a new item. ShopRite supermarkets in the northeast United States offers such variety. Walgreen's, the United States's largest drug-store chain, also has impressive depth in its health and beauty care (HBC) products, while offering a convenient format for grocery fill-in trips.

- *High tech:* Metro Group's Future Store in Rheinberg, Germany, opened in April 2003 equipped with a variety of sophisticated technologies. The supermarket features electronic shelf labels; large overhead digital advertising displays; RFID-enabled smart shelves; product information terminals activated by scanning a product barcode; intelligent scales that identify fruits and vegetables, automatically weigh items, and print out a price sticker; self checkout; and a shopping cart with a bar code scanner and a touch screen that displays item prices, keeps a running total of the shopping bill, and notifies shoppers of promotions throughout the store.

  The new Bloom stores in the greater Charlotte, North Carolina, marketplace create technology touch points that enhance convenience for the shopper. The stores are operated by Food Lion, which is owned by Delhaize America, the U.S. division of the Delhaize Group in Brussels, Belgium. Bloom's experiment in convenience-oriented technology features personal scanners that consumers can use to scan products while shopping the aisles, informational kiosks in the meat and liquor departments, self-service produce sales, and moveable wireless checkouts. This high-tech format promises to simplify and shorten the shopping trip, while adding an element of novelty.

- *Loyalty:* Tesco, the U.K.-based international retailer, uses its loyalty card program as a central marketing tactic to build and maintain one-to-one relationships with its customers. Launched in 1995, the Clubcard enables shoppers to earn points in-store,

online, and with nonsupermarket partners. Cardholders can re-
deem Clubcard vouchers for discounts in stores or online, or even
use them to reduce their auto insurance. Tesco's loyalty program
meshes with its well-known strategy: "Our core purpose is all
about customers. Create value for customers to earn their lifetime
loyalty. This statement is at the center of all we do."

- *Customer service:* Stew Leonard's bills itself as the World's Largest
  Dairy Store. In its three stores in Connecticut and New York, the
  retailer entertains young and old shoppers in a festive atmosphere.
  But what distinguishes the stores operated by this well-known fam-
  ily-owned business is absolute dedication to customer service that
  has spawned legions of loyal shoppers. The company's philosophy is
  chiseled into a three-ton block of granite at each store's entrance:

  "Rule #1—The Customer Is Always Right. Rule #2—If the Customer Is Ever Wrong, Re-Read Rule #1."

  The retailer is also known for its management philosophy: Take
  good care of your people and they will take good care of your customers. Not surprisingly, Fortune magazine has listed Stew
  Leonard's as one of the "100 Best Companies to Work for in
  America" for four consecutive years. Is the retailer's strategy
  working? Stew Leonard's has been listed in the Guinness Book of
  World Records as having "the greatest sales per unit area of any
  single food store in the United States."

Retail Branding

The brand is often the only thing that separates two products. The
best brands stand for something in the mind of the consumer. For
example, there are all kinds of motorcycles, but only one Harley-
Davidson. What does that brand stand for? Rebellion and adventure.

In retailing, the way to stand out in an overstored and competitive marketplace is to make sure the retail brand means something to every shopper. What does Wal-Mart stand for? Low prices. What does Best Buy stand for? It's the best deal on electronics. How about Toys R Us? Consumers can find any toy they want.

There must be an element of trust in a brand if it is to be successful. Consumers know they can rely on Wal-Mart to offer the lowest prices in town. If that trust was violated often enough, shoppers would rebel by going elsewhere.

The brand is the center around which all of marketing revolves. Everything must contribute to what the brand stands for—from mission to strategy to tactics. Every category in the store must be managed with the spirit of the brand in mind.

Shoppers: Getting to Know You

Many factors come into play when analyzing shoppers. Who are they? Where do they live? Are they new to the neighborhood? Do they have children or pets? The answers to these questions provide the information that retailers need to develop and maintain a functional strategy that can endure.

Demographics: Who Are My Shoppers?

Understanding the demographics of the shopper base is critical to strategy. Not just the present shoppers, but also the potential ones. The demographics of neighborhoods—the size of the population, the ethnic patterns—change over time. It's important for retailers to monitor these changes and make adjustments accordingly. That leads to unique store sets and special assortments. What is offered in one store might not be in another store five miles away because the demographics of the neighborhoods are different.

Demographics drive certain wants and needs. Those shoppers with babies are going to buy diapers. Seniors have little use for the back-to-school aisle of the store. Those who live alone don't need family-size meals. Knowing if the shopper base consists of young families, seniors, or singles helps determine everything from strategy to assortments.

Geographics: Where Do My Shoppers Live?

Knowing where shoppers live is also key to an effective strategy. Some people move all the time. Consumers are traveling more and come across more choices for their shopping dollar. As new stores with extreme value formats proliferate, people get introduced to different shopping experiences. Retailers must study and understand this dynamic in their backyards. Having the most convenient location for a food store—for years the advantage of traditional supermarkets—is not good enough any more when dealing with value-conscious, demanding, mobile, knowledgeable consumers.

Other Factors

Demographics can indicate certain needs, but it doesn't guarantee that retailers can prevent shopper erosion or attract new shoppers moving into the neighborhood. Retailers still must understand other factors about their target shoppers—how they shop, when they shop, are they deal motivated.

Offering low prices can only do so much. Perhaps retailers could appeal to bakers with cooking contests or the opportunity to have their recipe prepared in the store's bakery. That's a better draw for this particular audience than saying, "Here's an item at a low price."

A consumer's personality also figures into his or her buying habits. For example, do certain consumers like to shop for deals and use coupons? Retailers are not going to reach a person who likes to shop for deals the same way that they're going to reach someone with the exact same demographic profile who isn't deal driven.

Appealing to the time-starved shopper has become more important to retailers who are interested in retaining the full load-up weekly grocery trip. Retailers must make sure that their stores are not out of stock on staples. But they also have to balance that with being more convenient for shoppers on fill-in occasions.

Maybe that entails a convenience section of the supermarket. Retailers should be testing these convenience centers that cater to the time-starved customer coming home from work. They don't have time to prepare a full meal and want to pick up something easy to prepare for dinner. Why does that customer have to walk throughout an entire big-box supermarket to figure out what to buy? Why not shop the convenience section or the deli with meals to go?

Drugstores are bringing consumers in for prescription drugs at the pharmacy. Many have started to satisfy customers' needs for some of the traditional grocery products that they might want to pick up, such as paper goods and dry groceries. Store traffic may warrant installing a dairy case.

Who Is the Competition?

About 13,000 stores open, close, or change ownership every month across all retail channels of distribution. In today's era of widespread mergers and acquisitions, it's therefore challenging to stay on top of who owns whom. Meanwhile, real-time accuracy is critical to conduct business effectively and efficiently.

To realize the benefits of category management, the right product must get to the right store at the right time. That is a lot more difficult than it sounds. Manufacturers today are challenged to keep track of their changing customers. In fact, this difficulty has given rise to a strategic industry initiative called Location Information Management (LIM). This systematic process maintains, integrates, and leverages customer location information. The process includes the ship-tos, bill-tos, plan-tos, sell-tos, and account hierarchies combined with other key intelligence about retailers. LIM is being spearheaded by ACNielsen's TDLinx division, provider of location information data and coding structure.

The grocery business has been the most volatile trade channel in recent years, in part because of the growing availability of food products in many other retail outlets, and in part because of a retailer with roots in Bentonville, Arkansas—Wal-Mart.

Channel Blurring

Once upon a time, trade channels had clear identities. Supermarkets sold groceries, drugstores sold prescription and nonprescription drugs, and convenience stores offered fill-in purchases and had a fuel outlet. Today, these retail stores aren't what they used to be. Groceries are available in the drugstore and shoppers can buy gas at their supermarket where they can also fill prescriptions. Meanwhile, there has been dramatic growth in warehouse clubs, limited assortment stores, and dollar stores offering value-priced staples.

This channel blurring has eroded shopper loyalty with regard to where customers buy food. Groceries are now sold in a wide array of retail outlets. It's convenient to pick up groceries here and there instead of relying on the traditional supermarket. Even home improvement, office supply, and electronics stores are selling some food products.

As a result, there has been a significant shift in where people shop, with supercenters and dollar stores gaining shoppers and traditional grocery stores and traditional mass merchandisers experiencing a decline in shopping frequency (see Figures 2.1 and 2.2).

FIGURE 2.1   Consumers Take Advantage of Channel Options

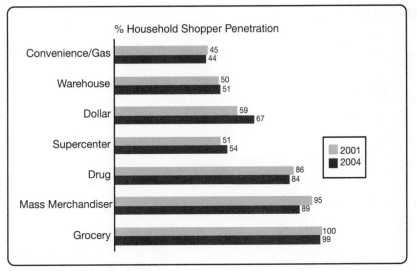

Source: ACNielsen Homescan.

FIGURE 2.2   Grocery and Traditional Mass Losing Trips

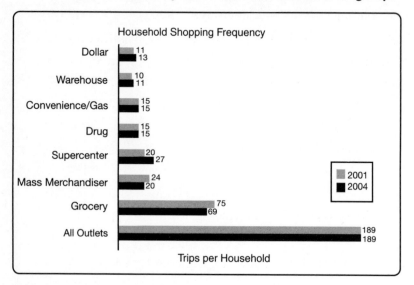

Source: ACNielsen Homescan.

Wal-Mart

Wal-Mart is in a class by itself. It quickly became the world's largest retailer since entering food retailing in 1988. Big and ambitious, backed by a world-class distribution system, and technically advanced, Wal-Mart changes the dynamics of every market it enters. Wal-Mart's powerful retail strategy is the very essence of its brand: "Always Low Prices. Always."

Wal-Mart has four retail concepts to meet the needs of various shopper groups on various shopping occasions, but it leverages its brand across all formats:

1. *Discount stores:* They average 98,000 sq. ft. and stock about 62,500 items such as family apparel, automotive products, health and beauty care products, home furnishings, electron-

ics, hardware, toys, sporting goods, lawn and garden items, pet supplies, jewelry, and housewares.

2. *Supercenters:* Wal-Mart supercenters essentially combine a discount store with a full-line grocery story under one roof to offer consumers the convenience of one-stop shopping. The average supercenter measures 187,000 sq. ft. and offers 116,000 different items.

3. *Neighborhood markets:* Wal-Mart's neighborhood markets are essentially grocery stores with an average size of 43,000 sq. ft. and about 38,000 items in stock. Launched in 1998, they are designed to provide convenience for the shopper who wants to park, shop, and leave quickly.

4. *Warehouse clubs:* Sam's Club, the country's leading members-only warehouse club, offers a wide selection of general merchandise and large-volume products at low prices. Though geared primarily for small business owners, the stores attract families looking for value.

Regardless of format or location, the company remains committed to the three basic beliefs that Sam Walton laid down in 1962 when he built Wal-Mart on the philosophies of excellence in the workplace, customer service, and low prices:

- Respect for the individual.
- Service to our customers.
- Strive for excellence.

Regardless of format, Wal-Mart stores offer a wide assortment, friendly atmosphere, and value in the form of quality goods and low prices.

Wal-Mart has made some of its store brands an important part of the product mix. This plays well to the customer base because Wal-Mart shoppers are typically value conscious. They are likely more prone to purchase private label products, and Wal-Mart has benefited. Ol'Roy, Wal-Mart's brand of dog food, is the leading store brand in America. Equate, its line of health and beauty care products, challenges the national brands.

But the retailer also attracts the more brand-conscious consumers because their prices on some of the traditional national brands are so low. The impression is that everything is less expensive at Wal-Mart.

Retailers looking for a positive spin from the dominance of Wal-Mart need only consider its premier distribution system that provides the best efficiency in the industry. It has made every other retailer in the country reevaluate and improve its distribution methods. Ironically, Wal-Mart has made many other retailers more efficient in shipping products to their stores.

Bringing Clarity to Channel Definitions

Even though the retail formats are blurring, CPG manufacturers need to understand the difference between these channels to conduct category management effectively. Such distinctions provide the framework with which to measure performance.

Having clear, agreed-to definitions is important for comparing apples to apples. The following definitions of key subchannels of grocery and other channels as tracked by TDLinx are endorsed by key U.S.-based industry associations such as the Food Marketing Institute, Grocery Manufacturers of America, and the National Association of Convenience Stores:

- *Supermarket:* A conventional supermarket is a full-line, self-service grocery store with annual sales of $2 million or more. This definition includes both chain and independent locations. Examples include Kroger, Harris Teeter, and Weis Markets.

- *Superette/small grocery:* A superette is a grocery store with an annual volume of $1 to $2 million. They are typically independent, but many superettes belong to groups like IGA, Inc. Small groceries, also known as "Mom & Pop" stores, include those stores with sales of less than $1 million annually. Some examples are Country Market and Superior Markets.

- *Supercenters:* A supercenter is a retail store with a full-line supermarket and a full-line discount store under one roof. This combination offers shoppers wide variety and one-stop shopping. Besides Wal-Mart, other operators are Meijer, Fred Meyer, and Target with its Super Target format.

- *Cash-and-carry warehouse store:* A cash-and-carry warehouse store has limited service and offers low prices. Rather than displaying products on the shelf for sale, they are offered in their original shipping cartons. These stores also sell bulk food and large-size items. They often serve as suppliers to smaller food stores. One example is Smart & Final.

- *Limited assortment:* A limited assortment store offers a limited selection of grocery products in a smaller number of categories than a conventional supermarket. Most of the items are private label with a small number of branded goods. Some operators are Aldi and Save-a-Lot.

- *Wholesale club:* Wholesale clubs include membership club stores offering packaged and bulk foods and general merchandise. The average store stocks about 4,000 SKUs, 40 percent of which are grocery items. Some examples include Sam's Club, BJ's, and Costco.

- *Convenience store:* Convenience stores are small units of 800 to 3,000 square feet and stock 500 to 1,500 SKUs. They have a small selection of grocery items including at least two of the following: toilet paper, soap, disposable diapers, pet foods, breakfast cereal, tuna fish, toothpaste, ketchup, and canned goods. Examples include 7-Eleven and Wawa.

- *Dollar stores:* Dollar stores are high-volume stores specializing in everyday household goods, including large quantities and an extensive selection of food, paper products, and health and beauty care items. Some examples are Dollar General and Family Dollar.

Aside from these recognized channels, there are other retail stores vying for the grocery dollar. The 39,000 drugstores in the United States largely sell prescription drugs and health and beauty care products. But they are stocking more and more dry groceries and many have refrigerated cases as well for dairy products, and some have freezers. Online grocers such as Peapod serve consumers willing to pay to have their groceries delivered to their doors. Take-out restaurants have chipped away at grocery purchases by offering time-pressed consumers meals to go as an alternative to food preparation.

Meanwhile, a very popular channel outside the United States is the hypermarket, which combines a department store and a supermarket. The result is a store with groceries and apparel under one roof. Carrefour, the French retail group, opened the first hypermarket near Paris in 1962. In Spain, the largest hypermarkets are Eroski and Hipecor.

Establishing the Mission

Every retailer should have a mission statement. The mission statement specifies why the company is in business and what its goals are. Most of these statements talk about providing value to shoppers by offering quality goods at fair prices and with helpful service. Ideally, retailers carry out the mission with a well-conceived strategy and effective tactics.

How often should the mission be reviewed? If the mission statement of the family business has been around for a half century, it might be time to refresh it. Some concepts and promises are timeless but demographics aren't. Demographics don't change weekly or monthly, and maybe not even quarterly. But it's a good idea to review the mission and its follow-through strategy annually to avoid drifting off target because of changing demographics or consumer needs.

Which Customers Will I Own?

The mission and the retail strategy must revolve around certain shoppers. The days of appealing to everyone are past. Successful companies today are finding a niche and trying to fill it.

If the target is the upscale consumer and the affluent families, the store will be quite different than if it were in an urban, low-income part of town. The mission and strategy are driven by the shoppers—who they are, what they want from you, and what you want from them.

What Shopping Occasions Will the Store Cater To?

There are all kinds of shopping occasions: the once-a-week food shop, the fill-in, the stock-up, holiday, special event, and the cherry pick where a retailer is practically giving away an item to compel shoppers to flock to the store to load up. Everybody who can wants to own the full shopping trip. The retailer has to decide which other occasions it wants to "own" (i.e., control).

Say the retailer wants to serve growing families with small children. With the right blend of strategy and tactics, retailers can earn the loyalty of these families for the full shopping trip (i.e., they purchase 80 percent or more of their needs for the week). But nobody owns every shopping trip. A competing retailer may target the same group for the fill-in trips for milk and bread. Another might target them for trips to prepare for their summer BBQ parties and back-to-school needs. These competitors will merchandise around those occasions the same way as all retailers do around the holidays.

If Wal-Mart wants to own the Valentine's Day purchase occasion, watch out. The stores will have flowers, balloons, cards, and gifts throughout. The whole store will be decked in red.

Financial and Performance Scorecards

Establishing financial and performance scorecards lets retailers measure themselves against their programs, plans, and expectations, as well as against the competition. There is nothing more critical for the success of a retail operation. Scorecards take the guesswork out of the equation and should be an ongoing process.

Retailers can use practical measures to analyze their day-to-day performance. Keeping track of consumers and their shopping habits provides a compass for a retail company. That's important because consumers are diverse and unpredictable today.

Retailers should measure what they want to manage. They have to select those measures that are most appropriate for their goals and retail strategy.

Degree of Capturing Target Customer Group Spending

If retailers aren't establishing their share of target customer group, they should start. Retailers should first identify their target customer group; that is, who they want to capture. If the target is families with young children, how well am I capturing their spending? Table 2.1 shows that Retailer A is performing especially well with such families, particularly households with children between the ages of 6 and 12.

TABLE 2.1   Retailer Dollar Index of Household by Household Size

DEMOGRAPHICS	Retailer A
SIZE - 1 MEM	53
SIZE - 2 MEM	110
SIZE - 3-4 MEM	129
SIZE - 5+ MEM	104
KIDS - NONE < 18	91
KIDS - ANY < 18	117
KIDS - ANY < 6	119
KIDS - ANY 6-12	133
KIDS - ANY 13-17	92

Source: ACNielsen Homescan Account Shopper Profiler.

A related logical next step is determining who else is serving those shoppers. Table 2.2 reveals that Retailers C, F, and G are prime competitors for households that are similar to those that Retailer A is targeting.

This measure refers to the number of trips as well as the dollars spent on those trips. If all the households in the customer group make a total of 20,000 trips to retail stores, the retailer aims to get a certain number of those trips. If they spend $20 million on party trips, the retailer targets a certain percent of the total.

Occasion and Category Contribution to Sales and Profits

If retailers want to own a store department or trip, they must make sure that the department or the category that supports the trip is a signifi-

**TABLE 2.2   Retailer Dollar Index Compared to
Other Retailers in Market**

Demographics	Retailer A	Retailer B	Retailer C	Retailer D	Retailer E	Retailer F	Retailer G
SIZE - 1 MEM	53	56	43	80	79	58	53
SIZE - 2 MEM	110	91	92	118	104	83	97
SIZE - 3-4 MEM	129	133	135	106	103	123	142
SIZE - 5+ MEM	104	130	151	86	126	167	101
KIDS - NONE < 18	91	84	83	105	92	76	78
KIDS - ANY < 18	117	131	134	91	116	147	143
KIDS - ANY < 6	119	117	125	111	87	146	97
KIDS - ANY 6-12	133	109	124	86	111	138	131
KIDS - ANY 13-17	92	152	144	87	119	126	151

Source: ACNielsen Homescan Account Shopper Profiler.

cant part of their operation. For example, a retailer focused on fresh foods should get a sales contribution from the perimeter departments that is greater than a retailer that doesn't focus as much on those departments. The fresh departments of a supermarket truly dedicated to fresh foods should generate at least 40 percent of total store sales.

Turns

Inventory turns are a measure of how quickly a company replenishes its entire stock of merchandise annually. The more turns, the less time inventory sits idle, which helps improve cash flow.

Meanwhile, there are different financial measures available. Here is a sampling:

- *Gross margin return on inventory:* GMROI is a measure that enables retailers to compare the performance of departments, vendors, stores, and customer groups. For example, a GMROI of $1.50 means a return of $1.50 in gross margin dollars for every dollar invested in inventory. It reflects the relationship between margins and turns. An increase in one or the other means that the GMROI increases.
- *Return on net assets:* RONA is a measure of financial performance calculated as net income divided by fixed assets plus net working capital. The higher the return, the better the profit performance for the company.
- *Net present value:* NPV is used in capital budgeting. The current value of cash inflows is subtracted by the current value of cash outflows. NVP analyzes the profitability of an investment or project. It compares the value of a dollar today versus the value of

that same dollar in the future, after taking inflation and return into account. If the NVP of a possible project is positive, then it should be accepted. But if it is negative, then the project likely should be turned down because the cash flows are negative.

- *Activity-based costing:* ABC is a model that identifies the costs involved in getting a product from its origin to the consumer. It attributes costs to products based on assigning costs of resources to activities and then costs of activities to products.

Communicate Strategy

Companies have different philosophies when it comes to communication. Some believe that if all of its employees know the company strategy, then it is easier to get everyone from top to bottom to make decisions in their specific jobs that support the corporate direction and strategy. U.S. grocery retailers have historically been a bit more publicity shy, fearing that the more they share, the more their competition may take advantage of that information.

These are two different cultures and ways of looking at things. It makes sense that sharing objectives and strategies with employees will enable them to understand what is happening and make decisions accordingly. It helps to enlist their support and generate momentum. It's a lot easier to manage people if there is clear communication and leadership. People generally are trying to do a good job. Why not give them the reasons to work hard and follow a certain path?

The culture of many supermarket companies goes back a long way. Grocers have always feared that competitors will learn their strategy. Today, most retailers know what their competitors are trying to do. They're checking out stores all the time. They do price checks, study assortments, and track the special services offered such as banking, coffee concessions, and so on.

Every competitor finds out the other store's strategy and tactics sooner or later. The focus should be on carrying out your own strategy.

Need to Know

Who needs to know and buy into the strategy? Everyone in the company and your suppliers, too. Unless they know, they can't contribute and may become an obstacle. It's especially important for a retailer to communicate a new strategy and direction to suppliers or the program might not be a win-win. The savvy suppliers will seize the opportunity to design new programs to support the new strategy.

Overcoming Political Hurdles

Unfortunately, some suppliers are more concerned with pushing their own agenda—that is, sales of their brands—than with practicing category management properly. Others support the process in theory, but then ask their subordinates to find a way around it.

A retailer's allegiance is not to the brand. It is to the category and to the shoppers. Their trusted trading partners will be those who sincerely believe in category management and design programs to complement the overall retail strategy.

Thumbs-Up: Here Are the Winners!

Retailers with clear and compelling strategies are the winners in the marketplace. They stand the test of time. They may dominate a trading area, but excellence in retailing doesn't just relate to size or the number of stores in a chain. It relates to the extent to which retailers fill a niche or satisfy shopper needs.

When compiling a list of these retailers, it's easy to name the well-known stars of the industry that have received much notoriety and publicity over the years—and rightly so. They include strong regionals such as Wegmans (Rochester, New York), HEB (San Antonio, Texas), and Schnuck's (St. Louis, Missouri), as well as multi-regionals such as Kroger (Cincinnati, Ohio) Wal-Mart Stores (Bentonville, Arkansas), and Target (Minneapolis, Minneapolis).

There are many other retailers with strong, winning strategies. Here's a look at some of them, each operating a different format:

• Save-a-Lot is a St. Louis-based chain of limited assortment stores that operates as a subsidiary of SUPERVALU, the country's largest wholesaler. There are more than 1,000 stores in the chain spread out over 36 states. About 25 percent of them are corporately owned, while the rest are owned by licensed operators who also have conventional stores.

  According to Bill Moran, president and CEO, the retail strategy is to provide a limited assortment of products for value-driven shoppers who seek the best values in any economic environment.

  Analysts have called Save-a-Lot the "crown jewel" of SUPERVALU and its growth is one reason why. The wholesaler opens about 100 new stores each year en route to a planned target of some 2,500 units coast-to-coast.

• Slater Bros. is a southern California–based grocer. Jack Brown, chairman, president, and chief executive officer, says there are no plans to expand out of southern California where the chain has operated conventional supermarkets for 69 years. Several large chains such as Hughes, Smith's, and Alpha Beta have left the area over the years. Today, Slater Bros. is surrounded by well-run operators such as Kroger, Albertson's, Ralph's, and Safeway as Wal-Mart enters the area with its supercenters. But Slater Bros. stays the course with a simple strategy:

"We're serving third-generation families, and we've kept our word to each generation about our prices," Brown says. "We are the low-price leader." Its signature product? Meat. When Brown joined the company, annual sales were $475 million in 72 stores. Today, sales exceed $3 billion and there are 158 supermarkets.

- Lund Food Holdings, a privately owned company in Edina, Minnesota, operates 20 upscale supermarkets in the greater Minneapolis marketplace under the Lunds and Byerly's banners. Some of the stores have sit-down restaurants. The delis offer gourmet take out prepared by a talented team of chefs in a large central kitchen.

  The retail strategy is to serve discriminating shoppers with high-end assortments, outstanding customer service, and a state-of-the-art décor.

  "We want to offer our customers sensational shopping experiences each time they visit any one of our stores," says Russell "Tres" Lund III, president and CEO of the 66-year-old family business.

- K-VA-T Food Stores is an Abingdon, Virginia-based chain that operates 85 Food City supermarkets in Kentucky, Virginia, and Tennessee. Steve Smith, president and CEO, wants shoppers to think of his supermarkets as being part of the community.

Food City, a conventional supermarket with an average size of only 34,000 square feet, caters to families in low- to middle-income areas. The retailer's operating philosophy is everyday low price with a blend of in-store promotions and big community events. The retailer stages the Food City Food and Cooking Show each year in Knoxville, Tennessee. Some 30,000 people attend the two-day event to try new products and collect recipes and coupons from manufacturers. The retailer also sponsors the Food City 500 auto race in March as part of the NASCAR Winston Cup Series. The Food City 250 is part of the Busch Series race in August.

"We believe very strongly in giving back to our communities. We operate in a lot of towns from 3,000 to 10,000 people, and we want Food City to be a focal point," says Smith.

- Harmons in Salt Lake City, Utah, operates nearly 70,000 sq. ft. superstores with a heavy emphasis on general merchandise and health and beauty care products. The 11-store grocery chain relies on world-class customer service to compete with Fred Meyer, Target, and Wal-Mart.

  The company's mission statement provides clear direction: "Value the associates and exceed the customer's expectations." The company invests in its employees with ongoing training programs, including a passionate emphasis on customer service. Harmons believes that quality people and first-rate service helps its fresh food sales because the personal touch is important.

  "People make all the difference," says Dean Peterson, president. "At the end of the day, they are the ones who are going to get the job done with the consumer."

Conclusion

Without a clear strategy, retailers would not be as successful as they could be. Customers do not automatically understand and respond to the promise of the retail brand. And perhaps loyal shoppers would be lured away by another operator with the vision, stamina, and wherewithal to execute with consistency.

Only the strong survive? No, only those with strong strategies survive.

THE EIGHT FOUNDATIONAL STEPS OF CATEGORY MANAGEMENT

During the second decade of category management, many retailers and manufacturers refined and tailored the process for speedier strategy fulfillment, smoother execution, and more robust results.

Where category management is executed well, these refinements are part of an evolution that is making stores—and the categories within them—more responsive to what shoppers want. The consumer is at the center of it all.

Retailers and manufacturers are reliant on tools such as demographic data that identify the customer populations around each store, panel data that provide a detailed picture of long-term purchase patterns by households, and a blend of retailers' point-of-sale (POS) data and manufacturers' category and consumer data that can be analyzed at any level to yield detailed insights. With these tools, retailers and manufacturers make smarter fact-based decisions that enhance sell-through, profitability, and the customer shopping experience.

The initial eight-step category management process, as originally conceived by The Partnering Group, has served the industry as a solid starting point; its sound principles have been demonstrated repeatedly:

Activities of the Category Management Business Process

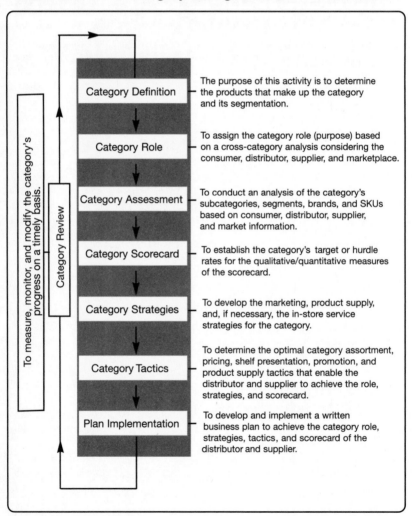

Category Definition — The purpose of this activity is to determine the products that make up the category and its segmentation.

Category Role — To assign the category role (purpose) based on a cross-category analysis considering the consumer, distributor, supplier, and marketplace.

Category Assessment — To conduct an analysis of the category's subcategories, segments, brands, and SKUs based on consumer, distributor, supplier, and market information.

Category Scorecard — To establish the category's target or hurdle rates for the qualitative/quantitative measures of the scorecard.

Category Strategies — To develop the marketing, product supply, and, if necessary, the in-store service strategies for the category.

Category Tactics — To determine the optimal category assortment, pricing, shelf presentation, promotion, and product supply tactics that enable the distributor and supplier to achieve the role, strategies, and scorecard.

Plan Implementation — To develop and implement a written business plan to achieve the category role, strategies, tactics, and scorecard of the distributor and supplier.

Category Review

To measure, monitor, and modify the category's progress on a timely basis.

Source: The Partnering Group, Inc.

No wonder there is an escalating trade allegiance to category management as a time-tested way to grow the total store by managing individual product categories as separate business units. The process aligns product manufacturing and marketing with retail merchandising and selling, as well as with consumer demand. How retailers choose to satisfy consumer demand serves to define their strategies and steer their category management focus.

Retailers and manufacturers report widespread use of category management and its various components, according to 2004 ACNielsen U.S. research (Trade Promotion Practices and Emerging Issues Study):

Category Management Tools

	% of Manufacturers That Use	% of Retailers That Use
Assortment Planning	90	86
Promotional Planning	84	86
Shelf Management	82	81
Category Business Planning	82	81
Everyday Low Pricing	76	67
Frequent Shopper/Loyalty Programs	41	43
Micro-Merchandising	31	43
Micro-Marketing	23	38

Source: ACNielsen.

While an increasing number of organizations are customizing or streamlining the eight-step category management process, before anyone attempts to do so, it is essential to fully understand the original eight steps, both their objectives and methods of execution. The next eight chapters provide that understanding. For each step, you learn state-of-the-art methods of execution and, where possible, a low-cost method. This part provides important context that will help you understand the case studies presented in Part III that illustrate how the industry practices category management today.

Whether customizing or sticking to the original eight steps, manufacturers and retailers unify around common local goals: growth through customer satisfaction and the culmination of retail strategies using sharper business processes with greater efficiencies. In the best of trade partnerships, manufacturers and retailers act as one, sharing information, working in tandem, and focusing on delivery of consumer value.

Step One: Define the Category Based on the Needs of Your Target Market

OBJECTIVE OF STEP ONE

Determine products that make up the category and its segments.

ANALYTICAL TOOLS USED

Market Structure

Preference Segmentation

BACKGROUND OF STEP ONE

Have you ever compared the ready-to-eat cereal category in different types of retail stores? How is the assortment at a mainline grocery store like Jewel or Kroger different from what Whole Foods offers? What about Costco? Jewel or Kroger may have the widest assortments, while Whole Foods has the greatest variety of organic products, and Costco focuses on best-sellers. And how are the cereals organized? By manufacturer? By type of cereal? By ultimate consumer, that is, children versus adults?

Ideally, decisions about what products to include in a retailer's assortment for a given category; and how to merchandise, price, and promote them; would be based on a clear retail strategy that states which consumers are most important to the retailer, coupled with both an understanding of how products within the same category interact with each other. (Does one cannibalize sales from the other, or does having both products raise overall category sales?)

Welcome to the powerful pairing of Market Structure and Preference Segmentation. Market Structure identifies the product attributes that define the category structure. It defines the product attribute hierarchy that drives household purchases and explains the competitive relationships between products. Preference Segmentation divides the market into distinct groups of households that share similar purchase patterns.

Historically, Market Structure and Preference Segmentation research were based on surveys in which respondents were asked about various product categories. Such an approach had inherent shortcomings, such as limited data points and insufficient respondent recall when asked about categories with long purchase cycles, such as many health and beauty care categories.

Today, actual consumer buying behavior, analyzed using consumer "panels," drives the research. Consumer panels are comprised of households equipped with in-home scanners that are used to record all of their purchases. They then download their purchase data to third-party market researchers for analysis. By examining such data over a year or more, patterns emerge revealing the product attributes that drive consumer purchase decisions.

In a simplified example, one carbonated cola-purchasing household may be observed to purchase diet colas primarily, mostly buying one particular brand, but often changing between two-liter bottles, six-packs of cans, and cases of cans. For this household, type of cola—diet versus regular—is the primary product attribute, followed by brand, followed by package size.

The salty snacks category illustrates why it's important to look at Market Structure and Preference Segmentation in tandem. Market Structure research may indicate that the first purchase decision within the category is size, with consumers preferring either small sizes or extra large sizes. The next decision is whether to purchase a branded product or private label. Consumers who prefer private label then choose between types of salty snacks, whereas those who prefer branded salty snacks then choose between products with a perceived health benefit such as baked products versus regular salty snacks (see Figure 3.1).

If the structure revealed that consumers who prefer baked salty snacks express the highest levels of loyalty to the category, a retailer might react to this insight and want to devote as much as half its display space to baked or low-fat varieties. However, Preference Segmentation analysis shows that consumers who are loyal to baked salty snacks represent only 2 percent of category purchasers. While it's important to stock baked salty snacks, it would not make sense to devote so much space to the segment.

The lesson is to shape categories around data of actual buyer behavior rather than what people say in surveys.

FIGURE 3.1   Salty Snacks Market Structure

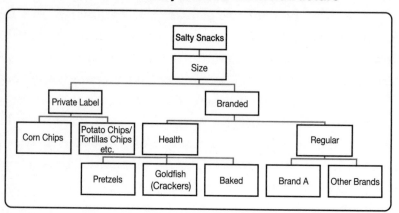

Source: ACNielsen.

Within the frozen pizza category on a national basis, Market Structure shows that price tier (economy, premium, super-premium) and meat type/topping are the first and second decisions by the average consumer, and brand and crust type are the third and fourth decisions. Preference Segmentation reveals many more ways that people shop the category, such as an economy purchaser who buys only pepperoni, or a super-premium buyer who prefers vegetables or thin crust.

While retailers may believe they need to offer frozen pizzas in every price tier to reach all consumers, a store in Beverly Hills may purposely abdicate economy-minded consumers just as a store in Newark might not assort for super-premium shoppers. They know their risk of losing these customers, but must prioritize by focusing on meeting the needs of their target shoppers.

Other influencers in the frozen pizza category are the shopping occasion (is the pie for personal eating or a Super Bowl party?), multiple users within a household (adults may want the premium brand for themselves, but a less costly alternative for after-school snacks for their children's friends), and diet (a group of consumers who might only buy vegetarian choices). Preference Segmentation defines small consumer groups that may not reflect the overall purchasing pattern for the category, but still represent valuable opportunities within the overall Market Structure.

The category of meal helpers provides another interesting illustration. Manufacturers used to believe that flavor was the key purchase driver for the category because people said that in focus groups. However, when consumer behavior was analyzed, it became clear that people buy the same protein over and over again—whether it is hamburger, chicken, or tuna—so these earlier efforts were misguided. Armed with new knowledge, suppliers focused their product development efforts on new protein sources such as pork, and secondarily on flavors. Some retailers started grouping products in the category by protein type instead of by brand, which had been more common.

Shoppers Come with Changing Missions

A cursory look at shopper behavior indicates that each time a shopper revisits a category over the course of a month, he or she might be on a different purchase occasion and behave differently. Does she need fruit-flavored yogurts in squeeze tubes for her children's snacks, or a plain container for an elderly parent who likes to mix in her own fruits? Are the candles for Christmas, Hannukah, Kwanzaa, aromatherapy, or a niece's birthday party? Is the shampoo for her colored hair or his thinning hair?

Perhaps she is pantry-loading items her family will eventually use, such as detergents and paper goods. Or filling in staples such as milk or bread between major store visits. Does she urgently need an over-the-counter remedy for an ill child? Or is she preparing for a party, making a rare purchase of expensive imported cheese? The variety of purchase occasions can be astounding.

However, when a household's behavior is monitored over enough time, patterns do emerge and those patterns form the crux of a category definition. The definition needs to be precise to be effective and encompass all the product forms, flavors, and brands to meet shoppers' needs on a variety of occasions. A category definition may last as long as a year because with so many categories under a roof, retailers can't typically revisit any one too often.

Market changes can occasionally prompt a retailer to consider redefining a category before its next scheduled category review. The surge of interest in the Atkins diet created the need to make room for everything from low-carb bread to beer. Yet, the interest has since subsided, requiring yet another refinement to many category definitions. Ready-to-eat cereal makers responded to consumers' health concerns by reducing sugar in children's cereals and adding function to adult cereals through new oat, bran, and antioxidant formulas. They also extended their category with portable cereal bars, prompting some retailers to group cereals and bars in a new "cereal solutions" category.

On the other hand, a newly launched eight-hour pain relief product by itself may be worth including in a retail assortment, but isn't a reason to redefine the analgesics category when consumers already have other similar choices.

While category definers years ago were traits such as main and secondary brands, premium and value products, large and small sizes, common and specialty flavors, today's newer, more effective definers are both behavioral and attitudinal. For example, purchasers of organic cereal packaged in boxes made from recycled paper are not just committed to eating a nutritious breakfast, but to taking care of the planet as well.

Learn what truly matters to consumers, and how they navigate a category. Are they Pepsi drinkers or cola drinkers who find alternate brands acceptable? Are they most "loyal" to a brand, a flavor or scent, a package size, a perceived nutritional benefit, or a value price? In this case, loyalty equates to the percentage of purchases going toward a specific attribute. For example, of 10 category purchases, if a household bought five of the small size and two of one particular brand, the household would be deemed to be more loyal to package size (50 percent loyalty) than brand (20 percent loyalty). Size would be higher on the market structure than brand.

By knowing these customer priorities, retailers could include them in their category definitions. A category manager could cull with insights and create room for potentially more exciting and lucrative new products. Should a retailer bring in new flavors if such variety doesn't mean as much to customers as other traits? Probably not.

The goal of using Market Structure and Preference Segmentation is simply to keep category definitions current with consumer demands. Their use is an essential first step in the journey to success with category management.

Manufacturers often bring retailers more detailed research about their category and brands, drilling down on these data streams to distinguish behaviors in all kinds of households—with or without children, in certain markets or regions, or even in different types of stores. Data differentiate consumers who shop a category, and empower retailers to define categories around their preferences. Data gives a full market view, so category managers can more accurately define categories for their stores.

A major canned food manufacturer provided an example of how manufacturers can effectively bring key consumer insights to retailers, on terms that retailers will embrace. The company identified 11 different consumer segments that buy its brand but differ in their preferences for flavor, form, use of deals, store type, and other factors. While the company's analysis hones in on specific opportunities, it realizes that some suit the strategies of certain retailers and others do not. For example, consumers who spend four times as much on the category as the typical category purchaser, and who spend three-quarters of their category dollars on the manufacturer's brand, are vital to both the retailer and the manufacturer. The research precisely discloses the flavors they buy, mostly at full price, so a retailer can assort appropriately and avoid giving away margin dollars needlessly.

However, deals sway brand switchers who buy the manufacturer's brand and its main competitor's brand equal amounts of the time. They buy the category on promotion 80 percent of the time, and their overall category consumption is far less than that of the other group.

Rather than overwhelm retailers with an array of choices, the company is selective and tailors presentations that mesh with a customer's go-to-market strategy. Is the retailer upscale or middle of the road, urban or rural, variety or value driven? Geographically, where is it strong, where is it weak? Which consumer segments might be interested in a specific proposition? Most important, which segments offer the category the best opportunity for growth?

This approach dovetails with the prevailing retailer trend to do more category planning at the individual store level to reflect the people who shop there and the category features they want. The goals are (1) a better shopping experience for consumers, (2) a higher return for the retailer, and (3) a preparedness and readiness to change as the market might require.

Retailers aren't likely to share all their insights, even with their category captains, but they're likelier to partner more closely with suppliers who understand their strategies and shape their consumer-based presentations accordingly. It makes the process more efficient and effective, and strengthens the platform for mutual growth. The key is telling the right story at the shelf for specific customers in specific markets.

When marketing and category management teams from both retailers and manufacturer category captains act cohesively, they're more likely to define categories as consumers want them to be. To create cohesion, both sides must be involved in planning so participants buy in to concepts early and agree at the end.

In this first step in the category business plan, retailers often rely on their manufacturer partners within a category to provide costly research and recommendations. However, these external recommendations need to be reconciled with sometimes conflicting views of how the retailer views its categories. The two sides recognize there's been an inherent tension between them. Retailers emphasize category growth, while manufacturers spend on valuable consumer research that faces retailer skepticism if it shows overt bias toward their brands. Ultimately, it falls to the retailer to decide how its categories will be structured using its best understanding of how consumers shop the categories.

Variations on a Theme

The premium approach to Market Structure and Preference Segmentation research tracks consumer behavior and attitudes simultaneously. Rather than layer separate attitudinal insights onto behavioral research, both sets of consumer insights are captured at once. However, most don't take the process that far.

At the other end of the resource spectrum, an operator's small size or limited budget shouldn't impede its ability to define categories appropriately. While it's likely that manufacturers aren't giving the operator much attention or bringing in third-party data, that doesn't mean single-store or small regional chain operators can't emulate what larger competitors nearby have created.

Go, look, and learn. This approach worked for Stew Leonard, namesake of his chain, who built a reputation for personalized service by listening firsthand to what customers told him. Any operator can spend an hour in the cookie and candy aisle to speak with patrons and understand how they want their sweets. By brand? By package? By form? By ingredients?

Moreover, visit stores of larger competitors, wander their aisles and watch how people shop categories. Observe closely in order to develop or refine category definitions. What to look for? Do consumers shop the entire store or head for certain aisles? How do the assortments in the competitors' categories differ? Which brands are people buying regardless of whether they're on sale?

Moving On

After defining a category, the next step is assigning it a role within the store that reflects both its importance and particular function. Because the definition stemmed in large part from the way consumers shop the category, the assigned role will be influenced by how the category helps shape the overall store image and strategy.

4

Step Two: Assign a Role to the Category That Best Supports the Retailer's Strategy

OBJECTIVE OF STEP TWO

Assign category role (purpose) based on a cross-category quantitative analysis that considers the consumer, distributor (retailer), supplier, and marketplace.

ANALYTICAL TOOLS USED

Basket Analysis

Frequent Shopper Data

Household Panel Data

Point-of-Sale Data

Occasion Analysis

Fair Share and Demand Gapping

Financial Analysis

BACKGROUND OF STEP TWO

What appears initially to be a simple and direct process, assigning category roles, actually has considerable analysis behind every decision. While many retailers create custom category roles that are tailored to their individual strategies and objectives, the four examples used in this chapter illustrate typical category roles (see Figure 4.1).

The options seem straightforward enough. Yet, ideal assignments only come after retailers consider category roles within their overall market position and strategy, and determine how each category helps them achieve their objectives.

With the right coordination, retailers can leverage the hundreds of categories they carry to maximize their total-store appeals.

Assigning roles delivers two primary benefits:

FIGURE 4.1   Category Roles

DESTINATION
To be the *primary* category provider and help define the retailer as the store of choice by delivering *consistent, superior* target consumer value.

ROUTINE
To be one of the *preferred* category providers and help develop the retailer as the store of choice by delivering *consistent, competitive* target consumer value.

OCCASIONAL/SEASONAL
To be a *major* category provider, help *reinforce* the retailer as the store of choice by delivering *frequent, competitive* target consumer value.

CONVENIENCE
To be a category provider and help *reinforce* the retailer as the full-service store of choice by delivering *good* target consumer value.

Source: The Partnering Group, Inc.

1. Greater consumer value by managing categories according to their importance to consumers
2. Maximal return on invested resources by retailers and suppliers through the efficient, intentional allocation of shelf space, marketing dollars, and manager time

There are a variety of analytical tools retailers may use, along with input from category suppliers, to precisely assign roles and revise them as competitive landscapes or retailer objectives change. They include:

- *Basket analysis:* What do people buy during the same shopping trip? How do you build bigger baskets through stronger cross-category connections?

- *Frequent shopper data:* What do your most productive customers prefer? Which categories matter most to them?

- *Consumer panel data, including penetration, purchase frequency, conversion, and more:* What percent of shoppers who buy wipes do you attract? What percent of a retailer's shoppers buy them elsewhere and how much do they spend with other retailers? How can you draw more of them, and grow their category transactions?

- *Point-of-sale data, including category size and sales trends:* How do national sales compare to local market sales? Is the category growing or declining? Are price increases driving category growth or are consumers truly buying more or less of the products in a given category?

- *Occasion analysis, to determine a category's contribution to holidays and other events:* Are your customers scratch bakers requiring flour and chocolate chips, or harried moms who simply want cookie mixes and decorating products, or both?

- *Fair share and demand gapping:* The difference between what sells and what you could sell. How many core consumers who like strawberry ice cream are in a trading area, how much do they consume, and how much should you be selling? Or how many party trips do soccer moms make in a trading area, and what percentage should you be capturing?

- *Financial analysis, such as sales, turns (the number of times a category's inventory rotates during the year); margin dollars (gross profit, or the difference between selling price and cost of goods sold); customer conversion (of people who buy products in the category anywhere, how many buy them in your store, and how much can you increase that); and activity-based costing (the full expense of carrying and selling a product, including costs of every kind such as shipping, warehousing, handling, marketing, and more), so a retailer's investments in a category reflect its role:* Manage from bottom-up to be realistic. If suppliers are managing, say, a 10 percent supermarket channel decline in diaper sales as volume migrates to mass, a food store can't realistically dictate a 5 percent annual category sales gain, so diapers may not be a realistic destination category by itself. If, however, the focus is on a baby department containing baby food, toys, and other products, and the retailer holds baby events during the year to differentiate the retailer, then diapers would play an important role in the greater destination baby category. In another example, if a chain objective is to increase share-of-wallet from 16 percent to 20 percent, that directly ties to specific consumer behaviors to be changed and, hence, different category roles.

This list of analytical components provides strong evidence that role assignment today is an increasingly consumer-based, analytic proposition, and a far cry from internal gut assumptions that once prevailed. To know the right role today is to first know your overall strategy as well as your customers and their purchase tendencies within categories. To bring to life store strategies that appeal to these customers, retailers carefully designate category roles, each with its own purpose in supporting the retailer's overall strategy and objectives.

A 360-Degree View Delivers Results

Four key questions provide the right perspective for assigning roles and managing categories:

1. How important is the category to the consumer? Look at household penetration, purchase frequency, annual spending, and degree of loyalty.
2. How important is the category to the retailer? The retailer's distinct approach will differentiate the category. How does it reinforce the retailer's identity and strategy? Look at its volume rank within store or department, growth trend, and seasonality.
3. How important is the category to the retailer's competitors? Look at its volume rank and trend within competing stores.
4. What is the category's outlook in the marketplace? Look at overall growth, new targeted opportunities, and impact of factors such as new brands, benefits, or packaging.

Answers will yield a complete picture for roles and their appropriate resources. It is powerful to learn that what you thought of as a destination category is really only routine to consumers, and so space, inventory, and advertising can be cut. That frees resources to develop alternate categories as destinations.

A classic approach might indicate cereal as a destination category because it has high penetration, high purchase frequency, and high volume.

However, by asking a tougher rhetorical question, a retailer can impose higher standards: What am I doing to differentiate my cereal aisle and make it a destination? If nothing much, perhaps it's routine.

By contrast, if a retailer merchandises a breakfast alcove with many related products, it has likely developed a meaningful meal solution section for hurried customers, and cereal, as the anchor of that effort, deserves the destination role.

Certain categories such as candy are able to fulfill multiple roles that coexist throughout the year at different locations—in line, check stand, or seasonal displays.

Others such as cough-cold-flu or sunscreens could vacillate between a convenience role in most months and a destination role during their peak sales seasons.

The Art and Science of Role Assignment

Experienced category managers typically have a good feel for their categories and a sense about what roles should be assigned for what categories. However, their experience and judgment need to be combined with an objective analysis of available data. A few examples will help clarify the process of role assignment. In each case, the classic characteristics of the role are summarized after the example.

In a destination role, a retailer strives to be the *primary* store of choice by delivering *consistent, superior* consumer value. Value takes many forms—not just low price—so retailers can enhance destination categories with the right blend of convenience, package forms, innovation, and other aspects as well. To be a destination category means that the category is central to the store's image and should link retailers and manufacturers in strategic partnerships.

As depicted in Table 4.1, Retailer A's comparison of the carbonated beverages and bottled water categories, for example, shows that carbonated beverages generate higher purchase frequency (11.2 trips per year) and dollar volume per purchasing household ($60.15) than bottled water.

Buyer conversion (of carbonated beverage buyers who shop in the store, what percentage buy the category in the store) for several types of carbonated beverages are not as high as the retailer would like, particularly when compared with the buyer conversion rates of some of its competitors (Table 4.2). However, a point in favor of a destination category assignment is that a dollar volume index analysis shows that carbonated beverage buyers are a good match with Retailer A's shopper base.

TABLE 4.1   Cross Category Comparison

	Item Trips Per Item Buyer	Item $ Per Item Buyer
Retailer A		
Carbonated Beverages	11.2	60.15
Bottled Water	4.8	14.63

Source: ACNielsen Homescan Consumer Facts.

TABLE 4.2 Buyer Conversion Comparison

	Carbonated Beverages	Cola Regular	Cola Diet	Lemon/Lime Regular	Lemon/Lime Diet	All Rem. Carb. Beverages Regular	All Rem. Carb. Beverages Diet
Retailer A	83	68	61	54	56	64	60
Retailer B	88	71	66	60	57	70	66
Retailer C	85	70	64	58	58	72	64

Source: ACNielsen Homescan Account Shopper Profiler.

A dollar volume index compares the size of a demographic group in the population with the size of that demographic group in another population group such as, in this case, people who shop in a certain retailer or buy a certain category. An index of 100 would indicate that there is an exact match. For example, if 20 percent of the U.S. population consisted of households that earn between $35,000 and $49,999 per year and 20 percent of all households in the United States buy carbonated beverages, the carbonated beverages dollar volume index for such households would be 100. Groups that index at 120 or above are considered to buy a disproportionate amount of the category in question.

In this example, one set of index numbers was created that compares the U.S. population to the population of shoppers at Retailer A. Another was created that compares the U.S. population to the population of buyers of carbonated beverages. Comparing the two sets of numbers indicates that buyers of carbonated beverages are fairly similar to Retailer A shoppers (Table 4.3).

Remember, role assignments are designed to be goal-based, not necessarily reflective of the current reality. Therefore, this retailer decides that carbonated soft drinks are a destination category.

Destination categories serve as the retailer's most compelling connection to the consumer, and so establish store standards for shopper satisfaction, sales, market share, service levels, and cost management.

TABLE 4.3 Demographic Comparison between Retailer Shoppers and Category Buyers

Demographic Segment	Retailer A	Carbonated Beverages
Household size - 1 member	53	70
Household size - 2 member	110	105
Household size - 3-4 member	129	120
Household size - 5+ member	104	124
Age/Presence of kids - no kids under 18	91	96
Age/Presence of kids - any kids under 18	117	109
Age/Presence of kids - any kids under 6	119	92
Age/Presence of kids - any kids 6-12	133	125
Age/Presence of kids - any kids 13-17	92	120
Household Income < $20,000	52	93
Household Income - $20,000-29,999	63	92
Household Income - $30,000-39,999	83	80
Household Income - $40,000-49,999	80	112
Household Income - $50,000-69,999	152	130
Household Income - $70,000+	139	111

Source: ACNielsen Homescan Account Shopper Profiler and Consumer Facts.

- Classic characteristics: Large dollar sales, high household penetration, high purchase frequency, differentiated from competitors.

In a routine role, a retailer acts as a *preferred* provider on a path to becoming the store of choice by delivering *consistent, competitive* consumer value. Sticking with the same example, bottled water shows lower purchase frequency and dollar volume per purchasing household. The retailer decides to make the category routine and, as a result, decreases the shelf space it devotes to the category in order to add more variety to its assortment of carbonated soft drinks.

- *Classic characteristics:* Large dollar sales, high household penetration, high purchase frequency—however, there will likely be related categories with higher scores for each of these measures.

In an occasional/seasonal role, a retailer acts as a *major* category provider by delivering *frequent, competitive* consumer value. A review of purchasing patterns throughout the year within several condiment and sauce categories shows that spaghetti/marinara sauce and barbeque sauce are especially seasonal, with spaghetti/marinara sauce selling best in cold weather months and barbeque sauce selling best in warm weather months (see Figure 4.2).

Assigning the seasonal role to this category means the retailer and its manufacturer partners will focus their promotional efforts on the spring and summer barbequing season. However, in regions that enjoy warm weather throughout the year, the category may be a routine or even a destination category.

- *Classic characteristics:* Seasonal or occasional dollar sales, average household penetration, seasonal or occasional purchase frequency.

FIGURE 4.2   Category $ Sales in Millions

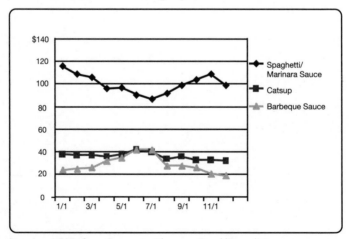

Source: ACNielsen Strategic Planner, Food/Drug/Mass (Excluding Wal-Mart).

In a convenience role, a retailer provides the catego.
consumer value, and reinforces its image as the full-service   ⌐r
choice. The store wants to make sure that it has batteries available,
for example, so that when buying the week's groceries a shopper who
also needs batteries doesn't have to go elsewhere to pick them up.

- *Classic characteristics:* Average dollar sales, average household
  penetration, infrequent purchases within a particular store.

Variations on a Theme

A more detailed category role matrix has been developed by Northwestern University Professor Robert Blattberg, PhD, who identified
six roles—from the high-volume, high-margin Flagship role to the
low-volume, low-margin Rehab role (see Figure 4.3).

Blattberg developed guidelines linking each category role to specific tactics, as outlined in Figures 4.4 through 4.9 on pages 88–93.

FIGURE 4.3   Alternate Category Role Matrix

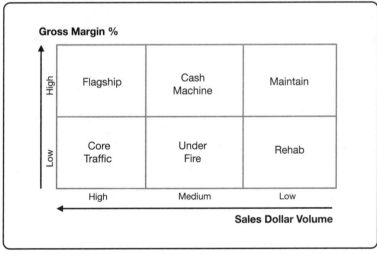

Source: Robert Blattberg, PhD.

FIGURE 4.4   Flagship

Goal	Option 1 Increase sales/ maintain margin	Option 2 Maintain sales/ increase profit
Pricing	• Match competition but do not lead. • Never initiate price decreases. • Maintain margins whenever possible. • Avoid EDLP pricing of items.	• Match competition but do not lead. • Never initiate price decreases. • Lead price increase if possible. • Maintain margins whenever possible. • Avoid EDLP pricing of items.
Promotions	• Match competition if they are aggressively promoting.	• Signal competition not to compete through aggressive promotions. • Avoid promotions that decrease profits.
Assortment	• Create as many subcategories as possible to increase the opportunity for consumers to purchase. • Add club packs as necessary. • Create high quality private label.	• Create as many subcategories as possible to increase the opportunity for consumers to purchase. • Avoid club packs. • Create high quality private label.
Planogram	• Place more profitable items in leading positions. • Allocate space to high volume, high profit items. • Avoid out-of-stocks.	• Place more profitable items in leading positions. • Allocate space to high volume, high profit items. • Avoid out-of-stocks.
Feature Ads	• Match competition. • Select items that increase sales and profits and feature frequently. • Run as A items but not as AA items.	• Avoid aggressive price points. • Select items that increase sales and profits and feature frequently.
Display	• Display as frequently as possible.	• Display as frequently as possible.
Positioning	• Multiply quality levels. • Provide wide variety. • Offer reasonable value.	• Multiply quality levels. • Provide wide variety. • Offer reasonable value.

Source: Robert Blattberg, PhD.

FIGURE 4.5   Cash Machine

Goal	Option 1 Increase sales/ maintain profits	Option 2 Maintain sales/ increase profits
Pricing	• Keep price points competitive. • Avoid using items as EDLP.	• Increase prices on selected items if they appear to be price insensitive. • Avoid using items as EDLP.
Promotions	• Promote profitably to increase sales. • Never run as loss leader. • Use coupon to offer price discount while mitigating loss.	• Promote only to increase profits. • Never run as loss leader.
Assortment	• Increase assortment in growing categories. • Prune less profitable items. • Create high quality private label using high volume items if economic return can be shown.	• Increase assortment in growing categories. • Prune less profitable items. • Create high quality private label using high volume items if economic return can be shown.
Planogram	• Increase space to category. • Place more profitable items in leading positions. • Allocate space disproportionately to high profit items.	• Place more profitable items in leading positions. • Allocate space disproportionately to high profit items.
Feature Ads	• Never run items as loss leaders. • Run items in A ads using coupons to generate interest in the category. • Try to use many items in B ads to increase profitability. • Use category often in ads to generate sales but avoid aggressive price points when advertising.	• Never run items as loss leaders. • Run items in B ads to increase profitability.
Display	• Use "shelf talkers" to emphasize best buys. • Display as frequently as possible to increase consumer interest in category.	• Use "shelf talkers" to emphasize best buys. • Display as frequently as possible to increase consumer interest in category.
Positioning	• Increase consumer trial. • Good assortment. • Priced so the consumer does not have an incentive to change stores. • Good value through promotional pass-through.	• Good assortment. • Priced so the consumer does not have an incentive to change stores. • Good value through promotional pass-through.

Source: Robert Blattberg, PhD.

FIGURE 4.6   Maintain/Grow

Goal	Option 1 Maintain sales and profits	Option 2 Increase sales/ maintain profits
Pricing	• Never use items for EDLP. • Make sure items in category are high margins. • Potentially price above competition.	• Keep price points competitive. • Avoid using items as EDLP.
Promotions	• Promote only as "budget buys" where margin is high on promotion.	• Promote profitably to increase sales. • Never run as loss leader. • Use coupon to offer price discount while mitigating loss.
Assortment	• Prune less profitable items in the line. • Reduce assortment by avoiding redundant items. • Avoid adding items to the category unless they will increase category volume or profits.	• Increase assortment in growing categories. • Prune less profitable items. • Create high quality private label using high volume items if economic return can be shown.
Planogram	• Place high margin items in prominent position. • Allocate space disproportionately to high profit items.	• Increase space to category. • Place more profitable items in leading positions. • Allocate space disproportionately to high profit items.
Feature Ads	• Run items as only B items.	• Never run items as loss leaders. • Run items as A items using coupons to generate interest in the category. • Try to use many items as B items to increase profitability. • Use category as often as possible in ads to generate sales but avoid aggressive price points when advertising.
Display	• Rarely display category. • Identify best buys with "shelf talkers."	• Identify best buys with "shelf talkers." • Display as frequently as possible to increase consumer interest in category.
Positioning	• Medium assortment. • Available when needed. • Good value through promotional pass-through.	• Increase consumer trial. • Good assortment. • Priced so consumer does not have an incentive to change stores. • Good value through promotional pass-through.

Source: Robert Blattberg, PhD.

FIGURE 4.7 Core Traffic

Goal	Option 1 Decrease sales/ increase profit	Option 2 Maintain sales/ maintain profit
Pricing	• Reduce number of EDLP items. • Reduce margins at shelf price to increase volume sold off deal.	• Use EDLP pricing for key items. • Reduce margins at shelf price to increase volume sold off deal.
Promotions	• Reduce aggressive promotions of items. • Decrease frequency category is used as loss leader.	• Aggressively promote items, often as loss leader.
Assortment	• Focus on profitable UPCs, often non-branded, and keep a broad assortment of these items. • Decrease the number of national brands in category and eliminate sizes that have relatively low volume. • Create high and low quality private label.	• Focus on profitable UPCs, often non-branded and keep a broad assortment of these items. • Create high and low quality private label.
Planogram	• Place more profitable items in leading positions. • Allocate space disproportionately to private label.	• Place more profitable items in leading positions. • Allocate space disproportionately to private label.
Feature Ads	• Decrease frequency of feature ads. • Use only AA ads when needed for variety. • Use as A items. • Feature items at price points that offer good value and provide profits to the category.	• Match competition. • Use items in AA ads. • Feature when necessary as loss leaders.
Display	• Display as infrequently as possible. • Display with complementary profitable items.	• Display as necessary to maintain volume. • Display with complementary profitable items.
Positioning	• Good price points. • Customer will not change stores to buy these items. • Good private label value.	• Excellent price points. • Worth changing stores to buy these items. • Good private label value.

Source: Robert Blattberg, PhD.

FIGURE 4.8   Under Fire

Goal	Option 1 Decrease sales/ increase profits	Option 2 Maintain sales/ increase profits
Pricing	• Raise price points where possible.	• Use EDLP pricing to increase non-promotional volume. • Match competition where necessary.
Promotions	• Avoid running loss-leader promotions • Decrease promotional frequency.	• Promote aggressively but avoid loss-leaders.
Assortment	• Decrease assortment by avoiding redundancy. • Prune low profit/low volume items. • Create lower quality private label for high volume items if economic return can be shown.	• Try to cannibalize sales of leading items with lower volume, more profitable items. • Prune unprofitable items. • Create lower quality private label for high volume items if economic return can be shown.
Planogram	• Place private label in leading positions. • Disproportionately allocate space to high profit items. • Decrease space to increase category profitability.	• Disproportionately allocate space to high profit items. • Use space location to cannibalize low-profit, leading-volume items.
Feature Ads	• Avoid running loss leaders. • Try to use as B item to increase profitability by only offering partial pass-through of promotions.	• Avoid running loss leaders. • Run as an A item when a coupon is available which increases movement and profits. • Try to use as B item to increase profitability by only offering partial pass-through of promotions.
Display	• Avoid using major displays for low profit items in category. • Use "shelf talkers" to push more profitable items.	• Display more items if they are profitable. • Use "shelf talkers" to emphasize best buys to support volume.
Positioning	• Good value through partial pass-through of deals. • Medium assortment.	• Good value alternatives are available to leading brands. • Highly competitive to other retailers. • Priced so consumers will shop at your banner.

Source: Robert Blattberg, PhD.

FIGURE 4.9   Rehab

Goal	Option 1 **Increase profits while decreasing sales**
Pricing	• Never use items for EDLP. • Raise prices to increase margins.
Promotions	• Promote only as "budget buys" where margin is high on promotion. • Limit promotional pass-through.
Assortment	• Prune less profitable items in the line. • Significantly reduce assortment by avoiding redundant items. • Avoid adding items to the category unless they will increase category volume or profits.
Planogram	• Place high margin items in prominent positions. • Allocate space disproportionately to high profit items. • Decrease space allocated to the category.
Feature Ads	• Do not feature category.
Display	• Do not display category. • Identify best buys with "shelf talkers."
Positioning	• Limited assortment. • Available to customer to offer variety for the retailer.

Source: Robert Blattberg, PhD.

Moving On

After assigning a category role, the next step is category assessment, which identifies growth opportunities—the gap between current performance and what could be—and sets the stage for development of strategies and tactics.

5

Step Three: Assess the Category to Find Opportunities for Improvement

OBJECTIVE OF STEP THREE

Analyze the category as well as its subcategories, brands, and items based on consumer, market, retailer (distributor), and supplier perspectives.

ANALYTICAL TOOLS USED

Point-of-Sale Scan Data

Household Panel Data

Space Management Software Data

Background of Step Three

Category assessment is the scrutiny of a category as well as its subcategories, brands, and items to determine their potential for generating growth. It is an ambitious attempt to leap from what is to what could be, to target and fill opportunity gaps, and to elevate categories to new performance levels.

This step also provides the fundamental base on which trade partners can form a comprehensive set of strategies and tactics (steps five and six). It focuses on the market research and analysis that is most relevant and actionable regardless of the source—from retailers, manufacturers, and third parties such as advertising agencies, brokers, and marketing information providers.

While retailers can effectively assess categories on their own, they typically rely on suppliers' deep insights of who their consumers are and how they buy and relate to their brands and the category, as well as their tracking of the market and category trends. When such valuable information is shared, and common templates are used to guide the joint assessment process, the best results occur.

This step is where the heavy lifting occurs in the category management business process. Data from many sources make it all possible, but also threaten to bog down even the most agile category manager who doesn't focus properly on the right business questions. The *right* questions relate to consumer needs and purchase behavior more than any other aspect.

For example, knowing that competitors carry certain SKUs compared with your assortment is simply descriptive and by itself answers no important opportunity-seeking questions.

However, by determining where else a consumer shops and why, you can begin to understand what is important to that consumer.

You can then quantify the opportunity of changing your assortment, pricing, or other elements. For example, if you get $15 a month of a shopper's yogurt purchases versus $20 that the shopper spends elsewhere, you can then begin to probe further to understand why. In other stores, the shopper may be purchasing newer product forms such as drinkable yogurt that has too little presence on your shelves. But this is just one possible reason. You need to understand why the shopper goes to the other stores, whatever the reason. This is the consumer perspective.

Four Perspectives

The consumer perspective is one of four prisms through which category managers must assess their categories. The other three are the market, the retailer (distributor), and the supplier perspectives. Together they provide a comprehensive set of insights that are invaluable in guiding marketing strategies and tactics:

1. Consumer information yields insight into who shops the category, and how, where, and why they shop it.
2. Market information enables a retailer to benchmark itself against a total market and its competitors within the market.
3. Retailer information details category pricing and profitability, item movement, and shelf placement.
4. Supplier information allows retailers to assess their vendors' past logistical, marketing, and promotional performance as well as future support of their brands to the public and to the retailer. Understanding the extent to which a brand (including private label as a brand) will be supported helps retailers forecast sales for the year to ensure category objectives are met (see Figure 5.1).

FIGURE 5.1   Category Assessment from Four Perspectives

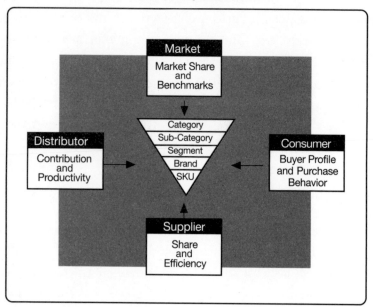

Source: The Partnering Group, Inc.

These four perspectives require equal attention because any one of them could uncover important opportunities or expose areas that need to improve.

The Search for Actionable Insights

The four-perspective analysis is best guided by a few simple parameters: Which questions to answer, in how much detail, and who is responsible for finding the information. The more precise the data, the more accurate the target goals, the stronger the category plan is likely to be and the more it is likely to resonate with shoppers. For example, knowing that 40 percent of households in certain communities follow dietary laws for Kosher foods could affect the roles, strategies, and tactics for many center-store categories and perimeter areas of meat, dairy, deli, and bakery. By understanding consumer behavior through data, a retailer could leverage opportunities to differentiate itself and turn many of these categories into destination categories through assortments, merchandising, pricing, and promotions that resonate with such households. By knowing the track record of suppliers, retailers could select their strongest trade partners.

It makes sense to base decisions on objective facts rather than assumptions or casual observations. Retailers should engage in purposeful rather than random searches for information, while keeping in mind that data can't always answer every question to a point of absolute certainty.

Again, analysis is best done as a collaborative effort between retailers and suppliers, with the output typically in the form of completed worksheets or templates. The perspectives, experience, and analytical skills of the parties involved help to fully connect the dots. Retailers follow their own set of "standard" templates that guide their assessments for each category, and these templates vary from operator to operator.

Retailers, however, still need to filter the suppliers' desire to promote or protect their own brands at the expense of the total category's management. Third-party software, such as Category Business Planner (CBP) from ACNielsen, can help reconcile any differences in category definitions before they become issues between manufacturers and retailers. The CBP tool enables manufacturers to view category data according to each retailer's unique definition of each category, allowing both sides to speak the same language. Does cereal include breakfast bars? Does yogurt include drinks? A manufacturer can click from retailer to retailer and see its category in each retailer's view.

Consumer Assessment

Greatest weight is given to the consumer assessment, which profiles category buyers and their purchase behavior. Household panel data is a key resource in answering such questions as:

- What percentage of households buys the category?
- How frequently do they make purchases in the category?
- How much do they spend per occasion and annually?
- Who buys the category? What is the demographic profile, lifestyle, or life stage? Where do buyers live?
- Where do consumers buy the category? What channels and what retailers?
- What drives the purchase? Promotion, impulse?
- When do they purchase? Day of week, time of day, time of year, purchase occasion?
- Are category purchases typically planned or impulse?
- Which categories are related? What else is in the buyer's basket?
- How loyal are shoppers to specific retailers' categories and brands?

It's crucial to not only answer these questions as they relate to shopper behavior in your store, but also in the stores of your competitors or the marketplace as a whole. That way, you have benchmarks that enable you to better evaluate your performance.

It's usually easiest to start broad and then drill down. For example, some of the basic metrics for understanding the category from a consumer perspective include item penetration (the percentage of households that purchase the category in a year), item dollars per item buyer (How much does each category-buying household spend on the category per year?), item trips per item buyer (average annual times that a category-buying household makes purchases in the category), item dollars per item trip (how much category-buying households spend on the category per purchase occasion), and the percentage of item dollars on deal (Of all the dollars spent on the category, what percentage involved some type of discount?).

You can see from Table 5.1 that within the "Shortening, Oil" category, salad and cooking oils are purchased by the highest percentage of households (67 percent), olive oil generates the highest annual spending ($12.46), lard is purchased least frequently (1.7 times per year) and generates the lowest dollar amount per purchase occasion ($2.03), and olive oil is the subcategory in which the highest percentage of dollars spent on the segment are via some type of promotion (25 percent). Such metrics could be used by a retailer to

TABLE 5.1   Basic Purchasing Metrics

	Item Penetration	Item $ Per Item Buyer	Item Trips Per Item Buyer	Item $ Per Item Trip	% Item $ On Deal
SHORTENING, OIL	**86.2**	**17.66**	**4.8**	**3.70**	**23.5**
COOKING SPRAYS	48.7	6.03	2.3	2.59	24.1
LARD	1.6	3.51	1.7	2.03	3.3
OLIVE OIL	35.8	12.46	2.0	6.18	25.0
SALAD AND COOKING OIL	67.0	9.72	3.1	3.13	24.8
SHORTENING	23.6	5.38	1.9	2.91	11.2

Source: ACNielsen Homescan Consumer Facts.

set objectives for the category. They could also become the bench-marks against which a retailer's performance is measured.

Basic first-cut demographics provide an average view of a consumer base, serving as a launching point for deeper understanding. For example, Table 5.2 indicates that, on a national basis, lard has a strong skew toward Hispanic households, with 13 percent of the dollars spent on the category coming from this segment. The dollar volume index of 364 indicates that a far greater percentage of spending on the category comes from Hispanic households than would be expected given their size in the population.

However, people with the same demographics might shop very differently and respond to different appeals. Furthermore, people within a demographic may be quite diverse in taste, ability to buy, or cultural influence resulting in very different shopping habits.

More sophisticated demographic data illustrate consumer diversity and help to segment customers and refine neighborhood marketing approaches. For example, it is easy to understand that marketing to Hispanics in Los Angeles, where emigrants from Mexico and Central America tend to live, and New York and Florida,

TABLE 5.2   Household Purchasing by Ethnicity

	Caucasian		African Amer.		Asian		Hispanic	
	$ Vol Index	% $ Vol	$ Vol Index	% $ Vol	$ Vol Index	% $ Vol	$ Vol Index	% $ Vol
SHORTENING, OIL	94	77	125	15	111	1	125	10
COOKING SPRAYS	105	79	85	8	54	3	83	14
LARD	84	73	55	15	23	2	364	13
OLIVE OIL	100	66	72	6	153	0	144	36
SALAD AND COOKING OIL	83	81	184	11	125	1	137	8
SHORTENING	103	83	96	12	30	1	81	6

Source: ACNielsen Homescan Consumer Facts.

where emigrants from Cuba and Puerto Rico tend to live, must differ because consumers have varying food preferences from their homelands. But there is quite a bit of diversity within the Hispanic population in a given market as well.

For example, Table 5.3 shows household penetration for the Shortening, Oil category in Los Angeles for the total market and then segmented by non-Hispanic households versus Hispanic households, and further segmented by the language preference of Hispanic households—language preference serving as a proxy for acculturation. Although less than 1 percent of non-Hispanic households purchase lard, 9 percent of Hispanic households do so. Looking further, it is clear that households where Spanish is the preferred or only language spoken are the appropriate target for manufacturers of lard and the retailers that sell the product.

Also, knowing where a consumer shops doesn't necessarily mean he or she spend a lot in that channel or retailer. As Table 5.4 shows, nearly 25 percent of category buyers make category purchases in supercenters ("supers") at least once per year, but just 13 percent of category dollars go to that channel.

TABLE 5.3   Household Purchasing by Language Preference Segment

	Total LA	Non Hispanic	Total Hispanic	Hispanic— Spanish Only/Pref	Hispanic— Bilingual	Hispanic— English Only/Pref
SHORTENING, OIL	79.8	76.9	86.0	88.2	83.0	83.4
COOKING SPRAYS	30.2	37.6	14.3	7.3	20.2	34.2
LARD	3.3	0.7	9.0	11.8	5.8	3.4
OLIVE OIL	29.6	32.7	22.8	20.1	27.6	23.8
SALAD AND COOKING OIL	61.2	54.1	76.4	81.4	68.6	71.7
SHORTENING	11.4	14.6	4.7	3.4	2.9	15.1

Source: ACNielsen Homescan LA Hispanic Panel.

TABLE 5.4   Retail Channel Share

SHORTENING, OIL	$2MM+ Grocery	Convenience/ Gas	Drug	Mass Merch Without Supers	Super-centers	Warehouse Club	Dollar Stores	All Other Channels
% Buyers	84.6	0.4	1.3	7.3	24.7	13.0	5.5	7.7
% Dollars	65.3	0.1	0.4	2.1	13.3	11.8	1.0	6.0

Source: ACNielsen Homescan Consumer Facts.

With deeper digging, a chain can identify which consumers are the best target for specific categories, subcategories, brands, and items—especially when also factoring in which consumers a retailer is trying to attract and serve.

Market Assessment

A market assessment evaluates a retailer's share of category, subcategory, brand, and item sales compared with the overall market where it competes and with specific competitors. Third-party data from marketing information providers answers questions such as:

- What are the sales trends of the category, subcategories, and brands in the marketplace?
- What is the retailer's market share?
- What are the specific opportunities for improvement at each category tier?

—How does pricing compare with the competition?

—How does shelf presentation compare?

—How does assortment compare?

—How does promotion activity compare?

FIGURE 5.2 **Category Opportunity Quadrant**

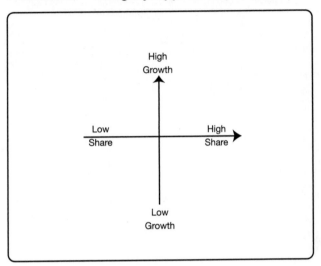

One way to identify opportunities is to use an Opportunity Quadrant (Figure 5.2), plotting where products fit based on an analysis of various factors such as the percentage growth of a category in the marketplace (vertical axis) and the retailer's share of category sales in the marketplace (horizontal axis). Figure 5.3 provides guidance for categories based on which quadrant the category is in. In separate comparisons, you could plot gross margin versus sales and gross margin versus turns.

Retailer Assessment

This is where the category manager takes an inward look at how well the category performs in its stores and how that category contributes to total margins, store image, and brand equity. Point-of-sale data and space management software data are primary resources used to answer these questions:

FIGURE 5.3   Recommended Action Steps

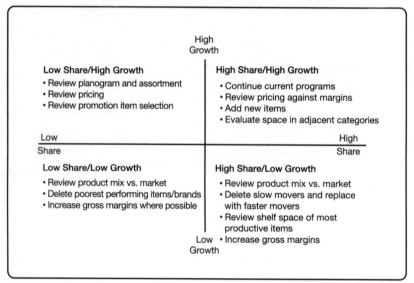

Source: ACNielsen.

- What are the overall sales and profit trends?
- How productive is the current assortment?
- How productive is the current shelf set/space allocation?
- What was the impact of any changes that were made to the shelf set?
- How productive is current pricing? Does it support the overall store approach of high-low, EDLP (everyday low price) or hybrid?
- How effective are current promotions for the category, including displays, features, and temporary price reductions?
- What are the inventory turns and days of supply?
- What are the profit margins, velocity, and inventory levels?
- What is the gross margin return on investment (GMROI) or return on assets (ROA)?

TABLE 5.5   Beer Category Merchandising Report

UPC	Lineal Space % Share	Dollar % Share
6177895643	2.8%	4.3%
7266654890	2.6%	3.7%
4455654778	5.3%	6.1%
6676778954	5.1%	3.5%
2215447869	5.3%	3.0%
9990076781	1.8%	0.7%

Source: ACNielsen Spaceman.

Other measures relevant to this analysis include: product acquisi-tion costs and trends, operating expenses allocated to the category, and service levels/fill rates on orders from suppliers.

Among the many reports a category manager would rely on are those generated by space management software programs that pro-vide analysis of space efficiency. For example, the analysis in Table 5.5 shows that the first three beer items are generating a greater per-centage of category sales than they are taking up space, whereas the bottom three are generating less revenue than one would hope based on their space allocation. A category manager may decide to reduce the space allocated to such items.

Supplier Assessment

During the supplier assessment, the category manager, in effect, eval-uates the performance of each supplier's products. Third-party data on categories and brands play a role in answering questions such as:

- What are sales trends for specific brands?
- How efficient and profitable are each supplier's brands?

- How quick and supportive is each supplier's flow of goods, information, and money (promotions and marketing development funds)?
- What product supply programs do suppliers offer, and does our chain take advantage of them?
- How powerful is each supplier's brand development in the market and relatively at our chain?
- Will suppliers launch any new products next year? Will they impose price changes? Will promotions and marketing support change?
- As a result, where are the greatest opportunities in merchandising, distribution, and promotion?

This view reflects how well individual suppliers support the retailer with demand-building excitement at the shelf and solid business processes. The product mix matters, and a category manager must understand that the forms, flavors, and sizes offered by manufacturers contribute to category profit and image and trigger purchases. The media and marketing messages of brands, including promotions, also affect performance and should be part of this assessment.

Assess Private Label the Same as Other Brands

When assessing the contribution of brands in a category, retailers need to measure private label in the same way. How does private label, as a retailer's own exclusive brand, add to its store's image with upscale packaging in an upscale category, or widen the category user base by meeting the needs of different customers, or generating higher profits per item?

Variations on a Theme: Lower-Cost Ways to Assess

Many small- and medium-size retailers who get less attention from manufacturers still seek access to third-party data to enrich their market and consumer views, and augment their own scan data, when assessing categories for growth opportunities. They're frequently turning to their wholesalers as sources for this information, and the wholesalers in turn are working with them to make their pricing, promotions, and assortments more competitive.

Others who can afford to buy the third-party data themselves are doing so in order to compete with larger retailers. When they pay for the data themselves, the smartest operators are also discoursing with third-party suppliers to outline the actions they took as a result of having the data, the results derived, and the return on investment.

Still other small- to medium-size retailers on tight budgets may rely on shopper exit interviews to glean insights. However, these interviews are unlike third-party household panels in two respects: they reflect shopper comments while panels capture actual buyer behavior, and their findings aren't trendable because the same respondents can't be captured months later for the next round of research, whereas panels are consistent.

Moving On

After identifying growth opportunities through category assessment, the next step is developing a scorecard that measures results against target objectives of the category business plan.

Step Four: Set Performance Targets and Measure Progress with a Category Scorecard

OBJECTIVE OF STEP FOUR

Establish target goals for retailer and key suppliers in support of the category business plan.

BACKGROUND OF STEP FOUR

As the name implies, the scorecard is how retail department and category managers and their manufacturer partners keep track of how they are doing. It's where tangible, quantifiable goals are established, against which progress is monitored. It establishes metrics designed to take a category where you want it to go, as established in step two (category role), from where it is, as established in step three (category assessment).

For example, buyer conversion in the carbonated soft drink category may not be what you'd like it to be, but you're committed to making it a destination category. That may be a metric you choose to monitor on your carbonated beverage category scorecard, with the goal of moving buyer conversion from 50 percent to 55 percent by the end of the year.

A scorecard's measures may include entries such as sales, profit, return on investment, market share, turns, gross margin return on investment (GMROI), penetration, purchase size, purchase frequency, conversion, service level, and more. When designed well and put into use, scorecards provide crucial feedback on how categories are performing, highlighting their strengths and weaknesses (Figure 6.1).

Here is a brief definition for each of the measures shown in the sample scorecard:

CONSUMER

Retention level	Shoppers you retain from year to year
Purchase frequency	Number of purchase occasions for that category
Purchase incidence	How often those trips occur relative to the 12-month period
Satisfaction rating	Qualitative measure based on a survey such as an exit interview

SHARE

Category of department	Internal view of the category's relative importance to the department

FIGURE 6.1   Sample Retailer Scorecard

	Current	Target
Consumer		
Retention Level	_____	_____
Purchase Frequency	_____	_____
Purchase Incidence	_____	_____
Satisfaction Rating	_____	_____
Share		
Category of Dept.	_____	_____
Category of Market	_____	_____
Sales		
Category $	_____	_____
Growth	_____	_____
Sales/Sq. Ft./Week	_____	_____
Profit		
Gross Profit $	_____	_____
Gross Margin	_____	_____
Gross Profit Sq. Ft./Week	_____	_____
Private Label		
Sales	_____	_____
% of Gross Profit	_____	_____
Gross Margin	_____	_____
Product Supply		
Days of Supply	_____	_____
Inventory $	_____	_____
Turns	_____	_____
GMROI	_____	_____
Service Level	_____	_____

Source: The Partnering Group, Inc.

Category of market	External view of the category's performance versus the market

SALES

Category $	Revenue the category generates for a stated time period
GROWTH	Percentage gain or loss year to year
Sales/square foot/week	A more precise measure of space productivity

PROFIT

Gross profit $	Absolute figure for a stated time period
Gross margin	Percentage difference between selling price and cost of goods sold
Gross profit $/square foot	A more precise measure of space productivity week

PRIVATE LABEL

Sales	Revenue for a specified line within a category over a stated time period
Percent of gross profit	Contribution to category profitability (should be a larger percentage than the sales contribution)
Gross margin	An absolute percentage figure

PRODUCT SUPPLY

Days of supply	Inventory on hand in both stores and distribution centers
Inventory $	Dollar value of what is on hand
Turns	Number of times a year merchandise rotates

GMROI	A way of measuring gross margin productivity versus your inventory investment. To compute, divide gross margin by the dollar value of average inventory at cost. A relative productivity measure.
SERVICE LEVEL	In-stock rate. The more substitutable items are in a category—say, soft drinks or toothpaste—the lower the service level that's acceptable. Some categories are too expensive to keep at a near 100 percent level, such as big screen televisions.

Retailers scrutinize such measures to gauge their advances and declines. Since no standard set of industry measures exists, retailers frequently examine other metrics as well, such as shopper penetration (the percent of households in a trading area that shop in your store) or basket size and composition.

One Size Does Not Fit All

A retailer may use the same metrics on every scorecard, or it may vary its scorecards by category due to today's focus on gathering less (but more pertinent) information overall and the fact that different categories are tasked with very different roles, which may require a different set of metrics.

Even when the metrics are the same, the goals may be different, again, usually because of differing category roles. A destination category may carry more lofty goals for sales growth and service levels although a convenience category may emphasize net profit (see Figure 6.2).

FIGURE 6.2   Different Roles Call for Different Goals

Category Scorecard	Destination Category		Convenience Category	
	Target	% Change	Target	% Change
Market Share ($)	32%	7	20%	2
Market Share (Units)	32%	7	21%	3
Sales ($)	$79 mil	10	$24 mil	5
Gross Margin (%)	11%	1	37%	7
Operating Exp. (% of Sales)	15%	(8)	27%	(1)
Net Profit ($)	$2.4 mil	5	$1.61 mil	13
Service Level	95%	6	81%	2
Inventory (Days Supply)	11	4	61	3
Inventory Turns	33	6	6	2
Return on Assets	27.2%	3	29.2%	5

Source: The Partnering Group, Inc.

Some retailers prefer more comprehensive scorecards, wanting a broader perspective and more detailed insights. They may add measures to see beyond their own frequent shopper club and point-of-sale scan data, wanting to monitor their share of wallet (the percentage of a household's total spending on a particular category, for example, the retailer is capturing) and their true stance in the market. Consumer data especially can disclose which items are important to niche shopper groups, even if the category's overall performance does not stand out; such items might be ethnic foods for consumers of certain nationalities or items unique to a particular geography.

As broad scorecards demonstrate, there are times to look beyond the basic numbers and identify category-lifting products that retailers would consider niche but important shopper groups would consider core. Scorecards that go beyond the typical views of sales, margin, and inventory paint a vivid picture of how well the retailer is connecting to consumers and creating a foundation for future growth.

Technology Helps

Technology is a key enabler of the effective use of scorecards. Information tools from marketing information providers enable data to be viewed in a great variety of ways. In a planning meeting with a manufacturer that offers products in many categories, a retailer may wish to start with an evaluation of that company's total performance across all of its categories such as that shown in Figure 6.3.

Then the meeting could proceed to a review of the manufacturer's performance in each of its categories compared to other manufacturers in those same categories.

Effective scorecards are those that encompass all of the elements needed to truly manage categories—including consumer,

FIGURE 6.3   Sample Manufacturer Scorecard

ACNielsen — Manufacturer Overview Scorecard

Refresh | RM | DOLLARS | MARKET | TOTAL CENSUS TRADING AREA | PERIOD | 52 WEEK ENDING 2005-04-16 | DEPT OPP GAP

MARKET: TOTAL CENSUS TRADING AREA
PERIOD: 52 WEEK ENDING 2005-04-16
PRODUCT: PARENT COMPANY = Company X

CLICK HERE for Opportunity Analysis

Parent Company sales are trending 3.7% up versus the year-ago period.

	Dollars	% Chg	Cat % Chg	Market Share RM	Pt Chg	% Increm	Pt Chg	Dollar Opp
PARENT COMPANY	$186,371,252	3.7	4.4	37.1	1.9	36.7	(5.5)	($7,925,232)
SOFT DRINKS	$74,552,106	2.1	6.4	37.4	1.8	57.0	(13.0)	($4,338,264)
SALTED SNACKS	$42,929,082	7.5	2.9	35.0	2.6	15.5	0.3	$284,963
REFRIGERATED JUICE DRINKS	$20,021,002	(5.6)	(2.4)	39.5	0.8	41.8	(9.6)	($2,277,360)
ISOTONIC BEVERAGE	$11,355,922	19.3	18.3	37.7	0.6	20.9	2.1	($753,622)
WATER	$7,229,056	20.3	22.1	53.7	5.2	37.6	(6.1)	($2,486,466)
HOT CEREAL	$7,008,906	10.6	4.0	34.3	3.5	13.7	(0.1)	$188,696
RTE CEREAL	$4,863,219	(2.2)	(3.9)	33.3	0.6	27.8	(0.1)	$284,247
SHELF STABLE JUICES AND DRINKS	$2,595,311	6.7	(0.5)	31.1	(1.7)	16.7	(14.6)	$336,987
MEXICAN SAUCE	$1,654,575	18.3	7.0	36.8	4.1	7.3	0.8	($69,817)
NEW AGE BEVERAGE	$1,259,264	(16.1)	14.0	41.6	0.5	9.6	(4.7)	($190,567)
PANCAKE SYRUP	$880,845	(10.2)	(4.9)	40.8	2.2	23.1	(21.9)	($120,670)
PANCAKE MIX	$704,063	(10.1)	0.2	35.5	(3.7)	9.6	(24.5)	($6,424)
FROZEN JUICE	$208,141	(11.0)	(9.9)	52.0	15.7	1.3	0.4	($62,502)
CRACKERS	$112,191	(54.1)	3.0	17.2	(11.0)	(2.4)	(30.8)	$117,104
NUTS	$94,354	25.4	22.9	22.2	2.3	(3.4)	0.6	$55,469
YOGURT	$67,013	(67.5)	6.8	42.1	(28.6)	(7.0)	(31.9)	($11,198)
PREPARED FOODS	$55,428	N/A	13.3	52.1	N/A	28.2	0.0	($17,959)
COOKIES	$42,672	(17.7)	1.5	23.3	1.4	(4.0)	5.1	$21,873

Source: Category Business Planner (CBP).

FIGURE 6.4   Balanced Scorecard

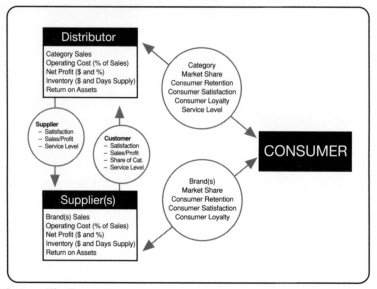

Source: The Partnering Group, Inc.

operational, return-on-marketing investment, competitive, and other metrics. They must also provide important feedback to both retailer and manufacturer, thereby fostering collaboration (see Figure 6.4).

A valuable tool in the hands of any category manager, the scorecard is a critical element in the dynamic process of satisfying consumers and maximizing results. More experienced merchants deduce more relationships between figures and speed the examination and improvement of any weaknesses.

Common Pitfalls

Given the complexity of a comprehensive category management process, it's tempting to skip the scorecard step all together.

However, failing to set measurable targets and check actual results against them could spur dramatic consequences for retailers and their key suppliers. In a too-common compromise, retailers succumb to time pressures of executing the rest of the category management process and entering the next business cycle without devoting ample effort to the scorecard. They often overlook the scorecard's full analytical opportunities when they review their organization's total results but ignore category details.

For example, children's outerwear should yield high gross margin because it is typically imported and private label. If internal reports show, however, that you're earning a much lower gross margin than expected, you could investigate, learn, and correct the causes, which could stem from many factors. Among them: incorrect pricing, or unauthorized markdowns taken at cash registers, as store managers try to sell products that have defects such as broken zippers. A category manager who doesn't tend to the scorecard would never investigate the source of the problem.

For others that do utilize scorecards, many should delve deeper by benchmarking such figures as shopping frequency from year to year, or household penetration within a trading area, or basket size or companion item comparisons, as examples. It can take time to obtain answers that would provide a complete multidimensional picture of the category, but it is time well spent.

Often, retailers live in a short-term world, setting their category-performance objectives as one-dimensionally as beating last year's numbers. To be most effective, budget plans and scorecard targets ought to be set within the context of the current selling environment as new competitors enter your markets and change your performance expectations.

Senior retail managers often express how data should look based on their snapshot observations during store visits—particularly at smaller chains with fewer research resources and a greater reliance on instinct. Scorecard targets are typically more accurate when based on actual performance data and consumer research indicating how a category performs. Scorecards are effective tools for keeping retailer strategies and tactics consistent over time, even in the face of high employee turnover.

The best retail department and category managers along with their manufacturer partners pay attention to details, and use the scorecard to indicate not only a starting point for the next year's goals but corrective actions along the way, updating targets as often as quarterly. These merchants understand the "why behind the buy," and can analyze reasons for a decrease—which competitor is snaring the business, whether they're losing shoppers, or the shoppers are visiting less often or buying less on their trips—to arrive at targeted solutions.

How Often Is Often Enough?

Reviewing the scorecard once a year or quarterly is appropriate, depending on the category. Generally, a category that turns faster and has an influx of new products, such as cosmetics or personal care toiletries, warrants a more frequent scorecard review. If a retailer's goal is to be perceived as first-to-market with new items, for example—say, the latest technologies in men's shaving or the latest toothpaste flavors—a quarterly review may be appropriate.

The scorecard alone won't make a retailer disciplined enough to say no to new products that don't meet customer needs but it should at least influence such thinking. Retailers should trust the data to guide decisions on both established and new items, rather than manipulate data to validate a preexisting belief or predetermined course of action.

By contrast, categories that change less often, such as ladies' coats, require scorecard reviews once or twice a year at the most.

Variations on a Theme: Top Shopper Scorecards

Some retailers are beginning to mine their loyalty club data in order to identify how their "top shoppers"—the small minority that account for a disproportionate amount of a store's sales—buy particular categories, and what items they buy storewide. Scorecards developed around these coveted shoppers have potentially greater value.

By linking frequent shopper program insights to third-party household panel data, chains can tie them back to identifiable demographic segments and extrapolate to a larger proportion of a market's shopper base. This gives a view of how these people shop one's stores versus competitors'. It also gauges share of wallet and more accurately depicts a category's true upside potential.

By applying consumer measures of the scorecard—retention level, satisfaction rating, purchase frequency, and incidence—to their top shoppers, retailers can understand where they are strongest and weakest in cementing loyalties with this most valuable consumer group, and develop strategies and tactics that help these relationships flourish.

Moving On

After committing to objectives for the scorecard, the next step is setting marketing strategies to attain them.

CHAPTER 7

Step Five: Create a Marketing Strategy for the Category

OBJECTIVE OF STEP FIVE

Develop marketing and product supply strategies to achieve the category role and scorecard targets, and plan for the efficient use of resources to fulfill opportunities.

ANALYTICAL TOOLS USED

Point-of-sale scan data

Household panel data

A retailer's internal data

BACKGROUND OF STEP FIVE

This is the step where an overall approach is determined for achieving the desired category role and meeting scorecard targets. We've defined the category, established its desired role, assessed its current state, quantified specific goals, and developed a scorecard. The strategy provides an overarching picture of how to achieve those goals. Done well, this activates sharp, focused marketing directions for individual categories, each with its own role and projected performance targets.

Marketing Strategies

Seven common marketing strategies prevail in retail today. They are:

1. *Traffic building:* Attracting consumers to the store, aisle, and category
2. *Transaction building:* Enlarging the size of the average purchase
3. *Profit generating:* Yielding profits
4. *Cash generating:* Producing cash flow
5. *Excitement creating:* Generating interest and enthusiasm among consumers
6. *Image enhancing:* Strengthening the view of the retailer held by the consumer
7. *Turf defending:* Positioning the category strongly versus competitors

Individually, and to the untrained eye, category strategies may seem randomly selected and uncoordinated—soft drinks build traffic, fresh seafood creates excitement, dog food protects turf. Collectively, however, when planned well, these strategies work in concert to support the retailer's overall strategy.

TABLE 7.1 Matching Category Strategies with Category Purchase Dynamics

Category Strategies	Category Purchase Dynamics
Traffic Building	High Share, Frequently Purchased, High % of Sales
Transaction Building	Higher Ring-up, Impulse Purchase
Profit Contribution	Higher Gross Margin, Higher Turns
Cash Generating	Higher Turns, Frequently Purchased
Excitement Creating	Impulse, Lifestyle-Oriented, Seasonal
Image Creating	Frequently Purchased, Highly Promoted, Impulse, Unique Items, Seasonal
Turf Defending	Used by Retailers to Draw Traditional Customer Base

Source: The Partnering Group, Inc.

While there is clearly an art to the process, hard science is required as well. Some general guidelines for using measurable category purchase dynamics to help in assigning category strategies are shown in Table 7.1.

A Multilevel Approach

Marketing strategies can exist at the category, subcategory, or brand level. Within boys' wear, for example, raising category-level margins may be an overriding goal (profit generating), yet certain brands provide opening price points to drive traffic or help a retailer enhance its low-price image. Soft drinks, on the other hand, are consistently messaged as high-volume/high-value (transaction building), yet the "new age" subcategory may include such an influx of hot new flavors that its most appropriate strategy is to create excitement (see Table 7.2).

TABLE 7.2   Differing Strategies within Categories

Category Roles	Category	Category Strategies				
		Turf Protecting	Traffic Building	Image Enhancing	Transaction Building	Excitement Creating
Destination To be the *primary* category provider and help *define* the retailer as the store of choice by delivering *consistent, superior* target consumer value.	Soft Drinks		Regular and Diet Colas		Specialty Flavors	New Age Beverages
Routine To be one of the *preferred* category providers and help *develop* the retailer as the store of choice by delivering *consistent, competitive* target consumer value.	Pet Care	Dog Food			Pet Supplies	
Occasional/Seasonal To be a *major* category provider, help *reinforce* the retailer as the store of choice by delivering *frequent, competitive* target consumer value.	Hard Surface Cleaners	All-Purpose Cleaners			Tub/Tile and Floor/Wax	
Convenience To be a category provider and help *reinforce* the retailer as the full service store of choice by delivering *excellent* target consumer value.	Shoe and Leather Care				Polishes and Protectant	

Source: The Partnering Group, Inc.

Under the broad category of pain remedies/analgesics, the subcategories of headache and sinus remedies can act as traffic builders, arthritis remedies can act as a profit generator, and children's liquid remedies can serve as transaction builders.

Depending on how actively a retailer would like to or is able to manage its categories, strategies may also change throughout the year, the result of a shift in the consumer base, emergence of a hot new trend, or new competitive pressures.

A retailer can apply category strategies uniformly across all stores, by store cluster, or on a store-by-store basis. Near a beach or bicycle trail where active people go, a store might display plenty of cold single-serve beverages (cash generating); or a store serving an elderly populace might use prune juice to build its image with that consumer segment and laxatives as a profit generator; a store shopped by young families may use kids' flavors and preferred brands as transaction builders.

In sum, retailers who assign category strategies to suit their local shopper base are likelier to market successfully.

Focus First on Consumers

What should never change is the unwavering consumer focus at the center of marketing strategies, since shoppers control where and what they spend. It's all too easy to become overly data focused, allowing the numbers on a spreadsheet to guide strategy development. The most successful retailers stay focused on understanding how shoppers view their stores so they can manage categories to meet consumer needs. It's always more effective to sell people what they want, in ways they want it, as Whole Foods does with healthy prepared meals (traffic building), or Trader Joe's does with exotic yet reasonably priced store brands (excitement creating and profit generating).

Product Supply Strategies

Deftly and cost-effectively moving product onto store shelves is essential to the smooth execution of category business plans, which is why this category strategy step involves both marketing and product supply strategies. Effective product supply strategies reduce costs while doing much to ensure that the products consumers want are in stock.

Common product supply strategies include:

- *Acquisition:* To improve sourcing practices not just to lower acquisition costs but to raise the quality and reliability of goods as well.
- *Inventory management:* To reduce total goods in the supply chain pipeline and their related expenses such as interest and storage costs.
- *Product handling:* To improve receiving and handling practices at warehouses and stores.
- *Order/payment transaction:* To improve order and payment processes.
- *Transportation:* To improve processes related to moving the goods.

Such procurement and distribution strategies can greatly benefit category performance. However, since they're conceived by logistics, operations, and warehouse experts, they need to be infused with sensitivity to marketing needs and coordinated with the rest of the plan.

Validate to Stay Relevant

Before committing to a strategy that merely sounds right, test its validity with hard questions that require specific quantitative and qualitative answers.

First and foremost, how will execution of this strategy benefit consumers? Will they save money, gain convenience, or have access to more variety?

Second, how will it strengthen the retailer? Will it raise sales or margins, or improve appeals to the target customer?

Third, how will suppliers gain? With exposure of more brands, higher share, or more efficient distribution?

Clear Communication Required

Good communication coordinates the process of setting marketing strategies, beginning with category/business reviews that ensure ample resource allocations and scorecard measures that keep efforts on track. Say a mass merchant targets high margins on soft goods and relies on consumables to build customer counts and unit velocity, these need to be not only category goals, but measuring sticks as well. Moreover, chains should base staff incentives on attaining individual category goals, with bonuses when category and overall corporate goals are met.

Good communication extends to business partners, too. Collaboration is critical to successful category strategies because retailers are generalists, and primary suppliers know their categories and consumers best. They especially know how people perceive their brands, and the roles they fill.

Clearly, brands affect every segment of a category. Some are bought more often, or have a higher dollar share, or shorter purchase cycles, or are "on deal" more often. Using the right information from manufacturers, retailers can effectively use different brands to drive different category strategies. For example, a supermarket seeking a high-end image would market upscale coffeehouse brands more aggressively than its own private label, which it would offer as a choice but wouldn't likely promote. The retailer could also create a high-end private label coffee.

Variations on a Theme: Including the Manufacturer Perspective

While this is still more the exception than the rule, strategy development is best done as a collaborative effort between retailers and manufacturers. Manufacturers can help themselves gain a seat at the planning table by being prepared for their category to fill any role for a merchant.

For example, a consumables manufacturer might develop alternative strategies for a supermarket that assigned the manufacturer's category to a destination role, a drug chain in a convenience role, and a mass merchant in a routine role.

Even better, the manufacturer would anticipate the need to coordinate the marketing, product supply and in-store service strategies for maximum effect at the shelf, and support its suggestions by sharing relevant consumer and market data on the category and its brands.

Even if manufacturers and retailers disagree on what's appropriate, by working toward agreement, the retail marketing strategies that evolve from those discussions become more refined. Initial differences are expected. However, too many retailers today not only don't involve manufacturers in the process of developing marketing strategies, they often fail to tell them the new direction, and that disjoints efforts going forward.

In today's environment, retailers must open their minds, and manufacturers must rein in their self-interest. While past behavior may have spawned distrust, by agreeing on sell-through rates or other specific goals, retailers and category captains can link their fortunes and create a more positive, productive dynamic.

Moving On

The crisper and more well thought out the strategies, the better the direction they provide for the next step—the development of specific tactics that will bring the category strategy to life.

8

Step Six: Choose Tactics for Category Assortment, Pricing, Promotion, Merchandising, and Supply Chain Management

OBJECTIVE OF STEP SIX

Decide on the specific activities that will achieve category strategies.

BACKGROUND OF STEP SIX

Once marketing strategies are set, category managers focus on what it will take for categories to meet or exceed corporate objectives. To succeed, detailed tactics that will shape categories for the coming year require successful orchestration of many disciplines within the retail organization and supply chain.

Tactics are the mechanisms for improvement in five aspects of category management: assortment, pricing, promotion, merchandising, and supply chain management. They literally change how consumers experience categories and affect category performance and store image.

Select the Right Tactics

How do category managers know that their assortment, price, promotion, merchandising, and supply chain decisions support their retailers' overall go-to-market strategies? By filtering options through their desired customer demographics, psychographics, and shopping behavior, their stores can appeal to consumers their companies most want to attract and serve.

For example, the use of plastic jars for baby food gave birth to a new segment of multipacks, with which retailers can service larger families and people who shop less often, and excite sales with a greater variety of everyday and promotional price tactics. The less fragile plastic reduces breakage having a positive impact on shipping, warehousing costs, and damage reclamation costs.

Assortment

The first tactic—assortment—answers the fundamental question of what a retailer wants in a category's mix. Product mix is the most tangible part of the category to consumers, so assortment serves as a mainstay differentiator for retailers trying to meet their needs.

Methods of attaining the right assortment have evolved over the years. Buyers used to decide on assortment based on how they perceived what sales representatives offered. This was too subjective, however, and later space-to-sales ratios became the primary tools.

Recognizing that sales measures alone weren't the best to rely on, retailers began to look at the incremental contribution to the category of each item. They began to ask: What is the unique contribution and value that this product brings to the mix?

To reach this point, retailers need to understand how consumers shop a category: Would they purchase a substitute or abandon the category or even the store? For example, the retailer already offers two brands of creamy peanut butter. By adding a crunchy choice, or perhaps a low-fat creamy, rather than a third brand of regular creamy, the shelf display may provide more incremental value.

Incrementality also ties to the category role, making it a more refined, usable, and value-driven sales measure than others. For example, cigarettes are a destination category in convenience stores, so retailers who follow standard sales rankings in a market might want to carry the top 95 percent of SKUs, and drugstores, which sell cigarettes primarily as a convenience, might carry only the top 50 percent. However, retailers savvy in the use of incrementality can more powerfully assort cigarettes based on how people shop the category's various segments and subcategories.

At the pinnacle of assortment intelligence, activity-based costing—in which retailers and suppliers know the true cost of every product at every step of the pipeline, from the point of initial manufacture to consumer purchase—is more of an unrealized dream than an attainable goal for most retailers who lack the infrastructure and resources to do such analysis. For those who do it, the process leaves few details unanalyzed. Costs associated with products range widely from media and promotions to space allocations in warehouses and shipping, and more.

Activity-based costing becomes part of the assortment process when a category manager decides how to fill an available shelf slot—

with a particular brand or private label. The retailer may assume more profit from the private label, but activity-based costing figures in the higher costs of manufacturing, packaging, and shipping associated with the product. In a direct-store-delivered category such as salty snacks, there is also the added cost of delivering to stores. Retailers with efficient supply chains have lower activity-based costs. With this discipline, retailers can compare the true profitability of products on the shelf.

Decisions to Make

Category managers shape category assortments through five types of decisions, including:

1. *Maintain:* Keep the current mix with no changes.
2. *Decrease:* Lessen the number of SKUs in the category, subcategories, and segments.
3. *Increase:* Raise the number of SKUs in the category, subcategories, and segments.
4. *Swap/exchange:* Replace items with new ones.
5. *Private label:* Develop, abandon, or expand its category presence.

Some common tools are new product and product deletion checklists, on which every item falls into one of four buckets: add, drop, keep, or ignore. Drops and keeps represent the current assortment; adds and keeps are the recommended assortment.

When making assortment decisions, category managers address these questions:

• What will meet the variety needs of target consumers at the category, subcategory, and segment levels?

- How does my current variety image compare with competitors'?
- Is my marketing strategy consistent with our company's overall marketing approach and my assigned category role?
- What are the cost/benefit ratios of different levels of variety? How great are the opportunities compared with the risks of sub-par performance?
- What are the new product acceptance criteria?
- What are the product deletion criteria?

They answer these questions by viewing the category from different perspectives. Smarter tactical choices follow analyses such as:

- Item performance rankings by sales, profit, and other measures, and indicators such as sales and profit per cubic foot
- Market comparisons of variety and sales contribution
- Sales/profit quadrant
- New product checklist
- Product deletion checklist
- Product segmentation analysis
- Consumer loyalty to particular brands or items
- Consumer switching and substitution patterns

Pricing

Pricing used to be much simpler when retailers were either high-low promotional or everyday low price (EDLP).

Today, in an unprecedented squeeze between rising costs of goods, labor, and energy, and sharp pricing by the big boxes, retailers such as Marsh and Meijer are part of a burgeoning movement to hybrid price and differentiate in their markets. With hybrid price, some key items that are EDLP earn operators an image for reasonable prices storewide, and different products on promotion generate 10 percent to 15 percent of a store's volume.

Still other retailers use another pricing strategy: They favor loyalty cardholders with regular, deep discounts that manufacturers fund.

Whichever method they use, retailers typically aim to offer reasonable everyday prices that appear to be low—and non-EDLP operators punctuate these with circular discounts on bellwether items or categories to reinforce value. These specials benefit stores most when centered on categories that address their best shoppers, say, cereals and candy where many households have children.

Retailers frame their big-picture strategies through two perspectives:

1. How can we differentiate and establish a position of consumer value versus the competition?
2. What role will pricing play for particular stores or categories, depending on local competition?

Staying true to their vision, retailers can look good in this dynamic pricing dance. That's why category managers constantly monitor the penny differences between their stores and competitors; they know consumers start to switch stores when they see a 5 percent to 10 percent differential. It clearly matters more on a $10 detergent than on a $1 pack of gum, but consumers think of the difference on their total baskets. They know prices of items they buy most often, but each consumer has a different list and he or she doesn't even buy the same items each week. Therefore, retailers need to price with complete categories in mind rather than item by item—especially since 70 percent of items in a store sell less than one case per week.

Competitive price checks are surprisingly courteous affairs at food retailers. Sometimes stealthily but usually open, price checkers scan each other's complete stores as often as once a week. They use these prices as essential context to avoid making incorrect pricing decisions.

Computer programs are available, showing how a retailer's prices compare with individual competitors. An index of 100 means their prices are exactly the same. In Table 8.1, Retailer A's Baking Mixes category prices are slightly higher than ours, while Retailer's B and C are offering prices that are somewhat lower.

Having wrung excess supply chain costs out of the system, retailers increasingly rely on pricing to deliver profits. Some use price optimization software to gauge consumers' price elasticity and no longer "leave money on the table," so to speak. Retailers frequently

TABLE 8.1   Comparing Prices with the Competition

Sales Index Report	Retailer A Sales Index	Retailer B Sales Index	Retailer C Sales Index
Baking Mixes	100.85	99.17	97.88
Mixes - Cake/Layer	100.75	99.25	97.80
Mixes - Brownies	100.85	99.15	98.02
Mixes - Muffin	100.91	99.09	97.82
Mixes - Bread	100.76	99.31	97.79
Mixes - Rolls & Biscuits	101.02	98.98	97.98
Mixes - Cookie	101.02	98.98	97.95
Mixes - Frosting	100.72	99.28	97.84
Mixes - Pie Crust	100.98	99.02	98.15
Mixes - Pancake	101.12	98.88	97.92

Source: ACNielsen Priceman.

build other rules into their use of these programs, such as: percentage difference between national brand and private label; the same price for all items of the same brand, size, flavor, or form; or prices per ounce when selling different sizes of the same product. For now at least, retailers see this software as proven technology, yet many feel they can neither afford implementation nor support it yet with an adequate information technology infrastructure. As powerful as these programs may be, they don't replace retailers' true understanding of the interrelated mechanical and emotional aspects of pricing.

With such insights and close connections to category strategies such as turf protect and transaction build, and powered by a top-down senior-level commitment to system-wide pricing disciplines, retailers can make their stores more compelling to consumers and increasingly productive.

To stay competitive, retailers typically take conservative price increases—more creeps than jumps. As they manage prices up for margin, they want to maintain velocity. Manufacturers do too, so they'll often discuss with retailers how prices should change. One recent exception was when two major manufacturers raised coffee prices 14 percent because of costly crop shortages, retailers passed the hikes along and consumers understood the nature of commodity swings. By contrast, when the cost of butterfat rose on premium ice cream and then abated, manufacturers funded promotions to manage the price volatility. Clearly, retailers and manufacturers never want to be perceived as taking advantage of consumers.

Besides pricing, other consumer outlays can have profound effects on different parts of the store. People stung by higher gasoline prices and overextended on credit have less money for food, and that may prompt a shift away from costlier fresh choices to more economical canned goods and frozen foods. These could be new opportunities for retailers to convey center-store values through the right pricing and promotions.

Decisions to Make

Category managers dictate pricing through three types of decisions:

1. *Maintain:* Keep the current pricing approach with no changes.
2. *Decrease:* Lower prices of all or selected SKUs in a category.
3. *Increase:* Raise prices of all or selected SKUs in a category.

When making pricing decisions, category managers address these questions:

- How great is the value we're providing to target consumers at the category, subcategory, segment, and SKU levels?
- Are we competitive with other retailers and are we seen as the category price leader?
- Which pricing approach is most consistent with our overall marketing strategy—high-low, EDLP, hybrid? Which is best for our category role and strategies?
- Are we achieving our pricing goals in the market by category, subcategory, segment, and SKU?
- How is our pricing affecting gross margin?
- Will price increases or decreases significantly affect category sales and profits?

- Are the category's leading items priced correctly?
- Which items in the category have the sharpest price image?
- Is private label priced appropriately?
- How aggressively should we price new items?
- How should items whose velocity is falling be priced?
- What price changes can we make to help both ourselves and manufacturers?

They answer these questions by viewing the category from different perspectives.

Smarter tactical choices follow such analyses as:

- Profit in dollars and percentages, sales, market share, and other fiscal measures
- Contribution to margin and quadrant analysis
- Pricing gap analysis
- Price elasticity/sensitivity analysis
- Retail pricing audits

Promotion

"Show me the money" goes both ways. For consumers, the phrase equates to "show me the savings so I'll buy." For retailers, promotions grow traffic and sales and satisfy Wall Street. That gains are short-lived matters little to retailers who want to post advances. However, promotions are fast becoming quick fixes that excite consumers but may weaken a retailer's long-term price integrity. When retailers are promotion-driven rather than equity-driven, they lose their ability to price-manage categories. People learn to pantry-load items like paper towels, detergents, canned vegetables, and bottled water during sales and wait for the next event.

High-low operators have little choice but to promote; people see low prices in the multiple channels they shop. Depending on the category, manufacturers spend between 10 percent and 20 percent on promotions, and trading partners are coming up with new ways to improve yield from their investments.

Brand bundling in feature ads leverages costs for manufacturers. Where eight brands might have run separately in the past at $10,000 for each ad, by grouping them a manufacturer pays only about $40,000 to be in a retailer's circular. The money saved is redirected into a better cost of goods for the retailer to help it compete. More brands at hot prices—such as five boxes of cereal for $10— appeal to more consumers and build traffic. Other possibilities: breakfast brand bundles such as juice, pancake, and syrup brands from a single manufacturer, or entertainment brand bundles surrounding an event like the Super Bowl.

Cents-off coupons are getting shorter dates because their incremental effect occurs within the first few weeks; people who hold coupons beyond that buy the product anyway. Coupons induce trial of new products and flavors, cause brand switching, and remind shoppers to buy the product.

With no advertising or display, temporary price reductions (TPRs) work best on products bought regularly such as potato chips, and least well on long purchase cycle items such as floor cleaners. They yield the least on dollars spent when used alone, and lift sales more when linked with circular features and displays (see Figure 8.1).

Circulars are increasingly strategic vehicles that communicate a retailer's price competitiveness with big boxes. Front pages have

FIGURE 8.1   Sales Lift by Promotion Tactic

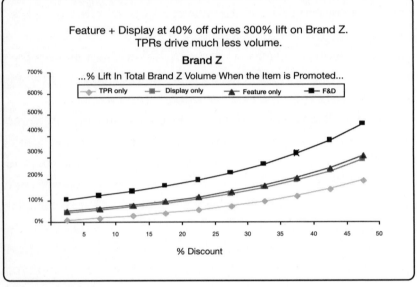

Source: ACNielsen

screaming hot deals in destination categories, and subsequent pages have other deals that help shoppers round out their trips to the store.

Promotions that have a double edge are becoming more common. For example, 10 bottles of a 32-oz. sports beverage for $10 may attract people who'd otherwise buy 64-oz. bottles. This gives retailers a hot price and a special package configuration they need to compete with big boxes, but it could decrease category sales. Although a manufacturer's sales force would push it to grow velocity, a retailer would be right to question how it truly benefits its category.

Stores themselves host a growing tactical presence of in-store television and radio networks, floor ads, coupon machines, product demonstrations and samples to enlarge baskets, while circulars and coupons stimulate trips to the store.

Such promotional efforts inside and outside the store aren't necessarily chain wide. Retailers create clusters according to the degree of competition they face or the type of consumers they serve and refine promotional strategies for the head-on categories. For example, jumbo packs of paper products bring supermarkets to a price-per-roll that compares well with big boxes. By promoting these packs, supermarkets gain not only volume but category market share, because consumers who buy them won't need to buy them again for some time.

Plenty of people cherry-pick hot deals like these, which retailers don't mind because it takes share away from competitors. The real prize, however, comes in building promotions with appropriate tactics that help the most loyal customers, the frequent shopper cardholders, and induce them to buy more. Some retailers large and small, from Kroger and Tesco to Greenhills to Dorothy Lane, are earning reputations for their smart mining of frequent shopper data. They stand out compared with most retailers who are just scratching the surface of this enriching information.

The push to lift sales and market share compared with promotional events of the prior year is unmistakable. Software tools enable pre-event forecasts of sales gains, case allowances, return on investment, and other important measures, as well as post-event analysis of what actually occurred. It's becoming more important to manage trade promotions, since events win consumer attention and retailers and manufacturers are devoting more resources to them.

Decisions to Make

Category managers dictate promotions through seven kinds of decisions:

1. *Vehicle:* Type of promotion, including price reduction, coupon, ad, display, demonstration, sample, theme
2. *Product:* Items promoted
3. *Frequency:* How often to promote
4. *Duration:* Length of promotion
5. *Timing:* Scheduling of promotion
6. *Location:* Where promotion occurs
7. *Cross merchandising:* Tie-ins

Retailers typically involve category captain manufacturers in the analysis of promotions and hold them accountable during quarterly reviews. At least six months in advance, category managers also expect suppliers to develop promotional plans that suit their image and marketplace context. Questions retailers pose range widely. Among them:

- What promotions are consistent with our overall marketing strategy and the category's role? How deep does that role allow price points to go?
- How will target consumers respond to various promotions? What will lift sales, traffic, or profit the most: price, feature, or displays, or some combination? Which products are most responsive to each of these methods? What is the impact of each promoted item on the category?

- What are consumers' key decision points? How important are brand, flavor, and size in what we promote?
- Will the promotion attract new consumers, and will they buy other products as well?
- Which promotions build consumer loyalty? Which ones create unfavorable purchase behavior and erode brand and store equity?
- How do competitors promote, and how will they react?
- Do I have promotions or events to attract customers who are not motivated by price discount?
- Do my promotions make the shopping experience more enjoyable?

They answer these questions by viewing the category from different perspectives.

Smarter tactical choices follow such analyses. For example:

- Sales, profit, market share, return on assets, and other fiscal measures
- Effect on customer counts, market baskets, and impulse sales
- Days of supply on hand and out-of-stocks
- Promotional activity relative to competitors

Merchandising

Selling space is a key determinant in how retailers present categories because, as a finite asset, footage is one of the few constant figures in retailing. The savviest retailers in managing space-to-sales ratios are frequently the ones with powerful categories, subcategories, and segments—sized right, located well, and in stock.

Each store has a fixed amount of space with no give. Expand one category, subcategory, or segment, and another has to shrink. Errors made while calculating or ignoring this simple fact end up on the selling floor and disrupt categories. For example, when a larger item replaces a delisted one, where do those extra inches come from? Stores may compensate at first with an off-shelf display, but there's an excellent chance that the new item may never make it to the shelf. ACNielsen data show that between 8 percent and 12 percent of sales throughout North America are lost to out-of-stocks, and that's often due to inadequate space.

Shelf presentation is so critical that it either drives purchases or drives people away. To maintain control, retailers need to manage every detail of space usage down to the placement of product. Otherwise, inexperienced stock clerks might inadvertently upset planograms and undermine plans. This could happen as easily as placing the top profit maker in detergent on a bottom shelf rather than at eye level because placement instructions weren't understood.

Miscalculated category space can leave stores trying to compensate by replenishing more often from the backroom. However, this escalates labor costs and exposes product to more damage due to more handling—and damaged product never makes it to the shelf and leaves detrimental space gaps in presentation.

This is just one example of what happens when individual store managers decide by default how to populate categories on the shelf. Yet, it happens all the time. Say a category manager wants 200 items in a set for a certain store cluster, but some of these stores have space for only 170, the store managers are making the final choices. After all, they're responsible for the bottom lines at their stores.

Today, planogram compliance hovers at around 60 percent—due to the complexity of more than 100 category planograms per store, and the diversity of store size, with some individual chains ranging as widely as 4,000 to 80,000+ square feet. The result: Retailers frequently issue "guideline planograms," and store managers do their best to follow them.

Category managers also conflict with retail operations on another aspect of space management: changing planograms. To change one takes two people one day, or 16 hours at $10/hour ($160). In a chain of 1,000 stores, that's $160,000. If another shelf is required, add $30 per store or $30,000.

One of the nation's largest retailers recently completed an internal study that showed initial compliance decreases the cost of redoing categories at the shelf by 32 percent. Despite this compelling finding, compliance at this chain stands at only 80 percent.

What's new in planogramming? As part of dynamic databases today, planograms can be reconfigured with reports on space-to-sales relationships. Retailers can act quickly when a manufacturer brings them key performance insights on item placement, such as high velocity elsewhere when in the second row corner rather than the fourth shelf middle.

Also, retailers can load market and demographic data into their business systems to help them allocate space better. Using such relational databases, one major retailer recently replanogrammed a hardlines category and raised year-one sales by $70 million chainwide, on an investment cost of $250,000.

Automated updates enable faster inclusion of demanded new products. While it's possible to further automate math-based decisions, the numbers alone shouldn't dictate planograms because aesthetics also affect how consumers feel about categories and stores. Successful merchandising strikes the right balance between math and art.

ACTIONABLE TIPS

- How high is high? The top gondola shelf should probably be no higher than 78″ because women at 5′ 4″ already need to be on their tiptoes at that height. Some categories lend themselves to merchandise above the top shelf, such as ready-to-assemble furniture or kayaks, as identifiers. It's probably wise to avoid the temptation of storing excess inventory on the uppermost shelf for several reasons: It's counted as inventory and gives false illusions of a category's performance in the store; it tends to become outdated and expire because it's not readily rotated into displays; and if heavy, few workers can lift it easily.

- Where do shoppers look? People come around a corner into an aisle and commonly look first to the gondola on their right. Their second look as they progress is to what's directly across on their left. The dead zone is the first four-foot section to the left, which requires a high-profile brand to get them to notice. Once standing in an aisle facing a gondola, people see a width of three four-foot sections, or 12 feet, with their peripheral vision. Eyeing a category, people first look at eye level, then to the top, then left to right and top to bottom, which makes bottom right the absolute worst spot in a shelf set. Placement makes an astounding difference in product and category performance.

- Seasonal merchandising is critical. Mess up Christmas, Easter, or Halloween merchandising and you may have to write off the entire season for the store because people will shop elsewhere. The stakes are greater than the actual season at hand; retailers risk losing customers forever. It takes six weeks for people to consider switching and another six to completely switch.

- Pinpoint displays that produce sales. Use handheld units to track the actual number of items in specific displays, by adding an extra field onto the unit's screen and assigning a digit to primary, secondary, tertiary, or cross-merchandised displays. Particularly useful for magazines, batteries, candy, and some other categories, such tracking could demonstrate the power of women's magazines near cosmetics or fitness/health magazines near vitamins.

Getting The Basics Right

What goes into space decisions is complex and endlessly varied. Retailers first decide where to locate categories within the store, creating a logical flow and solution adjacencies. The combined effect is hopefully one of a store that's easy to shop, committed to meeting consumer needs, and one that has some measure of distinction.

Operators then allocate space to each category, subcategory, and segment to attain the assigned role and scorecard objectives, and then drill down to arrange every element of a category, down to the brand, SKU, and package form levels. If the first steps in the category management process are done well, the impact is seen in how products are displayed. For example, in Figure 8.2, this shelf set organizes cereal by manufacturer. However, harkening back all the way to the category definition, if it is determined that consumers actually shop the ready-to-eat cereal category by type of cereal, the shelf set shown in Figure 8.3 on page 153, which groups all raisin bran cereals together, would make more sense.

However, even the best plans can go awry. Planograms designed with great specificity unfortunately end up that way

FIGURE 8.2   Merchandising by Brand

at the shelf only 6 times in 10. That doesn't prevent retailers from trying their best to customize planograms to the demographics surrounding stores, and so they develop clusters that arrange space and layout differently. These add to the challenge of executing tactics, but the payoff usually makes the effort worthwhile.

While assortment should be tailored to shoppers' tastes, shelf sets should reflect the category strategy. A low price image can be reinforced by putting low priced items at eye level. If the objective is to increase basket ring, put a larger size item or gourmet item at eye level. High profit items at eye level support a profit-generating strategy.

FIGURE 8.3 Merchandising by Type

Questions to Ask

Category managers should pose many kinds of questions, such as:

- Does the shelf presentation meet the needs of the target consumer, and does it seem logical and appealing?
- Does it differentiate our stores?
- Is it consistent with the assigned role, strategies, and scorecard objectives? Does it maximize the profit, sales, and velocity possible while following our strategies?
- Does it reinforce the variety and price images we seek?

- What is the potential of out-of-stocks, and will consumers substitute an item or leave the store?
- Which operations issues are relevant?
- What should the planogram contain if all core items can't fit?
- Where on the selling floor should we locate the category to maximize category and store performance?

They answer these questions by viewing the category from different perspectives. Smarter tactical choices follow such analyses as:

- Category scorecard measures
- Service level constraints, among them days of supply on hand, case pack outs, and product facings
- How competitors present the category
- Out-of-stock levels

Supply Chain Management

The behind-the-scenes activities that move product from suppliers to retailers may be unsung, but they are absolutely pivotal to successful category management. Without addressing supply chain flows, costs, and potential efficiencies, after all, how could retailers manage categories as business units and customize them store by store to meet consumer needs?

The most recent Grocery Manufacturers of America Logistics Study notes the widespread shift to inventory systems "pulled" by consumer demand rather than "pushed" by what the trade aims to sell, and shortened order cycle times. The study further reports on how leading retailers are taking steps to: improve product availability; synchronize data with trading partners; make product order and delivery more flexible; raise forecast accuracy and cross-functional collaboration.

Their aim is to speed distribution and reduce costs. Activity-based costing systems exert controls that minimize product movement and storage costs throughout the supply chain, regardless of who owns the goods at any point. Even more efficiencies come from today's environment of real-time data sharing among trading partners: Whoever has the best information available can best manage product movement between firms. Category managers making decisions that alter supply chain performance of suppliers responsibly base them on timely, accurate data because they realize, for example, that changing product mix at one store could cause a delivery truck to go over its capacity, or reduce efficiencies at a distribution center.

Numerous studies this past decade prove that companies excelling in supply chain processes have fiscal superiority—in higher margins, lower inventory investment, and shorter cash-to-cash cycle times—and use these disciplines to differentiate themselves.

As primary points of contact with suppliers, category managers are the ones to negotiate beneficial logistics arrangements. With retailers and suppliers evaluating and charging the other, both are motivated to maximize efficiencies and lower the cost of goods in the process. Indeed, lowest product cost is frequently the focal point of category managers' decisions.

Logistics are part of many dynamic decisions. Among them:

- *To carry an item or list a product:* This can enable a retailer to move to a more favorable pricing tier with a supplier, or can create a full truckload that lowers the price for new and old items, or can lead to more efficiencies with one supplier and the culling of another.

- *Promotion plans:* These require knowledge of product availability as well as price and associated purchasing and shipping options. For example, a retailer can't promote apple cider at a low price if the apple crop is bad and cider costs more than consumers expect to pay.

- *Global sourcing:* May give a retailer an advantage if the retailer can access product produced where expenses are lowest. Also, when shipping from abroad, air freight might cost 5 to 10 times as much as ocean conveyance. On the plus side, air freight reduces inventory in the total pipeline and is less likely to result in losses or damages.

- *Package and shipper design:* This needs to work from both logistics and marketing perspectives in transit, distribution centers, and stores. Specifically, packages and shippers must support stacked weight in the warehouse and meet other warehouse, trucking, and in-store standards for maximum safety and efficiencies. Cut cases can save on store labor in stocking shelves. Any exclusive packs sought by category managers to differentiate, of course, incur additional costs. And category managers need to be as savvy in sourcing, manufacturing, shipping, and all other aspects of logistics as branded suppliers when overseeing this aspect of their private labels.

Moreover, category managers' performance is often tied directly or indirectly to logistics, so they are personally motivated to maximize product turns and profit, minimize product damage and out-of-stocks, and accurately plan to meet consumer demand without excess inventory.

A Bevy of Decisions

Coordinating the supply chain requires close supervision of many diverse elements.

Acquisition (Sourcing)

Retailers need to represent all products, brands, and forms to meet consumer needs, and however many suppliers it takes to source them is the minimum they need. They can protect category assortment with contingent sources of substitute products in case primary manufacturers run short, and they can streamline their vendor base by asking, for example, an established honey supplier to make a creamed honey that is currently supplied by a small, niche company. They can protect category marketing and merchandising by having enough suppliers to support plans, which manufacturers might otherwise disrupt for various reasons. For example, suppliers wouldn't fund promotions for cranberry juice if a crop shortage made it difficult to supply amply for everyday consumption, or a particular supplier who overspent on trade funds may insist that a retailer earn more accruals before committing to a larger order. Multiple sources provide for contingencies.

Diverters are valuable sources of low-cost product as well. For example, if there is excess product, a manufacturer might sell product for less on the West Coast than on the East Coast to penetrate a market. An East Coast retailer might get a better price from a diverter than from a manufacturer's representative. When doing this, however, it's important to compare not only case cost but the benefits of advertising, rebates, accruals, labor, and support from manufacturers. Some categories are less likely candidates to be diverted, such as produce, with a short shelf life that is vulnerable to extra transit time—although wariness should extend to all consumables, even canned goods. One precaution available is radio-frequency identification (RFID) technology; sensors will be able to tell if a temperature ever went above or below a certain point. Also, retailers who back haul expedite product receipt and lower costs.

Supplier product grouping programs save energy resources by grouping items from different warehouses that require either trucks with freezers, refrigerators, or none.

Retailers typically impose product quality and performance standards on brands and private label, and enforce them through their own quality assurance test labs.

The degree to which retailers vertically integrate, or take on many of the sourcing steps themselves, depends on their individual strategies and economies of scale. Do they want to make their own private label and ship it as well? How many of the responsibilities do they want to assume?

Retailers can certainly innovate when making private label, rather than simply emulating brands. If trends indicate opportunities for rosemary olive oil or blueberry-flavored bread, for instance, they can develop product with these flavors even though the major brands have not yet done so.

Acquisition (Purchasing Practice)

Contract pricing is one approach, where a retailer and manufacturer agree up front on a net price for product without bill backs or other factors. Price brackets are more common; higher volumes earn retailers more favorable prices per case. Manufacturers may offer 10 cases at $10 each, or 20 cases at $9 each. However, simply buying more to get a better purchase price may not make sense if inventory carrying costs (Inventory cost × Cost of capital = Carrying costs) exceed the up front savings. Retailers often form buying consortiums and then split up the truckloads to qualify for more favorable price brackets.

Purchase terms state when retailer payment is due and provide an incentive for earlier payments. A term may be 30 days but often a retailer can negotiate paying in 60 days if both partners find benefit in the extended terms. This is most often done with seasonal product where the supplier benefits by ensuring the timely delivery of product and smoothing the last-minute shipping, while removing the extra carrying cost that would be incurred by the retailer for taking earlier delivery of that product.

Cash discount is related to terms and another source of income for the retailer, but benefits the supplier by providing an incentive to the retailer to pay promptly. A typical cash discount would be expressed as 2 percent, net 10, meaning payment is due within 30 days but if paid on or before the tenth day, the retailer will receive a 2 percent discount off the total invoice. Volume incentive agreements relate to predetermined bonuses when retailers reach certain purchase thresholds. The Robinson-Patman Act governs what can be offered to any particular retailer.

Order/Payment Transaction (Management)

Wal-Mart's Retail Link system is one of the most advanced examples of how exchanging information online can keep stores in stock and supply pipelines efficiently. As soon as a product scans at a cash register, the manufacturer knows that the unit sold and needs to be replaced; this is known as continuous replenishment or perpetual inventory. Their system illustrates how far data sharing has come since electronic ordering and price changes were the first online forays. A lot of transactional data remains routine today—such as purchase orders and acknowledgments, advance ship notices, invoices, promotions, and price changes.

However, item maintenance has the power to make other aspects of logistics more efficient and accurate. By coding the Universal Product Code (UPC) to product characteristics such as package count, price, and dimensions, trading partners can determine how many cases fit on a pallet, and how many pallets can be stacked while still fitting into warehouse bays. An industry entity called UCCNet aims to be a clearinghouse for such information.

DEX/NEX stands for Direct Exchange/Network Exchange. DEX is a process in which direct-store-delivered (DSD) suppliers use handheld technology to transmit invoices and credits to stores through a DEX port in the store's receiving area. The store verifies the delivery or return and issues acknowledgment. Or using NEX, manufacturers issue invoices to retail headquarters, which then retransmits to appropriate stores. This all happens before delivery so the stores' receiving departments know what to expect and more simply verify on delivery. This eliminates the need for handhelds, identifies any price-cost differences, prevents unauthorized items, and keeps store-level inventories accurate.

Electronic funds transfers are secure direct deposits.

Product Handling (Warehouse)

The goal is to schedule trucks one after another with no waits and efficiently stage their loads to minimize product movement. That's why prescheduled appointments for trucks to be at designated dock doors at specific times often have no grace period. You're bumped if you're late. That's just a fundamental of an efficient warehouse operation.

Cross-docking represents the ultimate streamlining. Say a manufacturer drops a truckload of paper towels at a wholesaler's warehouse, and no single retailer wants a full truckload. Rather than store the product deep in the warehouse, it is immediately divided and staged for delivery to retailers, according to their individual orders and truck schedules at specified dock doors.

Unit load programs conform pallet loads to the dimensions of retailer and wholesaler warehouse bays; no industry standards exist, so heights and widths vary greatly. Even further efficiencies come from pallet/case/unit packaging, where product is prepackaged to the volume a store needs.

Pallet exchange programs reduce the environmental waste of discarded pallets. Suppliers of heavy-duty reusable pallets charge for the number used over a certain time, and old ones are returned on otherwise empty trucks.

Damaged product programs typically reimburse retailers for broken or damaged items, although the burden of payment should hinge on who is responsible for the damage.

Group slow- and fast-movers in a warehouse (or in different warehouses) based on velocity to avoid pickers having to pass by slow-moving items to get to the fast-moving ones, which wastes steps, energy, and time. Proper grouping makes picking orders more efficient.

Warehouse automation reduces human/product interaction even more. Cases automatically travel down conveyor belts to the staging area to then be loaded on the truck to the store.

Product Handling (Store)

The last leg before products reach the selling floor requires careful handling and speedy set up. Sales-ready cases and units help, because cases have perforated fronts that tear off for easy and neat display of the units inside. Often used for promotions, retailers would like to have this benefit all the time. Pallet/case/unit packaging carries the added meaning that packaging must relate structurally to the product; for example, weak boxes wouldn't support heavy frozen foods. Retailers have developed other labor-saving devices such as gravity-fed cooler racks.

Prescheduled appointments and dedicated carriers/doors maximize the number of deliveries a store can receive, and should be part of the everyday discipline.

Transportation

Back-haul programs have been used for a long time to increase efficiency and reduce costs. Say a wholesaler delivers a truckload to a store, rather than travel back empty it goes to a manufacturer and picks up product for its warehouse. The category manager saves the shipping expenses the supplier would have otherwise charged.

Whether retailers, wholesalers, and manufacturers use their own truck fleets or outsource the driving depends on the controls they want and the costs they're willing to bear.

DSD programs reduce labor and transportation costs in categories such as soft drinks, beer, snacks, and breads. However, these savings go just so far in stores with unions, where staff must actually touch every product that comes in. And since DSD drivers manage their own inventory, retailers must watch they don't alter the category planogram.

With drop-ship programs, manufacturers deliver directly to stores, leaving more space on trucks from the wholesaler's or retailer's warehouse.

Inventory Management

As stated earlier, continuous replenishment, also known as perpetual inventory, is enabled by shared data. It is a fast, accurate way to keep stores in stock with a minimum of days of supply on hand.

With the right pallet/case/unit packaging, warehouses create pallet loads with strong foundations of the heaviest product at the bottom; they separate food from chemicals, and frozen product from refrigerated and nonrefrigerated.

Warehouse space needs to parallel category direction in order to properly support category manager decisions. Categories, subcategories, or segments that are growing, for instance, need more space in the warehouse, or stores risk out-of-stocks and missed opportunities.

Service level is the percentage of all products ordered that was delivered on time. Maintaining service level standards to the warehouse and to the store are key to support the elimination of out-of-stocks. Service level is a key measure that category managers use to evaluate their suppliers.

Vendor-managed inventory is sometimes known as comanaged inventory, where suppliers help determine an optimal level of supply on hand that's enough to meet consumer needs but isn't so much as to escalate carrying costs.

Supply chain decisions today reflect a mind-set that every sale matters and a retailer never wants to disappoint a customer. Far different from a decade ago when tactics might have varied with category role or strategy, the goal is clear and the supply chain questions that remain are consistent and introspective:

- Did you maximize efficiencies to bring the right product to the right consumer at the right time at the lowest cost?
- Did you make the most of all tools, resources, and programs available, even down to details such as extended terms, back-haul allowances, discounts, and favorable price brackets?
- Did you use activity-based costing to analyze your decisions?

- Did you plan your promotional support from manufacturers to coincide with events that are strategically important to you?
- Did manufacturers remove costs from the system to give you the lowest cost of goods?
- One of the best ways to account for manufacturer behavior is to create a supply chain scorecard and use it to monitor suppliers on such measures as: inventory turns, service levels, on-time truck deliveries, number of items they can cross-dock, support of advertising programs, and more.

Moving On

Once retailers decide on the tactics they'll use, plans progress to the next step of execution, where they become tangible and move closer to delivering results.

CHAPTER 9

Step Seven: Roll Out the Plan

OBJECTIVE OF STEP SEVEN

Implement the category business plan in a cohesive, structured way, by gaining approval of trading partners, assigning responsibilities and scheduling activities.

BACKGROUND OF STEP SEVEN

With strategies and tactics in place, retailers and suppliers are ready to enact the category business plan that they expect will bring opportunities to life, yielding positive results and competitive advantage.

By now, partners have fully briefed their teams so people understand their individual roles, and respect that category managers are the ones with the authority over distribution, pricing, space allocation, and merchandising decisions. To successfully implement the category plan, category managers need help and should willingly accept it (Table 9.1).

TABLE 9.1   Category Plan Checklist Example

Activity	Date	Responsibility
Promotion • Finalize promotion schedule • Review promotions quarterly • Develop seasonal cross category promotions (2)	10/1 * 11/15	Cat. Mgr. Category Analyst
Pricing • Input agreed to changes	10/15	Category Mgr.
Assortment • Delete selected items • Process selected new items • Finalize planogram • Implement planogram	9/15 10/1 10/1 12/1	Category Analyst Category Mgr.
Evaluation • Quarterly plan evaluation	1/1 3/1	Category Mgr.

None of this happens before the retailer approves four distinct components of the plan and has supplier funding and other resources lined up to support the plan:

1. Management teams of retailers and suppliers ensure that plans are consistent with their overall strategies. Retailers link to their corporate, departmental, and consumer strategies, and manufacturers connect to their brand and customer strategies.

2. They agree on the criteria, performance goals, and relevant measures in the scorecard, so they have a clear, early view of how plans can affect their business.

3. They reach accord on any further resources that may be needed to implement the plan, such as merchandising displays or more frequent promotions.

4. They anticipate the impact of the category plan on other areas of business and commit to manage this together. For example, how might store engineering be affected by plans for new fixtures or category relocation on the selling floor? How might storeroom operations be impacted by planned promotions?

Category managers can then begin to execute with checklists that detail activities, who is to do them, and by when. Much needs to happen simultaneously, so deft juggling is required.

Table 9.1 shows an example of a category plan checklist.

Execute and Reap Rewards

Nothing is more rewarding to category managers than to see their strategies and tactics pay off in sales and profit growth and positive consumer response. They'll see results quickly and when they fare well, they will need to thank countless store staffers and vendors who've successfully turned their concepts into reality. Execution is different from the rest of the category management process: Where category managers are typically hands-on and exert fairly close control over every step, execution is in the hands of many. That is both the power and the potential pitfall of execution. However, it can be mostly positive with the right coordination, the right training, and clear communications from corporate through field supervision and stores.

As the process unfolds from a close circle of motivated managers out to the field, one truth always holds: The better the store staff understands the category objectives, strategies, and tactics, the more effectively they'll execute them, the more closely they'll watch movement in their stores, and the more frequently they'll tweak the category to make it perform better. They'll be active and involved, insert high-demand items and cull slow sellers as directed, set up arresting signs and promotions that are visible and appealing, and make sure vendors stick to the plan and don't upset their shelves. When store staff is engaged, execution is improved.

Product: To Succeed, Keep Execution Simple

Despite the care and effort spent to develop strategic plans and tactics, retailers shouldn't be too surprised if store-level category execution doesn't fully represent the mock-ups at headquarters. Category managers may rightfully be upset because these gaps sap performance potential, but such gaps have been an unfortunate part of mass retail across all trade classes and categories for many years and will likely continue.

Retailers can apply best practices in category management to minimize the presence of such errors. Errors are seldom the fault of store associates, but reflect the many moving parts it takes to turn a category vision into reality.

Even a fundamental such as clear communication from corporate to stores can be confounded by a perennial trait at retail: the high staff turnover at stores, which frequently exceeds 100 percent annually. Because there is such a high proportion of new store workers, the staff on hand may neither fully comprehend category objectives nor the importance of their tasks, and this could impede crisp execution.

To manage the many moving parts of execution is easier said than done—with a backdrop of 40,000 SKUs in a food store and more than 100,000 in a supercenter, the simultaneous remaking of multiple categories, and the need to coordinate buying, merchandising, advertising, and logistics disciplines.

For example, say a mass merchant has reviewed consumer electronics for the past year. The chain knows every detail including sales, margins, inventory mix, and brand assortment. To establish what it will carry into the coming year, the chain has decided which brands or specific items to mark down and clear out in order to make room for the new. After analyzing such factors, the chain decides whether prices were in line with competition, promotional strategies were effective, and more. Thus, new planograms embody all that the chain wants.

In the instance of consumer electronics, this could mean more space for LCD televisions and MP3 players and less space for VCRs, as new technologies overshadow old ones.

This is when directives go to stores—to clear out, for example, which products to pull, where to display, and percent discounts. At the same time, the retailer authorizes new products to be sold and orders its distribution centers to flush out old items in order to make room for the new. If a synopsis of the category accompanies the directive, store personnel will be more likely to comply.

Planogram: Where Shelf Sets Can Go Wrong

Properly communicated, stores execute a markdown strategy that gives consumers a promotional deal and conveys which items will no longer be carried. However, if directions are unclear or badly timed, there may be no promotional support to move the product and stores can end up with residue forever.

This could begin a domino chain of events. Say stores anticipate new products arriving by a certain date, they staff appropriately to change over the category, remove all culled products from the shelves, and even relabel shelves for what is to come. They then go to the backroom for the new items, but they haven't arrived. The clerks fill the holes on the selling floor with products still on the shelves, but in the wrong places, and it's difficult to recover from this.

By avoiding certain missteps, corporate can provide stores with the greatest chance of success. Some of the most common missteps include:

- Issuing planograms with unintelligible images.
- Incorrect fixtures on hand, say if a planogram calls for replacement of shelves with peg hooks and they're unavailable.
- Store staff misunderstands the importance of new products, or how certain new products add significantly to the appeal of a category.
- Failure to monitor what direct-store-delivered (DSD) vendors, such as soft drinks, snacks, and baked goods, do at the shelf because stores lack enough labor.
- Failure to update fast-changing categories, such as health and beauty care, to include important new products. Stores that don't keep up the pace soon have categories that look very different from what corporate envisions.
- Being late for a season, say, licensed back-to-school children's wear.

Pricing and Promotion Must Synchronize

Price changes need to be visible at store level with the onset of plans. When they're not, items meant to be marked down and replaced may sit on a shelf for a long time. As a result, an expected inventory reduction doesn't happen, the idle goods continue to use valuable display space, and the retailer continues to pay needlessly and wastefully for the inventory investment.

Conversely, when a category plan calls for higher markups on some items to raise category margin, but stores don't make the changes, the desired margin mix/profit lift doesn't happen.

Also, in-store promotional signs and banners need to be organized well and displayed on time for maximum sales lift in support of many activities on the selling floor, such as changed endcaps, aisle stackouts for new planograms, and themed sales events. Signs from vendors or retailers' own sign departments that never leave the backroom do nothing for performance, and that has a dual financial impact on the retailer: no influence on sales, and frequently no proof of performance for earning vendor allowances.

Variations on a Theme: Raise Expectations for Execution

It is generally accepted that planogram compliance hovers around 60 percent, and an 80 percent compliance rate would be among the best—whether a retailer is a big chain or a smaller, local operation. While corporate messages are likelier to be lost downstream in a larger chain, more field supervision tends to offset that. What will help raise compliance? Try these:

- An open culture focused on getting work done rather than the blame game for what previously went wrong.
- Merchandising and reset calendars set a full month in advance so stores can anticipate what's coming and the amount of labor hours that tasks will require. Seasonal sets take priority when they're due, as do cut-ins of impactful new products such as

Rx-to-OTC switches, even during periods when stores are reset-ting several categories on the same day.

- Deploy reset teams to teach department managers within a dis-trict all the details of a category reset, about a week or two in ad-vance of rollout, so they can show their staffs and oversee execution in their stores. This approach is efficient and gives stores a sense of ownership over the category and its perfor-mance. Done right, category managers can lessen the surprises they see and the stomach roil they feel when they visit and view store-level execution of their lines of business.

Moving On

The next step of Category Review is actually an established part of the implementation plan. It is the mechanism for chains to monitor performance of their pivotal categories more often than the rest, on a scheduled, recurring basis.

Step Eight: Review the Category's Performance Regularly and Make Adjustments as Needed

OBJECTIVE OF STEP EIGHT

To measure progress of the plan against its assigned role and scorecard and to modify the plan when appropriate.

BACKGROUND OF STEP EIGHT

The review step revolves around the process of category management on a precise schedule. The recurring review monitors the progress of each step to keep a category on course. It is a vital evaluation tool that unveils problems and leads to fast corrections, and thus protects the integrity of the category plan.

With comprehensive reviews, retailers can better control all categories and support any underachievers that might hurt their own financial performance or the store's overall image. To be thorough requires examination of five key areas:

1. *Scorecard:* Current status against internal financial goals.
2. *Marketplace:* Any changes within the marketplace that could impact the plan, such as sales and consumption trends, strategic changes by competitors, new developments among the category's brands, and retail coverage. Despite media reports of weather affecting retail sales, that is really a cover story to consumers, tantamount to "the dog ate my homework." Internally, no one accepts this as a valid reason for poor performance.
3. *Status of the implementation plan:* What has been done so far? The review identifies any weak spots in execution, and the remedy depends on the source of the problem. Retail culture is one of urgency, not to wait for a problem to improve, but to act quickly.
4. *Activity summary:* A recap of activities within the category, such as promotions run or changes in assortment, pricing, supply systems, or space allocation. The list of tactics may seem endless, but they are the mechanisms for better results, so they deserve attention.
5. *Implications:* Next steps, recommendations for any changes, and thoughts about future prospects for the category.

Review frequency varies with the financial importance of each category to a retailer. Table 10.1 lists some general guidelines. Destination categories or those that, when ranked by dollar sales and

TABLE 10.1   Category Review Schedule

Category	Annual $ Sales	% of Total Store Sales	Cummulative Store Sales	# of Annual Reviews
A	1,000,000	17.2%	17.2%	3
B	800,000	13.7%	30.9%	3
C	785,000	13.5%	44.4%	3
D	650,000	11.2%	55.5%	2
E	600,000	10.3%	65.8%	2
F	540,000	9.3%	75.1%	2
G	440,000	7.6%	82.7%	1
H	420,000	7.2%	89.9%	1
I	390,000	6.7%	96.6%	1
J	200,000	3.4%	100.0%	
	5,825,000			

added together collectively drive approximately the top 40 percent of dollar sales, often undergo between two and three reviews a year. Mid-range categories, between the 40 percent and 80 percent level of contribution to dollar sales, have two annual reviews. The bottom tier of categories has one.

Retailers dictate the schedule of reviews and involve many people in the process: from department managers at stores up to store managers, through every level of field supervision, to buyers and category managers, and their divisional and general merchandise managers. After all, the financial plans of the company are a roll up of what individual category managers said they would achieve, and the reviews help keep performance on track as best as possible.

What Reviews Might Reveal

It's fairly common to check at least on unit and dollar sales, profit percentage and dollars, and turn rates and inventory levels as often as daily or weekly during the first few months after plan implementation and compare it to the category plan. Early numbers could disclose problems and opportunities. For example, low sales of a licensed children's clothing line might reflect lower than expected demand, or simply that merchandise is in the backroom instead of on the selling floor. Velocity that's higher than anticipated could soon outstrip a vendor's capacity to produce and could lead to inadequate inventory for an upcoming advertised promotion.

Once a season is rolling, anxiety subsides and these checks taper off to monthly reviews for regularly scheduled internal meetings among buyers, category managers, and vice presidents, as well as for less frequent and less structured meetings with suppliers to help them understand how their brands and products are performing within the context of the entire category.

For manufacturers, it appears as if no news from the retailer is good news. Suppliers are typically not part of the review process unless a problem exists that needs to be corrected—particularly one of their own making in manufacturing or distribution. This could range widely, from product recalls on a food product that unintentionally contains peanut fragments, a defective child's car seat, buttons that break on jeans, garments that don't hang crisply because the hangers are wrong, or incorrect or late shipments.

Wise are the suppliers who contact retailers as soon as they know of these pending problems, or as soon as they see that retail performance data for the products they sell aren't up to par. By being proactive, they can be part of the solution.

Variations on a Theme: Stay with Your Category, or Not

There's an irony to strong category performance year after year. Not only does it fail to protect a category manager's position, it often leads to turnover. Straightforward metrics are their measuring stick, and it is fairly impossible to ring up, say, 10 percent gains year after year. This explains why many retailers rotate their category managers—particularly those with good results—to different categories to establish new performance baselines. While this brings fresh eyes to established lines of business, which could be good, it also creates discontinuity and frequently means that category reviews aren't done by the people who initiated the plans or perhaps who understand their nuances best.

Retailers also frequently shift category managers to new categories to provide a fresh viewpoint and, in some companies, to keep supplier/category manager relationships from becoming too deep, causing the perception of impropriety.

Conclusion

With good records of plan objectives, tactics, and results to date, retailers can maintain integrity of their category review process and better ensure that assigned roles and scorecard targets are met.

11

Bringing the Consumer into Category Management—A New Take on the Eight Steps

ategory Management is a sophisticated process that maximizes sales and profits for a category across all stores in a chain. When first introduced, this was a significant improvement over the haphazard, undisciplined category review activities that preceded it. Just aligning category managers and vendors along the same process and data requirements was a great step forward.

Many retailers today have adopted the "classic" eight-step process mapped out by The Partnering Group and described in some detail in the previous chapters. The degree of implementation depends on the size and level of commitment of the retailer, and ranges from simply enhancing existing processes to establishing an internal organization to implement an ongoing fully featured program.

Category management, as it is commonly practiced today, achieves the largest gains in sales and profits the first time a category is reviewed. Thereafter, the returns tend to diminish. The key limitation of the standard approach is in the way a retailer's shoppers are viewed—as one single entity for which one category solution is assumed to be adequate across the chain.

This approach lacks the ability to target and track specific consumer segments. If the tactics implemented do not achieve the desired results, there is no easy way of isolating the consumer segment that is not responding. Typically, a chain will not even know that there is a group or two of consumers they have ignored. The usual approach is to start the whole process over again.

The single solution paradigm is rooted in the type of data that has been available. Until the early 1970s, shipment data was the primary information source. Point-of-sale (POS) data and the wealth of syndicated data that was developed from it allowed retailers to monitor and manage sales by store, flavor, package size, and more. As a result, the first version of category management took a decidedly product-centric approach.

The richer data sets available today—particularly, consumer data—allow us to view categories from the consumer's point of view. We now understand that each shopper sees our assortment, pricing, merchandising, and so on differently, adding a vital new dimension to the way we manage our categories.

With a consumer-centric process, key consumer segments can be identified with results tracked for each group. Goals for sales and margin can be applied differently for each segment so that expectations by store are more realistic. If results do not meet expectations, the chain can quickly identify which consumer segment is not responding. Adjustments to tactics can be made and implemented immediately. It is not necessary to start from the beginning of the process again unless there is a significant change in the demographic makeup of the chain's trade area consumers or in the category itself.

Seeing the diversity of consumer preferences allows us to quantify the differences in buying potential and better understand why some stores traditionally underperform. Identifying the gap between sales *potential* and *actual* sales provides new opportunities to optimize category sales and margins.

The consumer-centric process described in this chapter, developed by Spectra Marketing—a business unit of VNU and sister company to ACNielsen—and validated with several consumer packaged goods manufacturers and retailers, promises a dramatically enhanced return on the time and money invested in developing and implementing new category strategies. The process splits the first step in the classic eight-step category management process, adds a crucial new step, alters the order of several of the other steps, and adds important "checkpoints" along the way (see Figure 11.1).

The founding principle behind this modified approach is to allow consumer behavior and attributes to drive the process. Let's look at how it works.

Step by Step

The first change that the consumer-centric category management approach makes to the historic eight-step process is to split step one—Category Definition—into two steps. The first step in the new process, what we continue to refer to as Category Definition, takes into account the fact that all retailers do not define categories

FIGURE 11.1   Consumer-Centric Category Review

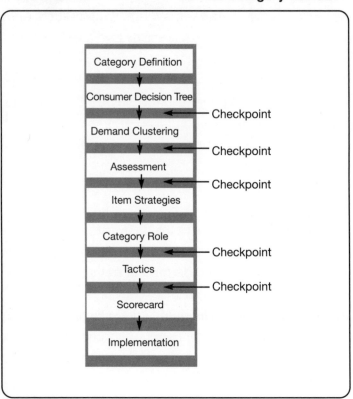

Source: Spectra Marketing Systems, Inc.

in the same way. One might include carbonated water in its definition of carbonated soft drinks, while another might not. When beginning the category review process, it's essential to start with an
understanding of what a category consists of at a given retailer.

The second step, Consumer Decision Tree, looks at how consumers shop the category. Here, analytic methods such as market
structure and preference segmentation, as described earlier, are used
to look at how consumers view a category. Is type of product—

Raisin Bran, Oatmeal, and so on—more important? Or, is brand—Post, Kellogg's, or others—more important? The resulting consumer decision tree, already consumer focused, is the same as what is typically used in the first step of the historic process.

This is where the first of five checkpoints is recommended. A *checkpoint* is a structured time for trade partners to compare notes and make sure they're on the same page with one another. It's designed to prevent category plans from being developed in isolation. More effective plan execution tends to come about when those tasked with the execution are involved in designing the plan.

Step three, Demand Clustering, is what really sets Consumer-Centric Category Management apart. Here we identify and locate unique customer groups and then cluster stores to reflect those groups. There are dozens of methods that retailers and manufacturers use to cluster stores to locate key customer groups. However, these methods typically rely on attributes that describe past performance.

Demand Clustering is a better method because it clusters stores based on the *future* sales potential for a category or brand. Spectra's Consumer Attribute Model (CAM), analyzes consumer panel data to determine which demographic attributes drive purchase behavior for each category or brand. Over 60 demographic attributes are examined to determine which ones most strongly correlate with purchasers of product categories or brands. That information is compared with the demographic makeup of the consumers living near a store, resulting in a Demand Index that shows how well the category or brand in question *should* perform in that store.

Demand-Based Clustering allows marketers to group stores that will benefit from the same marketing strategy for a given category. If one marketing strategy can be successfully applied for each cluster, more efficient than developing a strategy for each and every ....e.

Let's look at an example of how Demand-Based Clustering works. Table 11.1 is a profile of the consumers living within shopping distance of a chain that we'll call Joe's Food Stores.

Spectra's BehaviorScape Household Segmentation groups consumers based on their "Behaviorstage" (age of the head of household combined with presence of children in the household) and

TABLE 11.1   Joe's Foods Prospective Customers

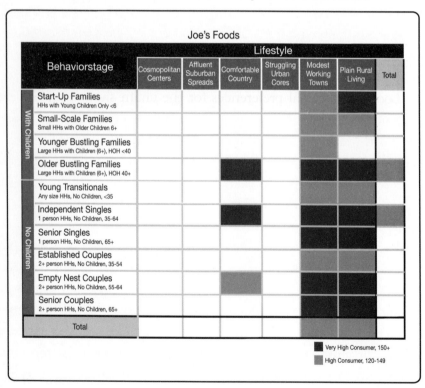

Source: Spectra BehaviorScape Household Segmentation.

Lifestyle (affluence combined with the location of household). The dark-shaded microsegments are consumer groups that index high—that is, there are high proportions of consumers in these segments living near Joe's stores chainwide. The lighter-shaded microsegments also index high, but not as high as the dark-shaded microsegments. As you can see, chainwide, people living near Joe's stores are mostly middle to low income and live in towns and rural areas. A few are a bit more upscale.

This is how Joe's potential customers segment on the whole. Joe's does a great job with the "average" customer, and has for years. While the segmentation you see is based on predictive demographics, that is, each segment has its own unique buying style and product preferences, this is still just an *average* representation that minimizes some of the smaller, key consumer groups around stores with whom Joe's has not been as successful.

Looking at cereal preferences for the chain shows Demand Indices that are relatively flat. For example, private label hominy grits shows a Demand Index of 112 (Table 11.2). In other words, there is a 12 percent greater potential for Hominy Grits sales among households living near Joe's stores than among the average of all stores in the states where the Joe's stores are located.

Typically, a category or brand would need an index of 120 in order to be thought of as having an outstanding level of upside potential. The indices seen in Table 11.2 are flat because Joe's total base of potential consumers has great diversity and the ranges in preferences offset one another when averaged together. So rather than seeing strong preferences for a few brands, we see only light demand for most segments of the cereal category. By tailoring their marketing to their average customer, Joe's can only hope to appeal effectively to those shoppers who fit the average profile.

TABLE 11.2   Cereal Sales Potential at Joe's

Product	Joe's DI
Private Label HOMINY GRITS	112
Qkr Frosted Shredded Wheat READY TO EAT	108
Qkr Cap'N Crn Pnt Btr READY TO EAT	107
Qkr Sweet Puffs READY TO EAT	106
G M Multigrain Cheerios READY TO EAT	106
G M Basic 4 READY TO EAT	105
G M Wheat Chex READY TO EAT	105
Qkr Honey/Nut Oats READY TO EAT	105
Quaker HOMINY GRITS	105
Kel Cocoa Krispies READY TO EAT	105
HOMINY GRITS	105
Kel Frosted Mini-Wheats READY TO EAT	104
Kel Smacks READY TO EAT	104
G M Frosted Mini Chex READY TO EAT	104
Kel Rice Krispies READY TO EAT	103
G M Honey Nut Chex READY TO EAT	103
Kel Special K Red Berry READY TO EAT	103
G M Oatmeal Crisp/Rsn READY TO EAT	103
G M Rice Chex READY TO EAT	103
G M Cinnamon Toast Crunch READY TO EAT	102
Private Label READY TO EAT	102
G M Lucky Charms READY TO EAT	102
Post Grape-Nuts READY TO EAT	102
Private Label CEREAL	102
Qkr Cinnamon Life READY TO EAT	102

Source: Spectra Marketing Systems, Inc., using ACNielsen Homescan Product Library (HPL).

Grouping Joe's stores into clusters based on purchasing preferences that are specific to unique segments of Joe's customers will allow Joe's to take a more targeted approach, improving its understanding of the needs of its average shopper, while also addressing the newly discovered unique needs of shoppers who are not so average. With marketing strategies designed for each unique group, Joe's can reasonably expect to grow penetration, share-of-wallet, and sales per transaction with these consumers. The effort required will be more than offset by incremental sales and profits. They will attract new customers, and existing customers will spend more. The more diverse the clusters, the greater the return will be.

In Joe's case a Demand-Based Cluster analysis identified five store clusters for cereal (Table 11.3). However, Joe's can only afford to execute against three clusters at best and only where there is enough potential return on investment (ROI) to justify the extra

TABLE 11.3 Joe's Food Stores Grouped by Consumer Purchase Potential

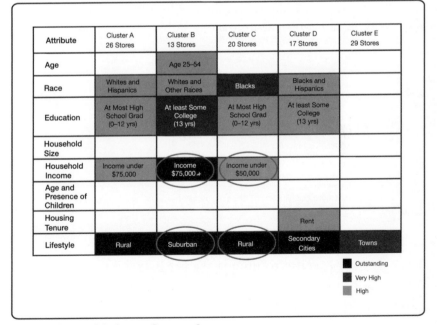

Attribute	Cluster A 26 Stores	Cluster B 13 Stores	Cluster C 20 Stores	Cluster D 17 Stores	Cluster E 29 Stores
Age		Age 25–54			
Race	Whites and Hispanics	Whites and Other Races	Blacks	Blacks and Hispanics	
Education	At Most High School Grad (0–12 yrs)	At least Some College (13 yrs)	At Most High School Grad (0–12 yrs)	At least Some College (13 yrs)	
Household Size					
Household Income	Income under $75,000	Income $75,000+	Income under $50,000		
Age and Presence of Children					
Housing Tenure				Rent	
Lifestyle	Rural	Suburban	Rural	Secondary Cities	Towns

■ Outstanding
■ Very High
■ High

Source: Spectra Marketing Systems, Inc.

resources. For this, Demand Gaps provide the needed input. Demand Gaps translate Demand Indices into dollars of upside sales potential based on the total size of a category in a given market. For Joe's, the high-income cluster, consisting of just 13 stores, has an upside of almost $1 million per year. Every day in each of the 13 stores, that's about 11 additional cases of cereal that are either not sold, underspaced, underpromoted, or priced incorrectly.

The low-income cluster also has a significant upside that is focused on a few brands and will be less expensive and easier to address. Since only the high- and low-income clusters have adequate upside, we will focus on developing marketing plans for three clusters rather than five. We can combine the three middle-income clusters into one and keep the low- and high-income clusters separate (see Table 11.4).

Let's look more closely at just how different the high- and low-income clusters are from the rest. While the majority of stores have

TABLE 11.4   Condensing the Clusters

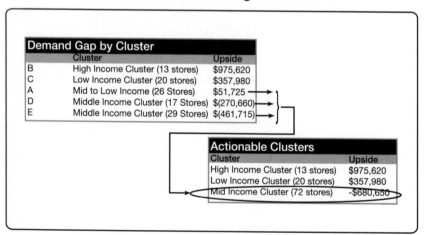

Demand Gap by Cluster		
	Cluster	Upside
B	High Income Cluster (13 stores)	$975,620
C	Low Income Cluster (20 stores)	$357,980
A	Mid to Low Income (26 Stores)	$51,725
D	Middle Income Cluster (17 Stores)	$(270,660)
E	Middle Income Cluster (29 Stores)	$(461,715)

Actionable Clusters	
Cluster	Upside
High Income Cluster (13 stores)	$975,620
Low Income Cluster (20 stores)	$357,980
Mid Income Cluster (72 stores)	-$680,650

Source: Spectra Marketing Systems, Inc.

TABLE 11.5 The Three Clusters

Household Income	Nation %	High Income 13 Stores			Low Income 20 Stores			Mid Income 72 Stores		
		Cluster B			Cluster C			Cluster ADE		
		Pct	Index	Actual	Pct	Index	Actual	Pct	Index	Actual
Under $10,000	7.5	3.8	51	963	11.6	154	3,439	8.2	109	11,248
$10,000–$19,999	11.8	5.9	50	1,495	15.3	129	4,536	11.8	100	16,186
$20,000–$29,999	11.8	7.5	63	1,901	14.7	124	4,358	12.9	109	17,695
$30,000–$39,999	11.3	7.1	63	1,799	13.2	117	3,914	12.4	109	17,009
$40,000–$49,999	10.0	7.3	73	1,850	10.5	105	3,113	10.8	107	14,814
$50,000–$74,999	20.2	18.5	91	4,689	18.5	91	5,485	20.9	104	28,669
$75,000–$99,999	11.8	16.9	142	4,283	8.4	71	2,490	11.1	93	15,226
$100,000+	15.6	33.0	212	8,364	7.7	50	2,283	11.8	76	16,186

Source: Spectra Marketing Systems, Inc.

middle-income customers, the other two clusters have dramatically different income levels (see Table 11.5). Income is one of the most important drivers of consumer purchasing.

Additional demographics reveal vastly different education levels and lifestyles. In chains where there are mostly high- and low-income groups with very few middle-income consumers, marketing to the middle can mean marketing to consumers who don't actually exist.

Consumer-Centric Assessments

In the Assessment step, Demand Indices identify what products consumers would be likely to buy if the products were made more available. In Table 11.6, the top of the reports shows the items with the highest potential for purchase for each group and the bottom shows the items with the very lowest potentials.

Looking at product purchasing potentials for total chain (left) and the 72 store middle-income group (right), the lists of products

TABLE 11.6   Total Chain versus Mid Income

	Total Chain 105 Stores		Mid Income 72 Stores
Product	DI	Product	DI
Private Label HOMINY GRITS	112	Private Label HOMINY GRITS	113
Qkr Frosted Shredded Wheat READY TO EAT	108	Qkr Frosted Shredded Wheat READY TO EAT	112
Qkr Cap'N Crn Pnt Btr READY TO EAT	107	G M Wheat Chex READY TO EAT	107
Qkr Sweet Puffs READY TO EAT	106	Post Grape-Nuts READY TO EAT	107
G M Multigrain Cheerios READY TO EAT	106	Qkr Sweet Puffs READY TO EAT	106
G M Basic 4 READY TO EAT	105	Qkr Honey/Nut Oats READY TO EAT	105
G M Wheat Chex READY TO EAT	105	Qkr Cap'N Crn Pnt Btr READY TO EAT	105
Qkr Honey/Nut Oats READY TO EAT	105	G M Multigrain Cheerios READY TO EAT	104
Quaker HOMINY GRITS	105	G M Rice Chex READY TO EAT	104
Kel Cocoa Krispies READY TO EAT	105	Kel Frosted Mini-Wheats READY TO EAT	103
HOMINY GRITS	105	Private Label READY TO EAT	103
Kel Frosted Mini-Wheats READY TO EAT	104	G M Basic 4 READY TO EAT	103
Kel Smacks READY TO EAT	104	Kel Smacks READY TO EAT	103
G M Frosted Mini Chex READY TO EAT	104	Kel Special K Red Berry READY TO EAT	103
Kel Rice Krispies READY TO EAT	103	Kel Cocoa Krispies READY TO EAT	103
G M Honey Nut Chex READY TO EAT	103	G M Frosted Mini Chex READY TO EAT	103
Kel Special K Red Berry READY TO EAT	103	Post Spn Sz Shred Wheat READY TO EAT	102
G M Oatmeal Crisp/Rsn READY TO EAT	103	Kel Hny Frst Mini-Wheats READY TO EAT	102
G M Rice Chex READY TO EAT	103	Post Spn Sz Frosted Shred Wht READY TO EAT	102
G M Cinnamon Toast Crunch READY TO EAT	102	Private Label CEREAL	102

Source: Spectra Marketing Systems, Inc.

with the highest purchase potentials are almost identical. Marketing to the average will serve these stores well.

Now let's look at the same report for the high- and low-income groups (Table 11.7). The report to the left shows the cereal purchase potentials for the low-income group. Jim Dandy Hominy Grits have the highest potential for sales in this cluster and Kashi has the lowest potential. The report to the right shows the cereal purchase potentials for the high-income group. Jim Dandy Hominy Grits have the second to lowest potential for sales in this cluster and Kashi has the highest potential.

And these lists differ significantly from the product potentials for the other 72-store group. Clearly, a one-size-fits-all approach to the

TABLE 11.7   Low versus High Income

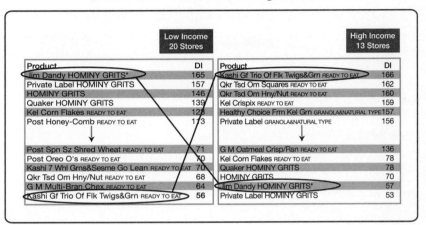

	Low Income 20 Stores			High Income 13 Stores
Product	**DI**	**Product**	**DI**
Jim Dandy HOMINY GRITS*	165	Kashi Gf Trio Of Flk Twigs&Grn READY TO EAT	166
Private Label HOMINY GRITS	157	Qkr Tsd Om Squares READY TO EAT	162
HOMINY GRITS	146	Qkr Tsd Om Hny/Nut READY TO EAT	160
Quaker HOMINY GRITS	139	Kel Crispix READY TO EAT	159
Kel Corn Flakes READY TO EAT	128	Healthy Choice Frm Kel Grn GRANOLA&NATURAL TYPE	157
Post Honey-Comb READY TO EAT	113	Private Label GRANOLA&NATURAL TYPE	156
Post Spn Sz Shred Wheat READY TO EAT	71	G M Oatmeal Crisp/Rsn READY TO EAT	136
Post Oreo O's READY TO EAT	70	Kel Corn Flakes READY TO EAT	78
Kashi 7 Whl Grns&Sesme Go Lean READY TO EAT	70	Quaker HOMINY GRITS	78
Qkr Tsd Om Hny/Nut READY TO EAT	68	HOMINY GRITS	70
G M Multi-Bran Chex READY TO EAT	64	Jim Dandy HOMINY GRITS*	57
Kashi Gf Trio Of Flk Twigs&Grn READY TO EAT	56	Private Label HOMINY GRITS	53

Source: Spectra Marketing Systems, Inc. using ACNielsen Homescan Product Library (HPL).

cereal category would not adequately address the consumer needs for these two store clusters. Once Joe's understands how different the preferences are for these unique store clusters, it will be hard to justify ignoring them in the future.

However, executing an additional set of planograms and a unique marketing plan may require incremental resources and spending, which is why it's important to have a checkpoint here to make sure that trade partners are in agreement about the potential return and required investment.

Setting Strategies

Item strategies take on new significance in a consumer-centric process. Turf protectors (based on demand, penetration, and market sales for the same demographic) in the category must be priced against the local competition, given the right shelf position, and must have enough facings to provide adequate holding power. If

Cheerios is a turf item in the middle-income group, and hominy grits is the turf item in the low-income group, and Kashi is the turf item in high-income stores, very different planograms, promotions, and pricing will be required by turf item by cluster. All item strategies can be adjusted by cluster, but many items will have the same role in all clusters.

Determining Category Roles by Cluster

A key change to the category review process, aside from clustering, is the sequence of the steps. In the consumer-centric version, the category role is determined by the collective roles of all the items in the category. This way, distinctions in item strategies by cluster can be carried forward to category roles. Categories where a large number of items have cluster-unique roles would indicate a need for assigning different category roles for each cluster as well.

In the low-income group, fewer ready-to-eat cereals have high indices. The focus is really on hot cereal such as grits. The hot segment may need to be considered routine while the ready-to-eat cereal segment is occasional.

In the high-income group, ready-to-eat cereal may include significant organic and natural offerings and could be destination.

In the middle-income majority of stores, cereal will probably be designated as routine.

Getting Tactical

All of the analytics developed so far can be applied to develop tactics, many of which will differ by cluster. The planogram in Figure 11.2 has been tailored to the average customer.

By adding demand indices for the low-income cluster we can demonstrate that there is an opportunity to grow sales in those

FIGURE 11.2 Ready-to-Eat Cereal Planogram

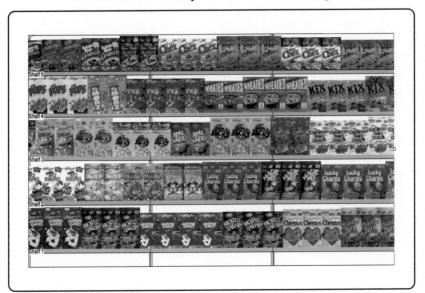

stores by reallocating space to some key items. For example, demand among shoppers in the low-income cluster is high for Frosted Flakes and Honey Smacks, and reduced for Lucky Charms, Chex, Kix, and Cinnamon Toast Crunch. The space devoted to such items could be altered accordingly (see Figure 11.3).

Adding demand indices for the high-income cluster shows an even greater sales opportunity since there are more items that index high. The adjustments to be made for this group would create a real departure from the average set and would be the opposite of what needs to be done for the low-income cluster. Specifically, space could be *reduced* for Frosted Flakes and Honey Smacks, and *expanded* for Lucky Charms, Chex, Kix, and Cinnamon Toast Crunch (see Figure 11.4).

Where possible, based on the geographic location of the store clusters, advertisements may be optimized for each group as well.

FIGURE 11.3   Low Income Indices

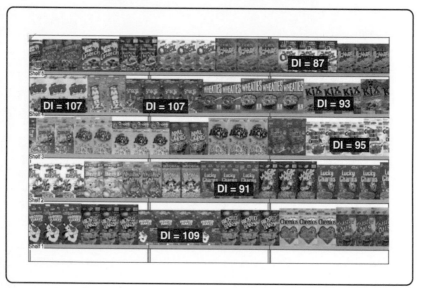

FIGURE 11.4   High Income Indices

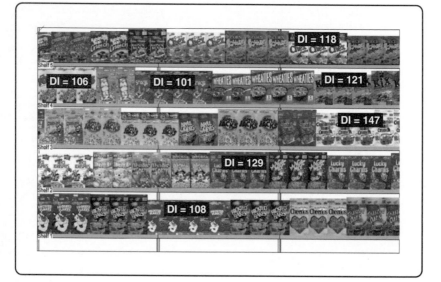

Figure 11.5 shows a typical newspaper advertisement with demand indices of the high-income cluster overlayed.

Many times a low-income cluster will be in the same ad zone as a high-income cluster. That's not necessarily an impediment to effective targeting because low-income groups are much less likely to subscribe to or buy newspapers or read direct mail but are much more likely to listen to urban radio. By using print for high-income groups and urban radio for low-income groups, two completely unique ads with different items can be delivered in the same geography to exactly the right households.

In this case, even an all-radio strategy can successfully target widely divergent groups while circulars can be used to address the main body of middle-income consumers. Table 11.8 shows the

FIGURE 11.5   Supermarket Advertisement

TABLE 11.8   Radio Preferences

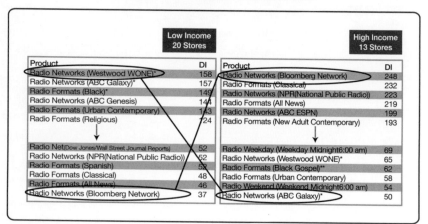

Low Income 20 Stores				High Income 13 Stores	
Product	DI		Product		DI
Radio Networks (Westwood WONE)*	158		Radio Networks (Bloomberg Network)		248
Radio Networks (ABC Galaxy)*	157		Radio Formats (Classical)		232
Radio Formats (Black)*	149		Radio Networks (NPR(National Public Radio))		223
Radio Networks (ABC Genesis)	144		Radio Formats (All News)		219
Radio Formats (Urban Contemporary)	143		Radio Networks (ABC ESPN)		199
Radio Formats (Religious)	124		Radio Formats (New Adult Contemporary)		193
Radio Net(Dow Jones/Wall Street Journal Reports)	52		Radio Weekday (Weekday Midnight6:00 am)		69
Radio Networks (NPR(National Public Radio))	52		Radio Networks (Westwood WONE)*		65
Radio Formats (Spanish)	52		Radio Formats (Black Gospel)**		62
Radio Formats (Classical)	48		Radio Formats (Urban Contemporary)		58
Radio Formats (All News)	46		Radio Weekend (Weekend Midnight6:00 am)		54
Radio Networks (Bloomberg Network)	37		Radio Networks (ABC Galaxy)*		50

Source: Spectra Marketing Systems, Inc. using Mediamark Research, Inc.

degree to which the low- and high-income cluster consumers tend to prefer certain radio formats and networks.

Keeping Score by Cluster

Scorecarding is saved for step eight because we cannot properly determine our goals until we've fully identified our store clusters, determined their potential, and come to an agreement about how much investment will be made in helping them reach their potential.

Scorecarding by cluster enables category managers to set much more realistic goals and then to monitor progress against these goals for each of the targeted consumer groups that characterize the three clusters (see Figure 11.6).

The middle-income cluster will have the traditional sales and margin goals. The middle-income cluster has traditionally been

FIGURE 11.6 Scorecards by Cluster

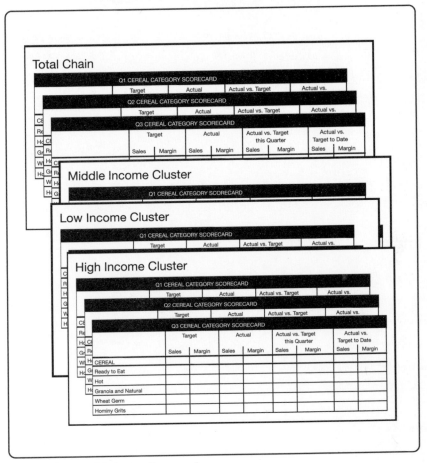

Source: Spectra Marketing Systems, Inc.

over promoted since it has been difficult to close gaps without addressing the unique needs of the other clusters. Promotional money may be shifted to promotions aimed at the high-income cluster. Some funds may move to other categories where there is a larger demand gap. There may be an expectation that sales will stay flat or decline slightly while margins will improve when promotional activity is adjusted.

The low-income group will have lower margin and sales expectations, with an expected upside in hot cereal. The high-income group will be expected to have higher margins, lower units sold, and higher dollars spent per customer, and a substantial sales and margin improvement.

Later, when results are evaluated, it will be possible to see which of the three strategies succeeded and which need adjustment by consumer type and store group. Since the consumer is well understood, remedies for specific underperforming groups are easy to formulate.

Implementation

The implementation stage has the added dimension of keeping track of which strategies are to be applied at which stores, and the task of making sure that vendors or store crews follow through on the different programs.

While there may seem to be additional work required to follow this consumer-centric category management process, it's actually more efficient than the original process because key consumer segments may be tracked individually, with adjustments made to limited numbers of stores. That prevents a lot of the rework inherent in one-size-fits-all approaches to category management.

Ultimately, Consumer-Centric Category Management is all about surfacing and focusing on consumer needs around which a category strategy can be developed that will deliver a better value proposition to the consumer, driving incremental profits for retailers and their manufacturer partners.

CATEGORY MANAGEMENT SUCCESS STORIES

General Mills—Going Beyond the Categories

Geneneral Mills is taking category management to the next level. Over the past few years, the company has expanded its scope beyond categories, and is now providing category management insights on aisles, departments, meal occasions, and even the total store.

"It is a natural evolution beyond categories," explains Al Fan, director of category management for refrigerated and frozen categories. "The question of optimal space allocation is at the top of the mind for many retailers. They want to know how to develop a competitive advantage in the marketplace while making sure there is enough space assigned for the categories in the aisles."

Such a sophisticated approach is not for everybody. The retailer must want it and be able to handle a great deal of information. The right organizational structure must be in place. Today, a considerable percentage of General Mills' effort goes beyond just the categories.

Operating on the cutting edge is nothing new for the Minneapolis-based company known for its leadership in the categories of breakfast cereal, baking products, and frozen and refrigerated foods. General Mills markets a product portfolio that includes more than 100 leading U.S. brands, as well as many category leaders around the world. Here's a sampling: Cheerios and Wheaties breakfast cereal, Betty Crocker baking mixes, Green Giant vegetables, Pillsbury refrigerated dough, Old El Paso Mexican foods, and Yoplait yogurt. Its products are sold in more than 100 countries on six continents. In the United States, the company is the number one or two brand in almost every category in which it competes.

Building on this solid foundation, General Mills serves its U.S. retail customers by developing consumer-driven recommendations to grow categories. The focus is simply to leverage its capabilities to create customer value.

"To develop the best category recommendations, we have to understand how the consumer shops the category and how retailers execute," says Fan. "We cannot keep the status quo. We have to do custom research and use innovative thinking to understand the future of the category. This is across all the tactical areas of category management, including baseline assortment, shelving, space management, and promotion management."

As such, the process is typically part of the retailer's business planning process. General Mills works within its retail partners' annual schedule for category reviews. The first step is building the category platforms with knowledge-based best practice recommendations. Then the job is communicating, analyzing, and developing a retailer-specific recommendation.

Fan was doing this work for General Mills six years ago in the cereal category. He is now working on frozen and refrigerated foods and has helped pioneer aisle management. For example, his yogurt category manager is not only focused on yogurt, but on the total dairy department. In other words, General Mills builds a platform of recommendations to optimize the entire refrigerated dairy section of the store.

It's not enough to recommend to a retailer that yogurt needs more space in the dairy aisle, they also need to know what category that space should come from. Retailers are also asking for recommendations on the optimal allocation of space across categories and ideal adjacencies to maximize total dairy sales. General Mills also provides insights about how consumers shop the entire dairy aisle by applying the same category structure segmentation techniques to the aisle that it uses for individual categories.

"This work requires more data and analytical capability, as well as investment into custom research," explains Chana Weaver, director of category management for dry grocery categories. "We've not only gone into aisle management, but also across categories into the area of meal solutions. Everyone is struggling with that opportunity for the consumer. Because our categories meet the consumer's breakfast, lunch, snacking and dinner needs, we had to develop recommendations for meal occasions which go across categories. We help the retailer understand how consumers view the meal occasion and what categories are included; that is, what is a traffic driver versus a transaction driver."

General Mills works with retailers to develop customized meal solution programs that cater to the needs of their specific shopper base. Retailers are using this information to create custom merchandising displays and in-store signage that promote cross-category purchases that ultimately generate a higher shopping basket ring for the retailer. "We are also helping retailers understand beneficial ways to manage the total store in terms of space allocation and layout," says Weaver.

That is a long way from the early days when General Mills began working with retailers. Ten years ago, Fan recalls, category management was just emerging. It was largely a decentralized and template-driven process that was practiced across the country by a few retailers and manufacturers. Research was confined to scan data, while the overall technology investment was minimal.

"The original templates always had the consumer front and center, but they had so much data that it was hard to see consumer impact," he says. "I also think there was limited investment at the time, in understanding the shopper. Not many companies purchased household panel or Spectra data. They didn't do custom research or category structure analysis. The consumer data available back then was very limited."

Consumer-Driven Approach

While category management at General Mills has always been driven by the consumer, the company has increased its emphasis in recent years by going beyond syndicated data into custom attitudinal and account-specific research.

"The core of our category management program revolves around our ability to understand how the shopper buys the category," says Fan. "The analysis we do with our research allows us to create category structures that define unique segments of the category in terms of variety and duplication. Because it is consumer- and purchase behavior-based, we believe this is the best approach to understand the consumer decision-making process for a category. The category structure will help identify which SKUs tend to interact with each other the most and those that don't. This information allows us to create category assortment recommendations that maximize incremental volume for the retailer."

Working with Retailers

General Mills does not prescribe or advocate any particular step-by-step process for category management. Managers work with retailers to meet their needs in whatever way the retailers want. Some of the largest retailers have developed a more formal and structured category review process and others still do ad hoc analysis based on changing market conditions or competitive threats.

"In some cases, retailers already have a process," says Fan. "In other cases, they have specific business questions or issues. If they want to talk about distribution, we will set it up by providing the background information on what the role of a category is and what the definition is, etc. But in many cases, they know all that and we will go right into an assortment analysis or a space optimization review. Other retailers who are just starting category management will defer to the traditional eight steps because it is comprehensive. As retailers become more comfortable with the process, they will become more ad hoc."

Because of its range of capabilities, General Mills is able to work at the retail level with key executives from the buyer up to the president. The functional partnerships at the retail level involve consumer research managers as well as marketing and merchandising executives.

Future

Fan believes it is General Mills' responsibility to build industry best category platforms—consumer-based best practices—to develop recommendations that will increase category growth. General Mills then works to communicate those insights to the field and works with customers to customize and implement those recommendations.

"Our philosophy is to be not just consumer-centric, but also customer-centric," he says. "We use facts and consumer data to develop recommendations that create customer value. But every customer is different—how they look at the business, how they define the categories, the data sources they have. So, we customize what we have to meet their needs. At the end of the day, we want to work very closely with our customers to make sure we can deliver against their needs. Whether those needs are standard category reviews or aisle management or total store reviews."

Big Y—Focusing on Implementation

Ten years ago, U.S. supermarket chains were just starting to implement category management. One of them, Big Y, went by the book with the original eight steps of category management as outlined by The Partnering Group, a pioneering consultancy in the field.

Category managers at the Springfield, Massachusetts-based chain now look back at the early days and shake their heads. There was too much emphasis on number crunching and not enough software to support the process. The consumer wasn't important enough in the analysis.

But Big Y had a vision.

"Our strategic vision was to gain a competitive advantage in the market through the use of category management," recalls Mark Rice, manager of space management and category development. "We wanted to be perceived by consumers as the premier supermarket in the area. We wanted to meet their needs better than the competition. We wanted to be the preferred one-stop variety shopping experience where consumers get superior value."

Today, Big Y practices a streamlined version of the original eight steps of category management. The category managers have eased off the data analysis, while enjoying the benefits of more technology. They focus more on the consumer now than in the past and make sure that retail implementation is a priority.

The chain's 52 food stores still joust for shoppers in Massachusetts and Connecticut with supermarket chains such as Stop & Shop, Shaw's, and Price Chopper. The competitors now include many other nonsupermarket retailers: warehouse clubs (Costco and BJ's), drugstore chains (CVS and Walgreen's), and Wal-Mart Supercenters. But Big Y's original vision endures, and category management is more important than ever.

"Ten years ago, we were looking at supermarkets as competitors," says David Foley, manager of several center store categories: household, oils, vinegar, condiments, and candy. "Today we look at everyone as a competitor—from drugstores to mass merchandisers. They are the ones really forcing us to be creative using category management."

Foley singles out pet food and baby care as categories that have benefited from this creativity. When pet specialty stores began cropping up in the trading area, Big Y made pet food a destination category by greatly expanding the space and assortments to prevent losing any market share.

For baby care, it developed "Baby Land" as a destination by merchandising formula, diapers, and accessories together.

"Category management forces you to think, collaborate, come up with ideas, and put it all together," explains Foley. "It's not just filling out templates. It is coming up with a plan that works, and then going back to modify it."

Foley calls such merchandising a form of aisle management. "We want a 'make sense' merchandising theme," he explains. "So, we are doing a little aisle management, but it is through the category management process. We want to make sure that not only are the categories managed, but our aisles are, as well."

Organization

At Big Y, category management falls under each department—from center store to perishables. It is coordinated by Rice, as the manager of category development. He supervises two field executives, three space management executives, and two data analysts. This team partners with the category managers to work with the data and develop a plan.

There are 17 category managers at the chain. Nine are responsible for perishables (produce and meat, bakery, deli, seafood, and food service), 6 for center store (dry grocery, dairy, and frozen foods), and 2 for nonfoods (general merchandise and health and beauty care). They make the decisions about their own categories.

"When we create the internal team for a category plan, we involve several departments, including someone from operations," says Rice. "In some cases, the operations person can be the grocery department manager from one of our stores; in other cases, it could be a store manager or a merchandiser. We include an operations member because they are the 'eyes and ears' to our customers on a daily basis. They help validate the consumer decision tree information that is brought into the meetings. They pass along frequently asked questions about items in the category, and they point out any operational issues, such as stocking, supply, and shelf management. We feel it's extremely important to have them involved."

Big Y reviews categories throughout the year with the help of one manufacturer partner for each category. Sometimes, more than one is used if a certain partner is not an expert in the entire category.

"We sit down with all the manufacturers in a category and see who would make the best partner. We have them bring all their information. Whoever has the best is the one we will pick," says Foley, stressing that it's not always the biggest company.

All of this work has paid off for Big Y. "We maintain scorecards for every category," says Rice. "On a dollar basis, you close a lot of opportunity gaps to increase sales and profitability. Monetarily, we've seen benefits. Some other things are hard to measure."

According to Rice, it is very important to have the top executives behind the category management program. Without their support, category management programs would eventually disappear because they require a big commitment from so many members within the company. It is also important to get their feedback during presentations.

"Initially, it was intimidating for category managers to present their plans to these executives," he explains. "But eventually they realized that executive feedback was also geared toward growing the category and satisfying our customers. They had a wider view than just the category, and over time helped bring our program to the next level with aisle and store management.

"It takes time and experience to get to that next level in category management," Rice continues. "Over the years, we have done hundreds of category plans in all departments. We've worked with numerous vendor partners and have seen many different reporting formats and presentation styles. Over time, experience allows us to see what works and what doesn't so we can make adjustments to our templates and program."

Big Y relies on internal category management advisory groups made up of members of the many departments involved in the process. After each round of presentations, the group discusses what is needed to improve for the next round.

The chain also asked a group of category management partners with previous experience to form an advisory group to critique the category management program. This has yielded many helpful suggestions for improvement.

"We look for feedback from whomever we can get it," says Rice.

Eight Steps

The chain still follows the eight steps of category management that it started with 10 years ago, but they are customized nowadays. Some of the steps were "too restrictive or time consuming," according to Foley.

"We needed to cut back the workload, but we didn't want to take away from the category management process. We all agreed with the process, but the data analysis needed to be streamlined," he recalls.

Managers spend a lot of time understanding consumers and how they affect the category, according to Rice. They rely on more consumer information that is now available from the category partners.

"Over the last 10 years, when you look at the 8 steps, we probably spent more time on strategy, tactics and now implementation than we did in the beginning," says Foley. "Everyone was getting caught up with the data in the beginning. By the time we got through the reams, which took 6 months, we were too tired to implement the plan. Now we know that the key is implementation, which is one of our last steps," he goes on to say. "When we are done, we want a plan in place ready to be implemented. We spend time on a new planogram in the process, and sometimes a new focus for the category, backed up by good strategy and good tactics. We want to be ready to go when the plan is done."

Technology Investment

Big Y's investment in technology is something else that has changed over the years. According to Rice, there wasn't a lot of technology in place a decade ago. The chain relied on manufacturer partners to bring in consumer panel data and other sources of information. The company invested in technology four years ago to enhance its category management program and now is more self-sufficient— something it likes.

"Now we can control our own data," he says. "A partner will usually bring in a lot of the information we need. But if we run into issues with a partner, we can fall back and rely on ourselves for the necessary data."

To upgrade its technology, Big Y is now using Category Business Planner from ACNielsen. "As a category manager I can pull up on my desktop demographics, Spectra information, market share numbers, and market information from Category Business Planner. Four years ago, I couldn't do that without having a resource," says Foley.

The investment has made a big difference in the practice of category management, according to Foley. Category plans can be changed faster because data is readily available, enabling the chain to stay one step ahead of the competition.

"When we implement a plan, say for salad dressing, we can follow it up, keep track of the category, and see the trends. In the past, we never identified trends and opportunities until the manufacturer came in or until a category review. Now we can see things happening from the desktop," he says, adding that planograms are distributed via intranet e-mail.

But everything is not as easy at Big Y. Foley says the biggest challenge in category management is dealing with all of the departments of a supermarket. Most manufacturers focus only on the categories in the center store. Big Y applies category management to other departments, as well.

"We don't always have the partners in the perishable departments that we do in grocery," explains Foley. "Occasionally, we have to do those plans internally. Our challenge is to execute a plan, say for stone fruit, within a seasonal format. With in-store bakery categories, if we don't have a partner, we'll still complete that category plan. But we'll customize it instead of being hung up with not fitting into category management templates and not having a partner."

Future

The new frontier for category management at Big Y deals with fully understanding the consumers of each category through available information provided by the category partners while staying ahead of current trends by practicing continuous category management now that technology has provided tools to make the process more efficient.

Category management has been a long road for Big Y over the past 10 years. The process has moved the industry away from relationships being involved in decision making to more fact-based decision making, according to Rice. It has helped Big Y compete better in a more challenging retail marketplace. It has enabled Big Y to understand the consumers of each category better so that managers can execute against the goal in the mission statement:

> Big Y is a family-owned and family-oriented retail food company serving people's at-home food needs. Our goal is to exceed our customers' evolving expectations by constantly seeking better ways to create and deliver world-class service and value.

A Step-by-Step Category Review

A category review at Big Y involves four meetings spread out over two months. Here is an outline for the Salad Dressing and Topping review:

Before the meetings begin, the chain selects a manufacturer partner after reviewing its capabilities for providing consumer and category trend information. The category manager then forms an internal team to develop the category plan. It includes the category manager, a category analyst, a space management specialist, a grocery manager (representing operations), and a store brand department member.

Meeting 1

- The team discusses, confirms, and comes to a consensus on category definition and Decision Tree, category role, subcategories, segments, and subsegments. Consensus is based on the consumer information provided.
- Assesses the consumer by reviewing consumer's category hierarchy of needs to be met (through manufacturer consumer studies), demographics (age, income, household size, ethnic, and gender breakdowns), and consumer behavior (household penetration, purchase cycle and size, on/off sale purchases, annual consumption, and expenditure).
- Reviews the remainder of the unpopulated template for concerns and analytical opportunities and determines the responsibilities of the partner responsible for market-level data and surveys. Big Y is responsible for internal data.

Meeting 2

- For the retailer and market assessment, the team reviews templates to understand and analyze trends, opportunity gaps, contribution, and productivity by subcategory, segment, subsegment, brand, and SKU.

- Reviews reports on other items and categories that have synergies and are affected by this category.
- Reviews the category scorecard.

MEETING 3

- The team analyses efficient assortment.
- Finalizes category strategies.
- Creates category tactics for shelf, assortment, promotion, price, and product supply.
- Schedules a separate, additional meeting with Big Y and vendor space management personnel to create and finalize a planogram based on new strategies and tactics.

MEETING 4

- The team rolls all findings and decisions into a polished category plan and creates a PowerPoint presentation.
- Presents the category plan to top executives for approval in a final presentation.
- If accepted, the category plan is implemented throughout the chain.

SUPERVALU—The Last Three Feet of Category Management

"If you're going to do category management, you need to be flexible," advises Michael Terpkosh of SUPERVALU, the largest grocery wholesaler in the United States. "Be able to change the process over time to make it easier and more efficient. Then move beyond the basics to be more effective on a much higher level. Don't lock yourself into one process and stick with it long term."

That's a bit of wisdom from the executive who runs the wholesale category management program for SUPERVALU's sprawling $19.5 billion empire of wholesale and retail operations that includes 24 distribution centers and 8 banners representing more than 1,500 stores that stretch across 41 states.

Terpkosh has directed the wholesale program for more than a decade. Along the way, he confronted the nettlesome problem of faulty execution in the store where the best-laid category management plans typically fall apart. Today, the Minneapolis-based company conducts over 80 category reviews per year. Each cycle of work involves category resets and new item cut-ins that go into a store every two weeks. With more than 1,200 stores on the program, that works out to a minimum of 96,000 category resets a year (not every category is reviewed annually).

It is the shelf set in the retail store—in the last three feet of category management—where the success or failure of the process is determined. How SUPERVALU fixed the problem of poor retail execution is a valuable lesson to any company practicing category management. It was part of the evolution of category management at SUPERVALU that began with small steps a decade ago and has culminated in a state-of-the-art process today.

Organization and Personnel

SUPERVALU handles its category management work with a clearly defined organizational structure. There are two main groups: one for general merchandise/health and beauty care and one for grocery, frozen, and dairy products.

All the category management work for general merchandise/health and beauty care—from review to strategies to tactics—is done centrally in Minneapolis. There are several category managers in this group who have support people to do category work and disseminate it to the regional facilities and other upstream general merchandise/health and beauty care distribution centers. The plan ultimately goes in the stores.

For grocery, frozen food, and dairy at headquarters, there is a staff of category managers who create category strategies and have major reviews with vendor partners to finalize those strategies. The category plan then goes to the regional locations where merchandisers create the planograms and the tactics that are executed in the stores.

A category manager oversees about a dozen categories with each being responsible for thousands of items. Each week the category manager reviews up to 100 promotion contracts submitted from the manufacturers/brokers and reviews hundreds of new products. Duties also include assortment, pricing, and space management work as part of the focus on strategy and tactics.

The groups at each region report to a management team there. Terpkosh's 10-person department of corporate, management, and retail pricing at headquarters is the development/training arm for the program.

SUPERVALU works with about 150 vendor partners. Several major manufacturers such as Kraft Foods, Procter & Gamble, Unilever, and others represent many categories. Smaller companies represent one or possibly two categories. They provide insights about the category, consumers, and the competition.

How are vendor partners selected? SUPERVALU picks the company in each category that will do the best job for SUPERVALU in that particular category. Typical questions Terpkosh might ask include: "Do they have the people resources to help get the work done? Do they have the data and the systems to make that possible? Do they have a commitment to retail execution that enables them to participate in the program to the level they need to?"

The largest manufacturer in a given category doesn't automatically become a vendor partner, but once a vendor earns that title, it's essentially a long-term partnership. SUPERVALU'S category managers informally evaluate the partners every couple of years. If both parties are pleased with the relationship, the partnership remains intact.

While there is only one partner per category, there can be one to three "category validators" who can be called on to give additional insights. Sometimes partners of one category opt to be validators on others. They want to give input, but don't want to provide the amount of work required of a partner.

"The validator role is actually discussed upfront in the review process," explains Terpkosh. "When we want a major review in a category, we'll have the vendor partner conduct the review. The validator can provide additional insights and perspective. That gets them in the game. The category managers will call on them and get their input just like they do from the partner. But it's a lot less intensive and a lot less time consuming."

Today's Process

Over the years, the number of people working in category management at SUPERVALU has decreased due to both retail consolidation and the increased sophistication of technology tools. While these changes have affected many companies, not all have learned how to do more with less and do it seamlessly like SUPERVALU.

SUPERVALU has effectively integrated category management principles and activities into the day-to-day work and business processes. The days of a major study of category management once or twice a year are long gone. The process is ongoing and involves merchandising decisions with manufacturers and sales agencies every day. This has enabled the wholesaler to stay more in tune with consumers in the marketplace and the competition than in the past.

"Because we have so much at our fingertips now, we can put programs together easily," says Terpkosh. "How is a manufacturer positioned within a given category? Are they growing their business for us at the category's growth rate? Or are they faster or slower than the category's growth? How is their business with us versus the competitive market?

"We look at a number of different factors, comparing our category results or our results with the manufacturer to what's going on with the rest of the marketplace or with our competitors in that category. Then, in discussions with manufacturers, we talk about how to drive the business at retail. So it all ties together."

According to Terpkosh, this way of doing business enables SUPERVALU to react to quick changes in the market. He points to the barrage of new "low-carb" products in 2004 that tested the ability of category managers to integrate them into the plan efficiently, and get them onto the shelf quickly. SUPERVALU actually saw the low-carb trend coming. A category manager was writing a position paper on how to handle the new products at retail when Unilever called to say they had 15 new items ready for shipment. Other manufacturers were right behind.

"So we were under tight deadlines," Terpkosh recalls. "The category management team had to rally folks, make decisions, put changes together, and get them to the retailers."

And they did. It was just another example of how important a working relationship with a manufacturer really is, and the experience served as a valuable lesson for all food distributors. A good distributor should always have his antennae up and be ready to sound an early warning about coming changes, whether in new products or consumer preferences or local shopping habits, partners need to work together.

"One of my favorite words is flexibility," Terpkosh says. "It's flexibility in how you structure, and it's flexibility in how you work with your partners in creating a real open dialogue. Over the last five years, about half of everything that we have developed has come from ideas that we've had internally or we saw somewhere else. But the other half has come from the vendor partners, either suggesting areas for improvement or offering ideas about new areas we needed to move into."

Vendors have been valuable SUPERVALU partners from the very beginning. Without specific software applications of its own, SU-PERVALU relied on vendor partners in the early days to help support the process. "Our vendor partners were doing 90 percent of the category review creation and work for us," says Terpkosh.

To change this, SUPERVALU began to purchase applications and tools for internal use. One of these tools was an effective planogram software package to maintain shelf sets. Another was a set of data mining tools to access information from data suppliers so that SUPERVALU could internally create custom trading areas to gauge performance versus the competitive market.

The wholesaler took a giant leap forward in sophistication about five years ago with the launch of several software applications and data sources from ACNielsen that made the process more manageable. One was Category Business Planner (CBP) that provided trading area information online and now sits on users' desks. The software gave SUPERVALU sufficient trend analysis for its needs, according to Terpkosh. Because it was online, category managers started moving away from big number crunching as they refined the process into what they use today for the independent retailers. CBP also helped SUPERVALU integrate category management into day-to-day merchandising activities and decisions.

The software essentially eliminated the need for vendor-partners to provide the same material in a category management presentation or deck. "It was redundant," Terpkosh explains. "We've backed away from around 70 to 80 percent of the trend analysis they were doing for us in the past. We basically said, 'There are a handful of tables and charts that we need from you for creating category strategies, and that's all we need you to provide us with.'"

Terpkosh points to CBP's ease of use, Internet functionality, and reliability as big pluses. "We have our trading areas online. We can do analysis at the trading area, category, manufacturer, and brand levels. This gives us real-time analytical power when we need it. Because CBP is so easy to use, it has helped us integrate category management principles and processes into day-to-day work activities, like negotiating with manufacturers and brokers."

Another valuable resource for SUPERVALU was Spectra data, which provided a look at the demographics of consumers living around stores.

"That was part of our evolution," explains Terpkosh. "Our first five years were devoted to getting the program up and running and getting folks comfortable doing category management work. And about five years ago, they started to make the switch to using more consumer information and using more ACNielsen and Spectra information. That really started helping us quite a bit. That's when we were able actually to fine-tune the process."

What followed was deploying in-depth tools to look at multi-channel data that tracks the performance of Wal-Mart, food, mass, drug, dollar, and other channels. The final piece was more sophisticated consumer insights.

"Consumer panel data was the latest step for us," says Terpkosh. "We ran it for the first time in early 2004. Our category managers needed to get a much better look and feel across multiple competitors and markets—across grocery or other channels—for what consumers think and feel. It made sense to try to bring in that next level of information."

Armed with sophisticated technology and new sources of data, category managers are now doing more of the pick-and-shovel work of the category review instead of the vendor partner. That is one way SUPERVALU has streamlined the process. And that is one of the ways that the process has evolved over the past five years.

SUPERVALU's category management work really begins by understanding the needs of their independent retailers. Across the SUPERVALU regional offices, a staff of field agents work with the retailers to execute the category management program in their stores. The field staff, with the category management staff in each region, gain insights and in-depth understanding into the strategy and needs of each retailer. This understanding is then applied to the creation of category strategies and tactics in the category review process.

SUPERVALU now practices a modified and streamlined version of the classic eight-step process. It includes five steps:

1. Analyze consumer data.
2. Review the category.
3. Develop strategies.
4. Recommend tactics.
5. Execute in the store.

Analyze Consumer Data

SUPERVALU has always been flexible when it comes to determining the category role: destination, routine, occasional, seasonal, or convenience. The corporate office sets up a role for each category based on category trends, consumers, and its importance with SUPERVALU, but regional merchandisers can modify the role based on local markets and shoppers.

"We spend a decent amount of time making those decisions, but we don't let it bog us down," says Terpkosh. "A role is set quickly based on the consumer, competition and our retailers' needs. We then evaluate the category role on a periodic basis with the category review."

Review the Category

When category managers look at category trends today, they include in the analysis what's going on with the consumer (trends, shopping preferences, consumer insight studies, and so on) and other channels of distribution (mass, dollar, Wal-Mart, or others). This approach is different than it was a decade ago when the focus was largely on category trends within the grocery channel.

SUPERVALU continues to refine its scorecard in terms of share, business trends, year-to-year changes, and the like. "They're sophisticated and let us know how we're tracking versus everyone else by giving us some comparative measures. But they're not too in-depth," Terpkosh says. "It is critical to understand our performance, and the performance of our retailers, in relation to all channels and in relation to consumer trends."

Develop Strategies

Category strategy has gradually become more detailed. Five years ago, a strategy document might have been 5 to 10 pages long, with the retailer's version only a couple of pages. Today, that document can be 40 pages long for internal use, while the summary for retailers remains about 2 or 3 pages long. The "Executive Summary Document" for retailers includes an overview of what's going on in the category, the plans for the category, and planograms that will be executed in the stores.

According to Terpkosh, the category management work done in Minneapolis has to be more in-depth for categories because strategies for food and nonfood are all done centrally. In the case of nonfood, tactics are also implemented centrally.

"Then we feed the information out to the people in each region who work with the retailers so that they've got a better understanding of what's going on in the category. They don't actually do a category review in each regional location any longer," says Terpkosh.

For the food categories, SUPERVALU does an overall category review at the corporate level working with vendor partners. They create the strategy and then communicate it to each of the regional locations where tactics are developed.

"The strategy has to be very in-depth because it almost works as an instruction manual or a recommended plan that goes to the merchandisers in each region who execute the tactics for that category," says Terpkosh.

Recommend Tactics

SUPERVALU has always spent a lot of time on the SKU mix and planogramming. As a result, there are few changes across the categories except for adding new items.

"Generally, we don't reinvent the shelf principles every time we do a category review," explains Terpkosh. "Retailers are comfortable with the plan. You do change your item mix over the course of time because you add new items and delete others. But you don't revolutionize the shelf set every year for all the categories. So we have shifted the emphasis now to spending much more time on promotion and pricing," he says. "Pricing for us has been the hardest piece to crack just because of the complicated nature and number of competitors in a given area. The emphasis is on what type of strategy to take—category by category or in an overall store—to drive the retail pricing at the store to help our retailers." SUPERVALU uses ACNielsen Priceman to help create retail pricing strategies by category.

Execution in the Store

Terpkosh says that retail execution is getting better, but that was not always the case. For years, the category management plan was short-circuited in the store with poor execution. The best strategy and tactics were essentially not being carried out.

"We buried all of our people into this huge cumbersome category management process because that is what the industry said you were supposed to do and what everybody said was going to work great. We ended up spending 90 percent of our time collecting and analyzing data and 10 percent of our time interpreting that information. Then at the end of the day, we were getting nothing done at retail," explains Terpkosh.

Other wholesalers and retail chains have wrestled with the same problem over the years. The way that SUPERVALU solved it serves as a model for others. Today, SUPERVALU spends 30 percent of its time on retail execution focusing on ensuring that what is planned and promised is actually delivered in the store. About 30 percent of its time goes to analyzing consumers and retail competition and 40 percent to strategy and tactics.

How did the wholesaler change its mix? The overriding principle that guided the change is that retail execution is the shared responsibility of all trading partners—the manufacturer, broker, wholesaler, and retailer.

"It's our responsibility to help get the job done in the store," says Terpkosh.

To ensure effective retail execution, SUPERVALU follows a three-step process:

1. *Pick a knowledgeable merchandising service organization (MSO):* SUPERVALU relies on Prism Retail Services to coordinate category resets, new item cut-ins, and other in-store work. The MSO works with SUPERVALU at corporate headquarters and in its six regional offices.

2. *Work with vendor partners that value retail execution:* With the help of vendor partners such as Procter & Gamble, SUPERVALU focused on increasing compliance and implementing the last three feet of the category management plan. The consumer products giant brought in best practices for retail execution and worked side-by-side with SUPERVALU.

3. *Invest in technology:* SUPERVALU does a "huge amount of work on the Internet," says Terpkosh. Applications used include ACNielsen Answers with Category Business Planner, a web-based tool from ACNielsen, which helps determine category management objectives in stores. The wholesaler runs its program for in-store execution on the Internet so retailers, manufacturers, and brokers have easy access to planograms and the packet of information containing their instructions for retail execution of updated planograms and new item cut-ins.

There is still a typical flow to the category management process. SUPERVALU provides information to the vendor-partner, who creates a consumer-based and action-oriented category review they both review together. Category managers write up the strategy for the categories and create the tactics. "Then it's handed off to the manufacturers, brokers and PRISM for retail execution," Terpkosh sums up.

But improved retail execution is not the only change from the way SUPERVALU practiced category management in the past. About a decade ago, it was a separate business process. The wholesaler and its retailers layered the weight of the category management process on top of the normal, everyday way of doing business. It simply became something else to do. Not so anymore.

"Now it's how we do everything every day," says Terpkosh. "There is still a review that happens once a year for the majority of the large- and medium-sized categories. But beyond that, the integration of category management principles into everyday work has been a major change."

Category management at SUPERVALU developed in two stages: the first five years when everyone was slow to learn what then was a complex process, and the last five years when they simplified the steps, focused on consumer insights, and deployed sophisticated technology to make the job easier.

Focus on the Consumer

The most important lesson for SUPERVALU was learning the value of market research that revealed consumer attitudes, characteristics, and shopping behavior. According to Terpkosh, this information, generally referred to as "consumer insights" in the trade, possesses more power than the detailed analysis of sales data. "Consumer insights tell the retailers and manufacturers what the consumers really want. When you know and understand consumer insights, the creation of the category strategy and tactics is much easier," he says.

Relying more on consumer insights and less on "number crunching" was part of the evolution of category management at the company. Everyone at SUPERVALU now admits that years ago there was just too much data internally and from manufacturers. It was clear that data overload was not going to provide answers or action in the store.

But there were plenty of questions five years ago for SUPERVALU: How do they get away from the "data dump" and move more into actionable information? Which insights will drive performance at retail? How do they simplify category management?

The answers became apparent about five years ago when SUPERVALU began to revise the process by fine-tuning its approach. The steps taken serve as a simple guide for companies still laboring under the weight of data overload.

"Our recommended review template today is much different than it was five years ago because we've moved away from a lot of that very data-intensive activity," explains Terpkosh. "Looking at numbers is fine, but I need to have a better understanding of consumer insights and what's going on with the competition to make decisions that are actionable rather than doing a huge amount of deep-dive analysis just involving numbers."

For example, SUPERVALU wanted to learn how its retailers could compete better with alternative-channel retailers. It welcomed input from a number of vendor partners to develop a program for its stores. One of the programs, the Center Store Program, is a key category management strategy retailers can implement to counter the effects of alternative channels taking away center store category sales.

SUPERVALU relied on consumer insights to create strategies. Vendor partners provided the research on changing trends and changing competitors to determine how they impacted various categories. "That was very big for us," says Terpkosh, who used the example of a hot retail format in the United States: the dollar store channel. When they were emerging as a retail competitor and couldn't be ignored, independent retailers asked SUPERVALU for advice. Will dollar stores last? Do we react to them? If so, how?

"A big 'Ah-ha' for us was the movement in dollar stores away from carrying discontinued packs or salvage items to carrying more of a regular, ongoing item mix across a number of grocery categories. Well, that was a huge insight for us," he says. "SUPERVALU started to work with our vendor partners to see how consumers perceived those items in dollar stores and why they were making more regular shopping trips there." The result is a program that enables retailers to put dollar sections in their stores.

Another example dealt with speed: making planogram changes more quickly and then getting new items on the shelf faster. A study of the existing process done in 2000 showed poor performance. SUPERVALU—like many wholesalers—took a longer time to get new items on the shelf than self-distributing retail chains. Self-distributing chains own and operate their own warehouses and don't rely on wholesalers like independent retailers do to get them new products.

"We would bring in a new item," Terpkosh recalls, "and then we'd suggest putting it into the planogram. It was up to the retailer to place the order. But when it came time to put the item on the shelf, a lot of times it just wasn't in the store."

Working with its vendor partners, the wholesaler put together an auto-distribution program which automatically ships new items to the stores when they are received into the warehouse. Retailers sign up for auto-distribution, and SUPERVALU determines the new items that automatically ship to the stores upon receipt into the warehouse. Of course, the planogramming process of category management is included to tell the retailers where the new item fits on the shelf.

This has been very successful for new products. The bottom line was an increase in speed-to-shelf and better retail sales of new items for the independent retailers. "Today, our retailers perform at the same level of speed-to-shelf as the self-distributing retail chains." says Terpkosh.

Challenge for Wholesalers

Over the years, SUPERVALU overcame a fundamental challenge: the lack of tools designed specifically for wholesalers. When it began the process a decade ago, all of the category management software was geared for retail chains that operated maybe one or two formats in a certain market. A wholesaler with, say, 300 stores in a regional trading area on category management had to improvise until special programs became available. In the case of SUPER-VALU, they started to develop their own software tools. Doing category management for a large number of independent retailers means dealing with many different formats and markets.

"That just adds a level of complexity: understanding the strategies of these retailers, the markets they're in, and trying to help them by producing a good quality category management program that will work for them," explains Terpkosh.

Of course, category management at SUPERVALU is not mandatory for the retailers. They must sign up for the program and pay a weekly fee to get the service. Today, over 1,200 stores participate in the program, representing more than 70 percent of SUPERVALU's independent retailer all-commodity volume (ACV). Terpkosh says this gives SUPERVALU an advantage over retail chains that other wholesalers can't match. Once a self-distributing retail chain headquarters decides to commit to category management, they have to "force-feed it to the stores," but independent retailers choose to take part in the SUPERVALU category management program.

"We have tried very hard to be better on the retail execution side," Terpkosh says. "We have to be a little more flexible. We have to get more information to the retailers about how we handle the category management and shelf reset program. It does make it more complex. But even though it's been difficult, I think it has paid off for us more than for a typical retail chain."

The logistics involved with a wholesale operation also differ from a self-distributing chain. Because of the number of formats served, it is always a challenge to have enough room in the distribution center to carry all of the products that a category management plan calls for. "You've always got an overabundance of SKUs and you are trying to fine-tune that mix between what you carry on the wholesale side and what the retailers need in the stores," says Terpkosh.

SUPERVALU's solution was to use alternative facilities, such as upstream warehouses. For example, most of SUPERVALU's retailers receive general merchandise and health and beauty care products from "upstream" facilities because all the products are not in every SUPERVALU distribution center. The upstream facilities provide GM/HBC products to several "downstream" distribution centers that in turn service the retailers. Alternate facilities helped SUPERVALU be more efficient and economical. It makes for a more varied product mix at a given retailer because the supply source is not just one distribution center.

Deploying a Centralized Process

When SUPERVALU began to practice category management, all of the work was done at the regional level. The vendor partner came in and did a review with each region, and each category manager determined a strategy and mapped out the tactics.

About six years ago, the wholesaler began to look at centralizing the process. The first steps were with general merchandise and health and beauty care. Because of the nature of the products—being nonfood—SUPERVALU was able to centralize the organization in Minneapolis and do all strategic and tactical category management work there.

Soon, there was discussion of doing the same in the food categories of grocery, frozen, and dairy, in order to develop an overall strategy in a given category. SUPERVALU tested a review calendar across the entire company for those food categories, leading to category reviews at the corporate level with a companywide strategy. The process ends with tactical processes at each region.

For example, a full-blown review is done with the corporate category manager of the pet category. A strategy is created and sent to the merchandisers in each region who are responsible for the pet category. The vendor partner's regional contacts understand that SUPERVALU category strategy and then work with the regional merchandisers on the tactics, which are then executed at retail.

"That's essentially where we've ended up," says Terpkosh. "It started out with a handful of categories and matured where today we have one category review calendar across all the regions. Everybody's on that calendar across the whole company. It's a great way to streamline the process, both for our folks and for the vendor partners. Information flows from corporate to the regions and then to the retailers."

In each store, SUPERVALU asks for a retail contact person. It could be the store manager, an assistant manager or a department manager. About a month before a reset date, the contact person receives a 2- or 3-page executive summary with the new planograms and an explanation of the category strategy. They can make some modifications before the reset team walks into the store. Manufacturers and brokers have the option of sending their own team or hiring the MSO to do their fair share of the reset work in the stores. Today, it's common for reset work to be done by labor from several sources.

"Beyond that, we just look for input from retailers on a regular basis about how they want to run their operation," says Terpkosh. "We have people in the field calling on them on a regular basis to talk about what's happening in the store with resets and the category management program. It provides them with the opportunity to give us feedback."

Retailers also receive store-specific reporting so they can track inventory, gross profit, and sales—category by category, subcategory by subcategory, and current year to last year. Basically, they can see how their retail business is performing with the category management program.

What's in Store for the Future?

Terpkosh sees this collaborative formula as key to the future, given the topsy-turvy, competitive marketplace that stretches out before the grocery industry. Two of the major changes in store for SUPER-VALU are "aisle management" and the Internet.

The wholesaler will be moving from "category" to "aisle" management, which literally means managing a whole aisle of the store as a unit rather than the individual categories in that aisle. What's prompting the change, Terpkosh says, is the need to remain nimble in the face of a sudden stream of new products and changes in how consumers shop.

"One of the things that trapped us with some of these trends over the last few years was the inability to adjust category size within the aisle," he explains "If you've got, say, 20 feet of a category, you're always going to have 20 feet of the category in a store. How do you expand or contract that based on what the consumers are seeing in that category and what they want to buy?"

So SUPERVALU is working with the broader practice of aisle management. Category managers expect to gain flexibility and the ability to make quick adjustments to the category shelf set.

The wholesaler is not a lone pioneer in this effort. Several major vendor partners—the first two were ConAgra and Unilever—have come to SUPERVALU with well-documented studies that called for a broader category management approach because "consumers are lost in the stores." Aisle management will help to realign categories more effectively.

Plans for the change are being prepared for the field staff by a team at the SUPERVALU corporate office with the help of the vendor partners. As stores are remodeled or reset, or when new stores are built, SUPERVALU field staff will recommend realigning categories so SUPERVALU category managers can move into aisle management.

"It going to do a couple of things," Terpkosh predicts. "It's not only going to give us the ability to make quick adjustments, but it's also going to help us be more efficient with execution. We'll do work in a given aisle one or two times a year versus eight or nine times a year because the categories today are spread over the review calendar over the course of the year."

The Internet has been a major change agent for SUPERVALU. It began as a convenient way to maintain information—mainly planograms and other category information—for the wholesaler, its retailers, manufacturer partners, and their brokers. Updates were relayed efficiently. Everybody had access and could stay on the same page of category management.

A lot of other activities such as new item introductions, promotions, and surveys are now going online, too. Terpkosh anticipates moving much of the merchandising activities with manufacturers and brokers onto the Internet. The change will extend to the stores and how SUPERVALU does business with its retailers.

"There's a huge potential there for a more efficient way of doing business together and driving sales," he says. "It's going to be something ongoing for a number of years to make the business better."

So goes the long and winding road of category management at SUPERVALU. From data overload to consumer insights, from a separate process to part of day-to-day operations, and from category reviews to aisle management, the evolution of the process continues.

RETAIL STRATEGY

Understanding a retailer's strategy is the linchpin of category management. This critical first step poses a challenge for wholesalers such as SUPERVALU simply because they serve many corporate and independent stores in various sizes and formats.

The obvious questions:

- What does each retailer want to accomplish?
- Who is shopping in the stores?
- What is the marketing strategy for each banner?

"They vary from a small independent supermarket to a large box, high-volume store, to an upscale supermarket—or something in between," says Mike Terpkosh, contemplating the variety of formats and the complexity involved.

What to do?

"We've found over the years," he says, "that it is very important first to sit down with retailers and understand how they're positioning themselves in the marketplace.

"There is some grouping you can do. People use the term 'clustering.' We have retailers with slightly different formats and in different locations, but they share the same strategies. We need to understand those strategies. It helps us to fine tune and be much more efficient in doing category management. That's a very critical piece for us."

But this dialogue is a two-way street. Retailers need to be open-minded when starting to work through their category process. Sometimes they need to modify their retail strategy because the marketplace or the competitive mix is changing.

"One of the foundational pieces of category management is to have the flexibility to fine tune how to go to market—in some cases, changing strategy—to remain successful or become more successful," Terpkosh says.

The strategy for SUPERVALU's corporate stores varies by group. They operate at different levels of category management and have different strategies depending on the format and where they're located. This is especially true for Save-a-Lot, headquartered in St. Louis. This very successful division of extreme value limited assortment stores is entirely different from anything else that SUPERVALU operates simply because of the nature of the format. They run their own category management program.

Cub stores better illustrates how SUPEVALU works with a retail group. This group of corporate stores has a mature category management program. It began building on its shelf management expertise at the same time that SUPERVALU was developing its category management process for the independent retailers. The two work together on many of the main category strategies. Cub handles the four Ps of category management: product, placement, promotion, and pricing for their retail stores, while SUPERVALU Wholesale coordinates the retail execution.

Terpkosh sums up: "Category management may be done by a category manager for independent groups, or it may be the category manager and merchandising folks doing it for a corporate retail group. But it ultimately feeds into the same retail execution program."

CROSSMARK—Just the Facts

Category management is simply fact-based selling. That notion guides the efforts of account executives at CROSSMARK, a sales and marketing agency based in Plano, Texas. It is a principle that they have been following for quite a while.

"We consider ourselves an early innovator of accepting category management as a way to do business with retailers and manufacturers," says Gary Bernius, senior director of category management. "We call it fact-based selling. We look at each category as a strategic business unit which aligns us with retailer goals as opposed to just meeting manufacturer sales goals at the category's expense."

As a result, every employee receives rigorous training in the category management process. CROSSMARK believes that account executives have an obligation to understand the process thoroughly. "If you call on a sophisticated retailer, you have to use those sharp category management skills," says Bernius. "The trick is to operationalize it so that it is practical in the real world and that is what we have done."

And that's the way it works at this sales and marketing agency whose roots go back to 1905. Over the past 100 years, there have been 55 mergers and acquisitions resulting in the CROSSMARK of today, with more than 17,000 associates throughout the United States, Canada, Australia, and New Zealand. The company provides consumer packaged goods manufacturers and retailers with integrated solutions in the areas of sales, marketing, merchandising, technology, and supply chain optimization. Primarily, its account executives represent a manufacturer's sales force in presenting to retailers and providing them with store-level support. Category management expertise grew naturally out of these relationships.

"When we get involved with a Kroger or an Albertson's in the official process, it is not unusual to represent multiple manufacturers," says Joe Crafton, president of strategic alliances. "In some cases, it is an advantage because it forces us to keep a focus on category results. Often we have multiple manufacturers in the same category. With massive categories like condiments or juice, there are multiple manufacturers who are soft competitors but choose to be represented by the same agency. This process would be impossible if every manufacturer weighed in with their own view of the category."

It was also hard to grow product categories prior to category management. The lack of a formalized process and data to support it led to a different working relationship than exists today.

"It was all about making numbers," recalls Bernius. "You were judged purely around the shipment. Then category management changed the whole industry. Now it is consumption tied closely to manufacturing. We make much better decisions on promotions. If we reset the front-end candy section of a retailer, we can measure it and see the lift. Before, it was who had the power to get things done." This change led to the emergence of fact-based selling. It meant that decisions about brands and categories had to be backed by facts.

"In the mid-1990s, category management created a common language and unity in our company," says Bernius. "The headquarters selling effort centered on a common dialogue and thought process. We could then talk to our divisions in a cohesive way and bind the company in the way we approach things. Along with retail coverage, it was one of the first things we put rigor into. It made us more fact-based sellers."

CROSSMARK expects all account executives to incorporate fact-based selling into their customer interaction. They are supported by category management analysts, who are divided into three roles. There are analysts assigned to manufacturer clients, top retail clients, or certain markets to work with local retailers, which are nonnational, number-three or below players in the local market.

CROSSMARK also works closely with executives assigned to them from ACNielsen. Working at headquarters, these executives ensure that there is continuity and consistency in the approach to category management across the country.

Working with Retailers

Over the years, CROSSMARK has learned how to work closely with retailers while helping them solve their problems. The keys have been customization and flexibility. Account executives realize that every manufacturer and retailer needs a custom approach—without violating the principles of category management. The aim is not to redefine the process, but to work within the retailer's process. For example, they worked hand in hand over the years with retailers who reduced the steps in category management from the traditional eight to five or six.

"It comes down to what the retailer has accepted," explains Crafton. "We have to work with them to customize an approach.

The 20 minutes we have on an appointment with a category manager is too valuable to argue about a template or debate if my approach is better. For the most part, we work with what they have established, take the manufacturer's approach and customize it with what the retailer does. We also incorporate a lot of consumer insights into to the template. Retailers are looking for manufacturers to bring in new learning such as consumer and shopping behavior. How it is influenced by shifts in the trade channel and how the consumer sees the category."

CROSSMARK breaks down the components of category management into steps that are easily executed. For example, its assortment tools are based more on business issues than the overall process. How many items do you need in the category to achieve optimal representation? Which items should they be? There needs to be flexibility to adjust to the retailer.

Among the many challenges is working with promotional schedules. CROSSMARK's manufacturer clients use a variety of incentives. They vary from two or three promotions to many more throughout the year. Some clients demand pre- and post-analysis for new item introductions, along with a full return-on-investment (ROI) analysis.

"The challenge is being everything to all people," says Crafton. "You can take the underpinning of the category management process and use it for your everyday business process. This allows us to take the lead in putting together promotional schedules which are the toughest things to put together when you represent many manufacturers."

CROSSMARK aims to conduct quarterly top-to-top reviews with the senior director of procurement or marketing and, in many cases, with the company's president or CEO. Other executives may get involved, including the directors of grocery, perishables, and general merchandise. During these sessions, the account executives look broadly at the total store in the context of the marketplace or they examine a specific retailer-defined trading area. They provide analysis for all categories first by department, and then by the categories themselves.

"We might take the top twenty categories, as well as the ones losing and gaining share, show the best practices, and develop a list of action steps to follow," explains Bernius.

Reviews can be total store in nature, with separate meetings held for each category manager and department head. In these cases, CROSSMARK provides a detailed analysis of the major categories. Other reviews may be more of an executive overview where only 15 minutes are spent presenting each category, and only senior executives are in attendance.

Although CROSSMARK schedules annual reviews for the major categories, the company believes in meeting with category managers any time there is a new item introduction or a new recommendation on space management. When they meet with retailers, CROSSMARK's account executives represent either one or several manufacturers. It depends on the opportunity being explored or the goal sought.

Category Captain or Validator?

Years ago, retailers used to designate a category captain to keep order in the vendor relationships. According to Bernius, "That captain got all the data and declared what the category set should look like. Everybody else danced to that tune."

But that is changing. CROSSMARK has seen a shift in the past five years away from the use of a category captain. One reason is cost. Many manufacturers are not willing to bear the costs associated with taking a lead role.

"If you are in an expensive category that is highly fragmented like household cleaners, you have to weigh the benefits before you commit to spending the money to be captain," Crafton says. "We go in armed with our assessment using category management principles and fact-based selling techniques. If we are successful in convincing them that our strategies work and the category results are achieved, we become a trusted advisor along with other trusted advisors."

"Category management today dictates that you take a role based on the value you get out of it," he goes on to say. "It could be validator, or the lead, or the role of a concerned supplier who has an idea for improving the performance of a category. The role we can best take with the retailer and get a return on the manufacturer's investment—that's how we best determine what we want to be as we enter the category management process today."

The Role of Technology

For nearly a decade, CROSSMARK has relied on technology as the foundation of its category management work. Its investment in technology has been designed to improve the speed, accuracy, and quality of data delivered to those who use it. CROSSMARK remains determined to set the industry standard for technology. As new tools are introduced, it wants to be the first to commercialize them.

Until 1996, the company relied on manufacturers for data. It then began buying data from syndicated providers. That meant getting tens of thousands of UPCs—store by store, week by week—in all categories for all reporting retailers.

"We were the first sales agency to convince syndicated data providers to sell data directly to us," says Crafton. "The previous model was based on our manufacturers providing us with whatever data they bought. We had a paradigm shift in the mid-1990s where we bought directly from the third-party data providers. It was never done before. That is a wealth of data that we can manipulate to look at by category or by retailer. With the granularity of the data and ease of use, we can now help retailers create marketing clusters and identify opportunities based on the unique behavior of the consumers of a specific store or group of stores," adds Crafton.

Purchasing data directly enabled CROSSMARK to reduce their reliance on in-store audits. Previously, a sales rep had to go into the store and figure out if he was missing product distribution. Audits actually took more time than it took to work those products in.

"We want to push out better data to retail reps in the store so they make better decisions," says Bernius. "As micromarketing becomes more commercially viable, the retail reps and store managers will actually have information on the SKUs in their stores to make informed decisions. We have store-level data so we know each SKU in the store, what it sold, and what the price was. We push that out to our folks to use."

CROSSMARK regularly scans the marketplace for trends that will enhance the category management process. For example, the company can do a gap analysis and develop base incremental charts that look at the effectiveness of promotions.

"Our account executives in the marketplace have tools at their disposal that are intuitive and quick," says Crafton. "Our more progressive salespeople use those tools on a regular basis. Reps assigned to our large corporate clients might have additional resources that manage the relationship. They look out on a national basis for threats and opportunities."

TrakSuite, a program that CROSSMARK created, allows account executives to look at assortments, promotions, pricing, and gap analysis. It is a PC-based tool that extracts insights from point-of-sale data then converts those insights into actionable solutions according to the principles of category management. As well as optimizing the category management process, the templates help buyers understand brand relationships and category performance. CROSSMARK uses this information to develop fact-based sales strategies that match up with the merchandising objectives of its retailers.

Over the years, one constant for CROSSMARK has been looking out for the health of brands from a category management perspective. That is, what are the gaps in the category and what are the plans to close them? Along the way, the company has helped its manufacturers and retailers meet their objectives.

Their secret to success? Just the facts.

WHAT'S IN STORE?

CROSSMARK sees opportunities in store for manufacturers and retailers, but there first needs to be a change in attitude and practices in three areas:

1. *Micromarketing:* There is too much centralized planning with the assumption that all stores have the same section size, configuration, and demographics. "The retailer today wants the right assortment, promotion, strategy and shelving because it is appropriate for that store," says Joe Crafton, president of strategic alliances. "We need to go from looking at the past 13 or 26 weeks to a more predictive method. For instance, we know the price elasticity by brand and by retailers. Why couldn't we build scenarios that tell retailers what will happen to their brand and category if they change the price?"

2. *Marketing mix modeling:* Everyone complains about the 40 to 60 percent of the $100 billion in promotions that is wasted. "If we can help a manufacturer understand the marketing mix, and help them

move money from trade to consumer to product development and give them a payout based on all these variables, we can really help a client. We do this by clearly demonstrating an ROI for each activity," says Crafton.

3. *Shopper data:* The privacy issues associated with loyalty clubs and shopper card data are huge obstacle to understanding the consumer and offering them more value. Retailers have a valuable data mining opportunity. "Consumers need to see how they can benefit," says Crafton. "Until consumers understand how it can help them, it will be hard to break through to the next level. Educating consumers that it is in their best interest to receive offers on dog food if they own a dog and not receive a cat offer when they have no cats. This education will take time and money."

Acosta—Multiplying the Impact of Category Management

When category management first took hold in the mid-90s, the manufacturer clients of Acosta Sales and Marketing Company wanted to be involved in every step of the process, especially at the larger retailers. As category management and capabilities in technology evolved, Acosta's role changed as well. Today, the agency takes charge of most of the category management work for their clients.

"Some manufacturers still want to be involved with the largest retailers, but for the most part our manufacturer clients only want to be involved in category management work when they have specific consumer research and insights they want to deliver," says Michael Bernatchez, senior vice president of corporate marketing for the agency based in Jacksonville, Florida.

Most retailers want to partner with the number one or number two brands to work on their category plans. The manufacturer or sales agency representing these brands helps the retailer with the category plan. Quite often manufacturers have invested in shelf-management resources to facilitate working with retailers on a daily basis. Acosta prides itself on working with grocery retailers in day-to-day category management as well as the "formal" category management review process. Acosta represents the category management interests of over 1,300 consumer packaged goods (CPG) manufacturers.

"A key difference at Acosta is our critical mass aligned with a single customer," explains Bernatchez. "We tend to be the retailer's largest 'vendor' in most cases. We also represent a lot of number one and number two brands. Because of this, we have category expertise that many retailers want to tap in to. In addition we have a lot of local resources to deploy against the category management process."

"We can also provide a much broader perspective to retailers," Bernatchez goes on to explain. "In some cases, category management is elevating itself to be department and aisle management. We have the ability to bring these solutions to the retailers because of our experience and depth of representation of big brands across multiple categories."

Company Background

Founded in 1927, Acosta bills itself as the leading full-service sales and marketing agency in North America. It provides outsourced sales, merchandising, marketing, and promotional services to about 1,300 CPG manufacturers in the grocery, drug, mass, convenience, and club channels of distribution.

Acosta operates as a field-based organization. Its sales and category management associates live and work in the markets where their retailers and clients are. To serve national clients such as Clorox and Heinz, Acosta relies on its category development managers (CDMs) positioned in every major market around the country.

The agency employs almost 400 CDMs and space technologists who are aligned with manufacturers or assigned strictly to major retailers. These people work closely on a day-to-day basis with Acosta business managers and the sales management personnel of manufacturer clients.

Acosta is a three-time winner of the Consumer 360 Award, which each year honors one retailer, one manufacturer, and one sales agency in the consumer packaged goods industry for demonstrating the best understanding of the consumer in their year-round merchandising activities. Winners are selected by the readers of *Brandweek*, *Progressive Grocer*, and *Convenience Store News* magazines.

Working with Retailers

The original eight-step category management process in the mid-90s was too unruly to execute, recalls Bernatchez. Since then, the process has been scaled down considerably. Also, technology and data deliverables from syndicated data providers have allowed many retailers to create a suite of customized category management templates that can be automatically populated.

"This has minimized the amount of manual data pulling and input required," Bernatchez explains. "Now we can spend more time analyzing the data and formulating recommendations instead of pulling and organizing the data. In short, it is now at a point where it's manageable."

According to Bernatchez, category management has become a very "calendarized" and rote activity by retailers over the past five or six years. That's also the view of Paul Mulvaney, an Acosta CDM who works with several leading northeast retailers.

"Customers today view the category management process as a menu from which they pick and choose the areas they want to see," says Mulvaney. "It seems most of our retailers do not want to do the full plan anymore. While it seems that our customers still believe in the process, they are definitely approaching it differently."

For example, one leading customer now does some of the hands-on work that Acosta traditionally did, such as pulling data. "Customers still ask for some consumer/panel data, but only occasionally," Mulvaney reports. "Another leading customer seems to like viewing general category, segment, and brand and promotional trends, but nothing close to what would be the traditional, full-scale plan. But I still do a good deal of assortment projects for all my customers," he says.

Because category management is a retailer-driven process, Acosta focuses its efforts on whatever the customer is familiar and comfortable with. That can mean falling in line with a structured process already in place, or it can mean taking a more leading role and guiding retailers through the process.

For instance, Safeway uses a category optimization program called SCOP (Safeway Category Optimization Program). Kroger employs a proprietary process called KOMPASS (Kroger Optimization Management Plan Aligning Store Sales).

"These retailers have a very strict and standardized process," says Bernatchez. "This tells us exactly what they want delivered and the format it should be delivered in. We fall in line with their templates and comply with their process. No matter what the approach however, the category management process basically tries to look at the consumer purchase dynamics and financial implications of merchandising, assortment, pricing and shelving (MAPS) decisions at both the category and brand level."

A typical meeting at a retail chain includes mapping out roles, responsibilities, timelines, milestones, and checkpoints, as well as measuring progress against each. These tasks are tied to a schedule for retail execution.

"Retailers have a very scheduled category plan," explains Bernatchez. "For example, they may do frozen entrees once a year and it will be done in March. The retail shelving will be done in September. It is very much according to a calendar at this point."

The Role of Technology

Acosta believes in conducting category management on a daily basis and consistently engaging the retailer with new ideas. To do so, the company has developed the Asset Knowledge Suite (AKS) of tools to leverage category management.

"We try to deliver fresh MAPS information to the field with the latest 4-, 12-, and 52-week category and brand information," says Bernatchez. "All of our people have quick easy access to information for their retailer and the retailer's competitive market. From there, we try to provide some consumer insights using Spectra and ACNielsen panel data," he says of the day-to-day approach.

Acosta has been very committed in the area of space technology at the retailer level. With nearly 100 percent of U.S. retailers now enforcing planogram compliance in their stores, Acosta has invested in a national team of 180 space technologists who create, develop, and update retailer schematics across the United States. In fact, 117 of these space technologists have a desk at the retailer's headquarter office and work very closely with category managers on a daily basis. These positions have been key to ensuring that the category plans are actually being executed by creating planograms that are consistent with those plans.

Creativity on Tap

One advantage of representing so many manufacturers is the ability to leverage related brands in a specific category to create merchandising themes. For example, Acosta represents Heinz ketchup, Kingsford charcoal, and Vlasic pickles. Combining them can make for a great barbeque theme.

"Grocery retailers have the opportunity to create consumer excitement by combining multiple brands and creating a big promotional event. This type of thinking is utilized as category plans are being developed. These events are not limited to brands represented by Acosta. It is what's right for the consumer and right for the category" says Bernatchez.

Acosta has dabbled with aisle management, but the work has been based on the retailer's ability and willingness to get involved. To date, there are very few retailers that are ready and willing to get involved at that level of category management.

Bernatchez believes that the next phase of category management will be fueled by data from frequent shopper card programs in supermarkets. There are a large number of retailers that have had these loyalty cards for years, he says, but haven't taken advantage of the data they accumulate.

That's changing. Retailers will be utilizing shopper card data to make category decisions. Kroger and Ahold have both embarked on consumer-centric retailing (CCR) initiatives that use shopper card data as the core to MAPS decisions, and others will follow, Bernatchez predicts. Grocery retailers are realizing the whole channel-blurring phenomenon requires them to take a much deeper look into the consumer purchase decision-making process, according to Bernatchez. The concepts behind the Coca Cola Retailing Research Council of North America study "The World According to Shoppers," which segments consumers into certain groups or characteristics and focuses on their "need states," are resonating with many grocery retailers.

But whether Acosta will be analyzing loyalty card data or relying on other customized data yet to be gathered, the agency will be ready for the next phase of the evolving category management process. It has been that way from the beginning.

"On an everyday standpoint, we manage our business under basic category management disciplines," says Bernatchez. "Whenever we go in with a business proposition for a retailer, we try to take category management principles into that dialogue."

A thousand or so manufacturers can vouch for that.

Chiquita—Extending Category Management to Perishables

Although category management emerged as a discipline for center of the store categories in the early 1990s, its application to the perishables categories such as produce, bakery, meat, deli, and seafood in the perimeter of the store did not begin until the late-1990s. Chiquita Fresh North America was the driving force in pioneering the application of category management principles and disciplines to the produce category.

"The banana category was the ideal category with which to build produce category management capabilities," says Sherrie Terry, vice president of category development for the company based in Cincinnati, Ohio.

She builds a convincing case: Bananas are the single largest selling SKU in the entire grocery store, representing nearly 1 percent of total store sales and 1.5 percent of total store profit. The quality of a retailer's produce department is the number one factor consumers consider when selecting their primary grocery store, and the quality of the retailer's banana program can make or break the quality image of the store's produce department. Eighty-five percent of households purchase bananas and nearly 50 percent purchase them once a week or more. Bananas are available year-round, and retailers typically work with a single banana supplier on an annual (or longer) basis.

"As the number one consumer preferred brand of bananas, with industry-wide recognition as the leader in consumer understanding, Chiquita was the first to identify category management as an opportunity to further differentiate itself as a value-added supplier in a 'commodity' category," says Terry.

Chiquita Brands International is a leading international marketer, producer, and distributor of high-quality bananas and other fresh produce sold primarily under the premium Chiquita brand. The company is one of the largest banana producers in the world and a major supplier of bananas in Europe and North America. The company also distributes and markets fresh-cut fruit and other branded, value-added fruit products. Chiquita products are sold in over 60 countries and Chiquita is one of the most recognized brand names in the world.

Since 1996, Chiquita has evolved its program from category *management* to category *development*. For Terry, "management" implies a less dynamic and proactive approach to the discipline, a focus on retail execution (versus the total supply chain), incremental improvement in performance (versus step-wise improvement), maintenance of the traditional retailer-vendor relationship (versus a fully integrated partnership), top-line performance measurement (versus bottom-line profit measurement), and less focus on the consumer than Chiquita is committed to. Chiquita defines category development as "innovative demand chain solutions that yield tangible results." It is a disciplined and comprehensive approach to business planning and performance measurement that delivers shopper satisfaction while driving profit for Chiquita and its retail partners. The process, which is consumer-centric, data-driven, and fact-based, integrates retail scan sales, supply chain ABCs (activity-based costs), extensive warehouse, retail, pricing, and promotion best practices, and consumer research through easy-to-use front-end software templates and tools that facilitate understanding of customer performance, key drivers of that performance, and identification of customer needs and opportunities.

The company's vision is to lead the industry in the successful, practical implementation of category development for produce, resulting in increased shopper satisfaction and profitable volume growth for Chiquita and its customers. The key elements shaping this bold vision are leadership, practical implementation, and value creation.

Initially, Chiquita's category management program was developed and managed as one of several value-added solution offerings within the Chiquita North American Marketing Department. A select group of forward-thinking salespeople with forward-thinking customers were chosen to help develop, test, and refine the systems, tools, and processes with marketing. As the data, systems, and tools became more extensive and sophisticated, as more customers saw value in participating in the program, and as Chiquita began to expand its category management expertise and offering into additional produce categories (fresh cut fruit, pineapples, and avocados), a separate category development department was established.

Because of its strategic role in understanding consumer and category dynamics and in securing and retaining customers, the department is led by a vice president who reports directly to the senior vice president of North America. Terry leads a team that consists of two full-time category managers and one category analyst. The managers both have category-specific (bananas, fresh cut fruit, etc.) as well as customer-specific (Albertson's, Kroger, etc.) responsibilities.

The Chiquita category development team works directly with field sales, marketing staff, and senior management to leverage information, insight, and tools to drive the business. They also work with The Perishables Group to drive the continuous improvement, development, and implementation of new tools, processes, and data resources to facilitate implementation of the Chiquita category development program.

"The Perishables Group has been our strategic partner from the very beginning," says Terry. "They are the exclusive supplier of random-weight retail scan data, and together we have developed integrated planning, review, and P&L templates and reports that make interpreting and presenting category and customer performance information and plans simple and meaningful."

The Perishables Group receives, quality checks, and warehouses' retail scan data and integrates internal shipment, cost, and promotion information. They have established and maintained an online portal for access to the most current software and data upgrades, along with capabilities for ad-hoc queries and analysis by users. A Perishables Group analyst is also dedicated to the Chiquita account and supports the Chiquita category managers in the preparation of regular and ad-hoc reports and analyses.

Produce Is Unique

Applying the principles, data sources, and tools of category management to produce brings a unique set of challenges that has required creativity, innovation, and tenacity to overcome.

Seasonality

Retailers generally work with different produce suppliers throughout the year because of the seasonality of fresh fruit and vegetables. In the case of bananas, it's generally one supplier for 52 weeks or, in some cases, longer. In the majority of other produce categories, however, retailers will have different suppliers from different source countries at different times of the year. For example, although consumers can buy grapes year-round, they are sourced from Chile, California, or Mexico, depending on the time of the year. There are multiple suppliers growing and shipping from each of these different source regions. Even within a given season, retailers frequently have two or three suppliers, in order to hedge their bets against weather or crop shortages and to create greater negotiating leverage with suppliers. "Occasionally one supplier will have a crop shortage, so retailers don't want to be dependent on only one supplier," explains Terry. Therefore, different brands and/or suppliers can be sold within a single retailer on any given week.

PLU *versus* UPC

Unlike consumer packaged goods that all include a 10-digit scannable bar code (UPC) that identifies both the brand and the specific SKU (item/flavor/size) that serves as the basis for coding the retail price into the retailer's scanning system (which is the data source for category management analysis), the vast majority of produce is sold on a random weight—that is, price per pound—basis. Each variety within a produce category has been assigned a price look-up (PLU) code that serves as the basis for coding the price per pound into the scanning system. PLUs are category/variety specific only. They do not include a reference to a specific brand or supplier. For example, PLU #4011 equals "bananas, regular," no matter what the brand. In fact, it has only been since 1994 that PLU stickers were required to be placed on produce by the suppliers. Although there is a movement to transition to a more robust, UPC-like, scannable labeling system for produce and other random weight items, at this point the front-end system of most retailers is not capable of handling scannable random weight product codes, even if produce suppliers could find a way to cost-effectively place such codes on bulk produce. Therefore, product is weighed at the cash register and PLUs are entered by hand by the cashier. The more obscure or unique a category (or variety within a category) is, the greater chance there is of entering an erroneous code, resulting in over- or understated volume and price by item.

The use of PLUs versus UPCs impacts not only the accuracy of the price charged consumers (and, therefore, the income to the retailer), and the quality of the data available to suppliers who leverage the potential of category management programs, it also prohibits the objective identification of the brand/supplier of the particular item sold by the retailer. For categories with several brands/suppliers during a given season, quantifying the performance of one brand over another requires the collection of extensive and timely competitive intelligence in order to track (manually) which brand/supplier was being sold by which retailer during which weeks. "We have to know who the brand or supplier is for each retailer that we're getting the data from," says Terry.

One Brand

In the case of bananas, retailers usually carry only one brand of bananas at a time based on annual or multiyear supply agreements. This makes it easier to "track" which brand is in which store at a given time. However, competitive comparisons between brands have to be made by comparing category performance at a comparable, but different, set of stores that carry a competitive brand— either at another division of the same retailer or at rival retailers—instead of being able to compare the performance of different brands being sold side by side in the same store.

Data Accuracy and Timeliness

As noted earlier, the manual nature of entering an item's PLU increases the potential for item mis-rings, and therefore data inaccuracy, particularly for complex, multivariety categories. As a result, establishing category hierarchies, intimate knowledge of each produce category and retailer, and quality checking, cleaning, and validating the data that is received by the retailer is an extensive, time-intensive, and collaborative process between The Perishables

Group and Chiquita. One consequence is that the time lag between actual sales and the availability of "clean," usable scanner data is too long. "But it is better this year than last," an optimistic Terry quickly points out. "I hope that next month is going to be better than this month. Prior to 2005, we received weekly data on a quarterly basis about 8 weeks after the close of the period. This year, we're targeting to get weekly data monthly, with a 6 week-lag time. Still, by the time we look at the data and analyze it, you're talking about being about 8 to 10 weeks behind. In a category that receives, ripens, and sells everything within 7 to 10 days of arrival in North America, that is simply not quick enough to impact near-in performance and remain relevant to the customer. We are also experimenting with receiving weekly 'flash' reports that are delivered about 10 days after the close of the week. Everyday is an improvement, but my sense is that we should be able to get clean data much quicker than that." For category managers, salespeople, and marketers who join Chiquita from the packaged-goods world with long-established data cleaning and delivery processes, this can be a very frustrating aspect of being a pioneer of this discipline in perishables.

Some History

Chiquita produced the first banana category management program in 1996, working with The Perishables Group (then known as Willard Bishop Consulting). It rolled out the process to the first wave of customers the following year.

At first, access to retail scan data was very limited and often came directly from retailer partners. A "cleaning" and "validating" process had to be developed in addition to leveraging the information. Unfortunately, data errors and omissions slowed progress.

"In addition to improving data resources, we also had to determine the best way to summarize and present the information in a way that was succinct, impactful, and allowed us and our customers to draw important conclusions and recommendations in a timely way," says Terry. "Because of this, we drove the design and development of the 'front-end' report templates and presentations at our software supplier. We also brought in the concept of a 'net profit customer P&L' based on activity-based costs unique to our categories and supply chain—something that traditional CPG category management programs did not provide, and the development of a weekly planning tool with the capability to project annual sales based on proprietary customer-specific or industry-wide pricing, promotion, and retail best practice history and models."

Since produce decision makers were not used to seeing this kind of data, Chiquita had to "sell" the value of fact-based decision making and the reliability and accuracy of the data, as well as the "solutions" recommended by the analysis. Also, integrating multiple data sources into a cohesive presentation was time-consuming.

Technology Improvements

The situation has improved steadily over the years. Data is now available for many more retailers in more categories. There are now more syndicated research services that provide information on consumer produce purchase and consumption behavior.

"When we were first starting," recalls Terry, "all the front-end software and the data tools had to be either emailed to us or sent to us on a disk that the users would put onto their laptop or desktop. If there was any change in the data or a mistake, correction, or update, we had to make sure that everybody who had that data got the new disk and got rid of the old one so that we were always using the most current information. Now you can actually go to a portal on-line and pull up databases. That's where they're all housed and re-freshed so everyone is always working with the most current available information."

The integration of multiple data sources—although still done in-house at Chiquita—has become more streamlined. Customers are more accustomed to the information and more customers are begin-ning to see the value it can provide to their decision making and overall category performance.

As system capability has grown, larger amounts of data can be handled more rapidly and a historical database can be created, thereby allowing Chiquita to detect, monitor, and understand meaningful trends.

"There are tons and tons of data," says Terry. "The warehousing, cleaning and management of the data is something that The Perish-ables Group does for us, and they are now able to handle bigger amounts of data than they were before. When we first started, we were doing a lot of things in Access databases."

The data is becoming more robust and "projectable," and as each year passes, the historical and trend databases become stronger, as well.

"When we first started," Terry reports, "we could only purchase data from retailers representing approximately 11 percent of the U.S. all-commodity volume (ACV); even when combined with data that was retailer-supplied, our maximum retail coverage was about 17 percent. Now, through The Perishables Group's alliance with AC-Nielsen, we have access to the retail scan data from retailers repre-senting 64 percent of the U.S. ACV beginning with January 2004. With this level of coverage, we are much more comfortable projecting total category performance and trends. And for customers we've been doing this with for six or seven years, we have pretty good history," says Terry. "Of course, we absolutely protect the confidentiality of individual retailer data; we never have and never will identify individual retailer performance to another retailer." (Note: All references to retailer ACV exclude Wal-Mart Supercenter data.)

Consumers First

At Chiquita, being "consumer centric" drives everything the company undertakes. Chiquita begins all of its work in a category with primary and secondary research designed to understand the consumer. What drives purchase and consumption, satisfaction and dissatisfaction, and habits and practices? What are the key satisfaction gaps and wishes for the future? Chiquita purchases secondary panel data (both NPD consumption data and ACNielsen Homescan purchase data) and commissions proprietary focus groups; quantitative concept tests, habits, and practices studies; purchases decision-tree research, concept/product fit research, and so on. In addition, Chiquita works with retailers to conduct store-level tests to validate positioning and product merchandising hypotheses prior to publication of best practices.

It is interesting to note that secondary panel data related to produce purchase and consumption habits has only become available since 2000. Chiquita starts with understanding what drives consumer purchase and consumption, and then reviews the entire supply chain backward to determine the best practices at the retail level, at the warehouse, and in transportation and logistics to ensure shopper satisfaction, while delivering profitable volume growth for trading partners.

"We start with the consumer for a couple of reasons," explains Terry. "At the end of the day, we sell a commodity. The only thing that really differentiates us is the consistency of our quality, our understanding of consumer behavior, and—most importantly—the power of our brand. We have to know more than our competitors about what consumers want in terms of quality, how they use our products, and the end benefits they desire from using our products. And understanding what consumers think and feel about our brand and the relationship they have with Chiquita is imperative. Why do consumers have such a passionate feeling for our brand and what must we do to keep that relationship alive? Superior execution against these drivers sets us apart from our competition."

Working with Retailers

Chiquita serves as banana category captain for 20 retailers in North America. Category plans are developed annually and updated monthly. Formal reviews are generally done quarterly. Chiquita strives to understand customers and their total performance by division, zone, and store. It works with retailers to develop, implement, monitor, and revise programs to achieve their annual business objectives.

Chiquita uses a 52-week planning tool it developed in conjunction with The Perishables Group both externally with its category management "partners," and internally for those 20 retailers, plus an additional 10 customers. Customer-specific baseline volume by week is loaded into the planner, and then price promotion, advertising, in-store merchandising, and other promotional programs are added by week. Based on customer-specific (or national default) lift models, the planner then projects annual volume, revenue, and profit by week. This is an interactive tool that Chiquita sales representatives can use with the retailer to develop and refine weekly plans in order to achieve annual objectives. The planner helps refine volume and revenue forecasts for the year. About 40 percent of Chiquita's banana volume in North America is impacted.

Chiquita implements its category development program on a customer-by-customer basis. Which information and tools are applied to each retailer is different, based on the needs of the customers' business and the value they place on it. "If you don't work the category development tools at a retailer level, the program appears to be a 'cookie cutter' and not relevant to the particular customer you are speaking to," says Terry.

Understanding the retailer's positioning, strategy, consumer base, and merchandising strategy is integral to determining the category definition and role, according to Terry. The goal is to prove that the Chiquita brand and the Chiquita program is the best choice for retailers to reinforce and optimize their positioning and strategy.

"It is very important that retail senior management agrees with the category definition and role and communicates that across the entire organization at all levels," says Terry. "This helps establish the level of financial and human resources that will be allocated to the category and the priority that others place on ensuring thorough program execution."

Given the importance of bananas to total store image, traffic, and profitability, Chiquita recommends that bananas are designated a "destination" category for the retailer. Although many retailers initially consider bananas as a "routine" or "traffic building" category, once they are presented with the facts that quantify the strategic, image, and profit importance of the category, they generally agree to designate bananas as one of the very few "destination" categories in their stores. As a result, significant attention, priority, and resources are allocated to proper execution of supply chain best practices and consumer support, thus ensuring improved category performance.

The retailers' division managers must participate in the development and agree with the annual plans. "They will set the priorities and resources for those under their direct control," says Terry. "Store-level personnel must comprehend the category role and best practices, and be aware of what the approved programs are. Training for store managers and produce managers is vital to success. We try to ensure that all levels are touched by the appropriate Chiquita people at regular intervals throughout the process."

Chiquita leverages the thorough classic eight steps of the traditional category management process. Retailers typically don't dictate a process or approach. They tend to dictate the specific forms and templates in which they want the data presented.

"Given the unique nature and the status of produce category management versus CPG category management, it has been our experience that traditional CPG templates don't work for produce," says Terry. "Rather than argue with the retailer over this, we try to figure what the retailer is trying to accomplish, and present it in the most efficient way possible given the data availabilities and limitations of our categories. To date, this has not created a problem with a retailer. They are more interested in content and results than format."

The company demonstrates its category development capabilities to customers new to category management or new to Chiquita itself in an overview presentation that generally follows the elements of the traditional eight-step flow. The eight steps also come into play internally when Chiquita sets out to understand a new category or when updates to existing category overviews occur. Finally, the company employs the disciplined process to identify what they know and what they don't know in order to fill in the knowledge gaps.

Execution and Compliance

Retail execution of produce plans is critical because the products are so perishable and handling at the warehouse and retail level has a significant impact on the quality the consumer sees at the point of sale. Shoppers buy fresh fruits and vegetables based on freshness, appearance, aroma, and color. Consequently, Chiquita and its retailers conduct regular audits for compliance to best practices. These audits are summarized and distributed to zone, region, division, and senior management, along with by-store rank-order sales, shrink, and other performance measures. Chiquita sometimes adds incentives and rewards to encourage rapid and consistent implementation.

"We also track actual versus forecast results for each program," says Terry. "This helps to establish a rich program archive and database which is then used to improve the forecasting accuracy of each customer-specific planner and strengthen the sample size of our best-practice database."

Proper training is at the heart of retail execution and compliance, according to Terry, who gives credit to Chiquita business development managers and Chiquita market technical services representatives with expertise in ripening and warehouse management and retail best practices. They audit and train warehouse and retail associates on best practice implementation and the impact proper execution can have on overall department performance.

"As we look to the future, Chiquita expects to expand its capability to additional produce categories and also to lead understanding of cross-category interaction and total department impact of various category-specific programs," says Terry. "We will continue to push for leading-edge data, software, and analytical modeling tools to maintain our competitive advantage in a discipline that will deliver increased consumer satisfaction and drive profitable volume growth for Chiquita and its customers."

The Hershey Company—
Linking Consumer Insights
and Customer Strategy

T he Hershey Company describes its category management process as a four-step process: knowledge base, trade tactics, consumer insights, and consumer strategy. In the mid-1990s, the company focused largely on the first two steps by training its category management team extensively on acquiring an expert knowledge base and then applying that knowledge in converting sales data into actionable trade tactics. Category management was only about the numbers, such as sales velocity, retailer profit, variety, and other measures of sales performance. Personal relationships with customers strongly influenced the process, while information about consumer purchase decisions was limited. There was plenty of data about consumer behavior and pricing strategies, but there wasn't much information about what motivated that purchase.

The process has evolved and improved since the mid-1990s, with the focus shifting to consumer insights and customer strategy. This focus has had an enormous impact on category management for the maker of world-class snacks such as Hershey bars and Reese's Peanut Butter Cups. The company is the largest North American maker of chocolate and sugar snack products, marketing such well-known brands as Hershey's Kisses, Reese's Peanut Butter Cups, Kit Kat, Ice Breakers, Twizzlers, Smart Zone, Snack Barz, and of course the famous Hershey's Milk Chocolate and Hershey's Milk Chocolate with Almonds bars.

"We build category knowledge and provide value through effective tactical work," explains Michelle Gloeckler, vice president of customer marketing for the Hershey Company. "Retailers have become more focused on consumer insights, and we have been able to increase what we have to offer regarding consumer insights, which helps generate potent strategies specifically designed around their consumer base."

This approach has enabled the Hershey Company to become a category leader that aims to improve the retailer's business from the tactical level to the strategic level for sustainable performance excellence. The Hershey Company faces the unique challenge of balancing the classic sales/marketing dichotomy of "usage" occasions and "purchase" triggers. This all comes down to the consumer: why, where, and how they buy snacks.

Usage occasions define how consumers interact with the product. That is, they need something to hand out for Halloween or something to eat as a snack because they've missed a meal. There is also an unwritten purchase occasion called the "need base," explains Gloeckler. "No one really needs candy, but people have a strong desire for it. If they are feeling happy, or hungry, or indulgent, they want treats. Unlocking the consumer's 'need states' and 'usage occasions' are the key to successful snack marketing."

Gloeckler explains how usage occasion-based purchasing is brought to life at retail by managing the purchase-based decision. This is done by working closely with retailers to understand consumer shopping behavior, where the product should be merchandised, and developing pricing strategies that trigger purchase decisions.

The Hershey Company's category management department allows the company to remain nimble and responsive to consumer desires. It provides ongoing market performance details to both internal and external customers. "We use syndicated data, customer point-of-sale data, and loyalty card data to identify and monitor trends," explains Gloeckler. "Internally, Hershey's communication process is optimized through the promotion integration department which provides a single source that links to multiple functional areas."

The objective is to analyze the data to identify and implement profitable retail strategies. Retailers want to find opportunities that are based on tactical data. The goal is to ensure that purely tactical data is based on historical sales and consumer insights, and then deliver a win-win plan for retailers and consumers.

Before the late 1990s, information about the underlying motivation for candy purchases was limited. Over the past five years, a wide range of new packaging designs have been introduced to address changing consumer needs. These changes were made possible by recognizing lifestyle changes, and understanding how, when, and where consumers eat Hershey's products. Consumers are demanding choices in packaging that give them convenience—letting them take snacks with them to eat immediately, on the go—or are suitable for home and candy dish use.

One of Hershey's first consumer studies in the mid-1990s was a proprietary shopping behavior study that was presented to the category management team. It provided a great deal of information and became a source of competitive advantage. "With the availability of panel data, we created powerful tools based on the consumer panel information," Gloeckler says. "We continue to invest in proprietary research, whether it's marketing mix modeling or a 'need' scope analysis. We also conduct seasonal proprietary research using ethnographic studies of what consumers purchase and why they purchase it."

Organizational Structure

Before 1998, the Hershey Company did not have a category management department. Regional analysts assisted the regional sales manager and analyzed data from all retail customers in a geographic area, but the analysts were not dedicated to a particular customer.

Today, the Hershey Company organizes its category management team members around trade channels with dedicated teams that focus on specific customers. These team members add value by garnering a significant amount of "face time" with large retail customers.

In July 2004, Hershey created a customer marketing department consisting of category management, trade management, and strategic communications under the leadership of Gloeckler. The new structure made sense, she says, because of the close links between trade investment strategy and category management.

"We've found that the best location for category management resources is to be aligned with the selling organization," Gloeckler said. "This strategy keeps category management resources close to Hershey's customers. Combining category management, trade management and customer marketing under a customer marketing umbrella provides Hershey's with even better cross-functional capability.

"Trade work deals with syndicated data," she goes on to say. "category management personnel were the keepers of syndicated data. The trade promotion people were the keepers of the 'spend.' In order to get true ROI, we had to pull those together." The structure has evolved to address both trade channel nuances and opportunity for growth.

The best way to understand how category management works is to compare the responsibilities of the sales team with the responsibilities of category managers. For some, the distinctions between these groups are blurred, and the sales team and category managers do work closely together. However, these are separate functions with very different responsibilities.

Hershey has a dedicated retail sales force with business managers and retail managers operating separately. Business managers sell programs and items to chain headquarters, while retail managers are responsible for ensuring that tactics are implemented in the store. They go where the activity is—building displays, getting items on shelves, and making sure the activities Hershey thinks should be happening are, in fact, being executed in the store.

Category management is focused on identifying opportunities. The category manager is responsible for looking at opportunities across the category; the sales person is responsible for selling Hershey-specific programs and promotions to customers.

The Classic Eight Steps

Although Hershey has worked with various category management processes, the traditional eight-step process is the cornerstone of training throughout the company. The business fundamentals that gave rise to the "template" process are relevant throughout the different business channels, according to Gloeckler, but the focus has changed recently. "Today, our proprietary tools and our experience allow us to quickly determine roles, strategies and appropriate tactics," she says. "This allows the customer teams to move quickly through the analytical process and focus on the opportunities by building solid business plans for each customer."

"We've become flexible in working with customers based on their needs," says Gloeckler, "whether a retailer rigorously follows the entire eight-step process or works with a modified version. Once you have the 'basic training' in the fundamental business drivers, you can adapt to any process."

Hershey deploys its category management managers in the field to work with retailers as snack category advisors. The managers are equipped with the knowledge to work with retailers, no matter what tools and systems the customer might use in its business. "It's not all about Hershey, but the right trade-offs to grow the snack category." stresses Gloeckler. "That is the cornerstone of our positioning and actions with our customers. We want to bring them the tools and insights to profitably grow their category."

Technology

The Hershey Company has made significant investments in technology to ensure that category management has the right internal resources. For example, tactical tools such as Efficient Assortments and Promotional Planning Tools are critical to Hershey, as well as to retailers, in order to quantify business opportunities.

Efficient Assortments offer the ability to combine basic sales velocity information with linear-inch dimensions to provide a sales-per-inch look at shelf efficiency. Hershey also employs a proprietary tool called the Navigator Order Projection System that enables category management personnel to order the right amount of product per store based on multiple, variable inputs. The tool generates a total category order by store and by item using historical inputs on sell-through. If a customer chooses to share information about profitability with Hershey, that data is included as well.

Another proprietary resource dedicated to retail execution is REX. This is a handheld computer that tells managers where the retail activity should be focused for a certain time period and creates the optimal retail plans for Hershey's retail sales representatives. REX provides Hershey's selling and management team with detailed results that are tracked throughout every promotion and product introduction.

Working at Retail

"Ultimately," says Gloeckler, "everything happens at retail. That's where consumers come face to face with our brands. How a product plan is delivered is critical to success. To ensure success, Hershey has built a superior supply chain and provided dedicated resources for retail execution."

Hershey provides three separate areas of focus for the confectionery business: front end, gondola, and seasonal/promotional. One of the keys to success is the emphasis Hershey places on making sure that its go-to-market strategy aligns with the customer's retail strategy. "There is a ton of complexity with seasonal promotions," she explains. "Customers want to do something with seasons, but how much? Will they build a big thematic Halloween display, or do they just want to have seasonal product in stock at full retail price to maximize profit margins? Before we offer our assistance, we need to understand customer goals; otherwise we'll make recommendations that are not in line with the customer's needs.

"The unique impulse and expandable nature of snacks make this area one of the most daunting. At the same time, this provides the greatest growth opportunity for most customers," says Gloeckler.

Hershey places a major emphasis on promotion because of the nature of the snack categories. Snacks have high household penetration, a low purchase cycle frequency (defined as the number of days between product purchases), a high percentage bought on impulse, and a high percentage bought due to tactical merchandising. "We spend a lot of our efforts with respect to trade promotions, quality of merchandising conditions such as advertising and display space, and purchase frequency," says Gloeckler.

The company applies its skills in the candy and snack aisles. The shelf planograms for confection and snacks are complicated because of various packaging designs including peg bag, lay down bags, multipacks, and giant bars. "We have good analytics on the front end," she says. "However, much of our volume is seasonal and off-shelf driven via displays, which cause the aisle sets to be much more challenging."

Gloeckler believes that retailers should identify opportunities through tactical information such as loyalty card data, even though such data techniques are still in their infancy. Certain retailers, such as Wegman's and CVS, "are so close to what they are doing with their data. Success depends not only on the ability to mine data, but on understanding how to best act on it after you have made the investment and drawn out some insights."

Working as Category Captain

Hershey has the opportunity to present traditional category reviews to most customers at least once a year. According to Gloeckler, "this allows Hershey to bring a continuous stream of category analyses to retailers to help maximize sales." Hershey continues to focus its resources on retailers with growth potential who value analysis and insight as the basis for making fact-based decisions.

Hershey uses an internal process called "cycle planning" to coordinate selling efforts with category management analysis. This involves conducting reviews of recent promotions and previews of new ones. Category managers determine performance as well as how trade promotions fit in.

"We gauge our effectiveness by the value that retailers place on our work," says Gloeckler, adding that Hershey plays an advisory role to its top customers. "Suppliers such as Hershey must be able to deliver the category and consumer insights to build winning business plans with the retailers. Hershey has received a high degree of recognition for our category management objectivity. We constantly strive to coordinate our efforts with the critical decision makers in the field in order to validate strategic direction and to clarify resource expectations."

And that is just fine with Gloeckler. "It's not about doing things the Hershey way; it's about being flexible, fitting into the retailers' language and expectations of what the snack category role is. Every customer organization and dynamic is different. Our goal is to fit in with the retailers' process and provide actionable insights and strategic recommendations."

What Does the Future Hold?

Hershey will continue to focus on turning customer strategy into retail execution by providing actionable information, according to Gloeckler. Ever nimble, Hershey is able to mine syndicated data and customer POS data and link it with production and forecasting.

As customers become more and more sophisticated and use their own data exclusively, there are opportunities for store-level analysis in the future. "Analysis at this level requires the ability to manipulate large data sets using standard analytical frameworks," Gloeckler says. "We'll continue to build the skills and expertise of our analyst teams to take full advantage."

The new applications of retail data create a wide range of opportunities. "There is the ability to employ regional clustering and targeted ethnic marketing as well," Gloeckler adds. "Retailers can better understand their audience and want to cater to it. Retailers are recognizing that what strategies work in Florida may not work in Oregon."

Miller Brewing—Tapping Category Management for Competitive Advantage

Beer drinkers are notoriously loyal to their brands, so it's critical for retailers to maintain a broad variety, ranging from imports to economy brews. But not having a particular brand in stock does more than disappoint a shopper.

"If the consumer's product is not in the store, they will often leave to shop somewhere else, taking their entire basket of purchases with them," says Jeff Schouten, group director category management and e-commerce for Miller Brewing Company in Milwaukee, Wisconsin.

Assortments in the beer category vary greatly from market to market and even store to store to suite local consumer preferences. The quest for efficient assortment has led Miller to a focus on consumer insights as a core competency. Understanding beer shopper makeup and behavior is key to effective category management.

"We use consumer information and our own proprietary research to paint a complete picture of the beer shopper and beer drinker," says Schouten. "We use this knowledge to help our retailers develop effective beer merchandising, assortment and promotions."

For more than 10 years, Miller has relied on category management to help retailers sell more beer, more profitably. The process enables retailers to understand the category, the shoppers, and the local market. With this knowledge, they can focus on programs that increase sales and reach category goals.

Miller also takes a strategic approach to category management. The beer marketer is forward-looking and intent on making changes to improve performance of the entire category. "We're trying to see how we want the category to perform for the retailer and for Miller in a two- or three-year time horizon, and we tend to be more all-encompassing. Other companies just focus on shelf sets, but we're really trying to look at the whole business.

"It's all about the retailer and improving their business and making sure that they can give better service to their customers. A lot of companies talk that way. I'm not sure how many really take it seriously. We do," says Schouten.

That's good news for retailers and their distributors who play a key role in the process. Since beer is a direct-store-delivery (DSD) product, distributors perform much-needed services in the store as part of the category management process. In most instances, they do the resets and maintain the integrity of the shelf. They know the local market, the consumer, and the store.

"They are the ones who will provide us and the retailer with on-going feedback on what's working and what's not working in the store, whether it's the set or the display," says Schouten. "At the local level, the distributors will be involved with our local people. They'll give input to plans and to the execution. Since they often have their own relationship with retailers, they'll be meeting with them on a periodic basis."

Over the years, distributors have played a key role in the success of Miller Brewing Company, which celebrated its 150th anniversary in 2005. Since Frederick J. Miller began the business in 1855, the company has grown into the second largest brewer in the United States. The brand portfolio is divided into three classes of beer: Mainstream (Miller Lite, Miller Genuine Draft), Worthmore (Leinenkugel's brands, Foster's Lager, Pilsner Urquell, and Henry Weinhard's brands), and Economy (Miller High Life, Milwaukee's Best, and Hamm's). Miller owns and produces over 50 brands of beer.

In addition to its on-premise business in taverns and restaurants, Miller sells products largely in four off-premise channels: grocery, convenience, liquor, and drug stores. Its relationship with retailers through category management has made a difference in the marketplace.

"Our main goal is to make beer work best for our retailers," says Schouten. "It works best when we understand the retailer's business and they collaborate with us and our distributors to create the best plan to optimize their category performance.

"Our efforts have aligned us better with retailers' goals and strategies," he continues. "They have helped us better understand our retailers and adjust our strategies to meet local consumer needs. We're executing better at each retailer and in each market as a result."

Schouten outlines Miller's category management process in four broad steps:

1. *Identify opportunities.* To assess performance opportunities, Miller's category management team conducts a thorough analysis of the total beer business: the retailer's business, the market, and the competition. After considering the retail mission, it's time to define the role that beer plays. Some examples:
   - *Destination/driver:* The retailer is the shopper's store of choice to buy beer.
   - *Routine/staple:* The retailer provides consistent service and remains in-stock for everyday customers.
   - *Convenience/fill-in:* Beer is another purchase during a normal shopping trip.
   - *Occasional/seasonal:* Beer is purchased for special occasions such as a party or holidays.

   After determining the role that beer plays in a store, Miller looks at local trends, sales, and distribution data. This analysis may include a strengths, weaknesses, opportunities, threats (SWOT) analysis.

2. *Develop opportunities and strategies.* Work begins with a deep understanding of the consumer. The team develops insights from the data to determine causal factors and looks for opportunities for improvement. Miller develops measurable objectives that drive category volume and profit. Then strategies are developed to support the objectives. Some examples:
   - *Turf protecting:* Set parity retail pricing on certain SKUs versus specifically targeted competition.
   - *Traffic building:* Discount popular brands to draw traffic.

- *Transaction building:* Aggressively price certain items to stimulate purchase of higher-priced brands.
- *Profit generating:* Vary margin based on consumer demand and price.
- *Cash generating:* Set price to maximize case and item/segment velocity.
- *Image enhancing:* Promote products that are in line with a desired image and develop appropriate promotions.

3. *Develop tactical solutions.* The team suggests tactical solutions that fit within the retailer's total strategy. The plan can include recommendations for assortment, merchandising, promotion, pricing, space, and store service/supply. Some examples of tactics:
   - *Availability:* Increase distribution of certain brands of packs for the cooler.
   - *Merchandising:* Add shelf-strips to identify package/price and simplify shopping for consumers.
   - *Pricing:* Review pricing of premium brands to remain competitive.
   - *Promotion:* Take part in promotions for Miller-sponsored music concerts to increase sales of sponsoring brands.
   - *Space management:* Review movement to ensure optimal days-of-supply without losing variety.
   - *Service and supply:* Increase deliveries to high-volume stores for holidays.

4. *Track and measure.* Miller follows up by tracking business results, communicating them, and recommending corrective action. The team recommends tracking actual performance versus plan at scheduled intervals.

"Our process is flexible," says Schouten. "It is applied according to the needs of the retailer and opportunities within the category."

Miller further breaks down this process to analyze the business, review a retailer's mission and strategy, review the category role, conduct a situation analysis, set goals and objectives, determine assortment and merchandising, develop promotions, design the space, track and measure results, and communicate and adjust.

Market Structure

To assist retailers in understanding how specific beers appeal to specific consumers, Miller has developed a market structure. This framework enables retailers to review each brand's consumer platform. There are three beer segments within this structure: Above Premium (Worthmore), Premium (Mainstream), and Below Premium (Economy). Other beverages complete the market structure (see Figure 19.1).

Organization

Miller's category management group includes national and regional sales teams. Several corporate departments also contribute to the program, including research and trade marketing.

Miller has placed its category management personnel throughout the country as close to its retailer partners as possible. Category consultants and space management analysts are assigned to chain customers. Distributors provide the local expertise and space management service to local retailers, as well as store-level execution of the category plan.

FIGURE 19.1 Beer Category Market Structure

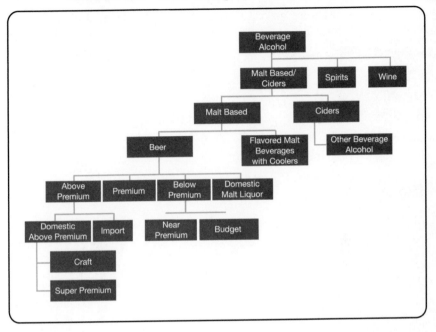

"Our network of nearly 500 distributors is critical in our category management strategy and serves as our arms and legs in servicing our customers," says Schouten. "As part of our direct-store delivery system, they work closely with our retailers on space management, merchandising and improving the supply chain for efficient deliveries.

"Our distributors know their local markets and beer drinkers' habits well, and therefore are that much more in tune with effective individual store strategies," he goes on to say.

"They are in most stores every week—in some cases every day. In addition to the category management initiatives, our distributors keep close tabs on product quality and in-store promotional effectiveness."

Technology Investment

Miller relies on several proprietary and syndicated tools and programs to make category management more efficient and bring a greater depth to category insights. These include a complete suite of ACNielsen-based tools and data, including PricePoint, a tool that provides insights to help evaluate pricing strategies, illustrates how prices are distributed throughout a market or retailer trading area, and suggests optimal pricing; and CoolerMax, which optimally allocates space across the entire beverage cooler in convenience stores.

"Our customized space management software allows for enhanced analysis and tracking, and greater efficiency in the process to allow us to complete tens of thousands of store-level sets annually," says Schouten.

Miller also uses several consumer data tools, such as the ACNielsen Homescan MegaPanel consumer panel that provides in-depth consumer shopping information for all available channels; and Spectra InfiNet, which is a series of databases that provide a variety of consumer- and retailer-specific demographic information and deliver insights into consumer behaviors.

"As a DSD company, we also have detailed data at the store level that enhances our ability to optimize performance at every store within the market," says Schouten.

What's on Tap?

Miller is looking beyond the beer category to determine how beer fits within the total alcohol portfolio and the total store. The plan: With the appropriate mix of beer, wine, and hard liquor, retailers can maximize the total alcohol portfolio, which also means more growth and profits. "We anticipate the need for continued emphasis and new learnings about the American beer drinker," says Schouten. "The better we understand the beer shopper, the better we can satisfy the beer shopper and our retail partners."

SPACE MANAGEMENT: KEY TO SALES

Beer is a fast-turning product, but shelf space is often limited. Moreover, consumers prefer cold beer, and refrigerated space is not easily expandable. Beer must jockey for space in the cooler with other beverages. As a result, space management is a critical component of beer category management.

"It's also critical to balance the days-of-supply within a consumer-friendly shelf set to minimize the chance for out-of-stocks," explains Schouten. "Miller has an effective, time-tested process to complete sets at the chain, cluster or store level. We have hundreds of space management analysts, all of whom have received extensive and ongoing training in beer space management."

Effective space management can optimize the assortment and space allocation, while maximizing volume and profits. There are three parts to Miller's strategy:

Price-level merchandising: Arrange products in the cooler based on traffic flow and on guiding shoppers to select higher-priced, higher-margin brands.

Days-of-supply (DOS): Each SKU earns space based on weekly movement; in other words, the higher the movement, the more space earned. DOS also creates a mix of holding power and brand variety, while minimizing out-of-stocks during peak selling times such as weekends and holidays.

Cooler space optimization: Ensure that the right amount of space is provided for the higher-profit beer category, which is typically underspaced compared to other beverages.

"We have customized space management software that makes the process more efficient and enables accurate analysis and measurement," says Schouten. "We also place an emphasis on executing and maintaining the sets in the store using our distributor network."

Miller's space management process aims to produce fact-based, profit-generating planograms. There are six steps:

1. *Prepare the data:* Use retailer data to understand the brand preferences of customers and market data to understand customer opportunities.

2. *Understand the consumer:* Use Spectra data to understand consumers living near the store, and retailer data to understand those who shop in the store. Miller's Behavioral Tracking Study data and proprietary consumer research provides insights about how consumers shop the beer category.

3. *Develop the assortment:* Use the Efficient Consumer Response (ECR) six-step assortment process along with an Efficient Item Assortment application and Space Planning software.

4. *Develop the planogram:* Use price-level merchandising and DOS strategies to develop the planogram. Distributors provide local market input.

5. *Implement the planogram:* Distributors set the shelf and cooler and affix customized shelf tags.

6. *Measure the project:* Use scorecards and roundtable meetings to measure success and find ways to improve performance.

"When it comes to space management," sums up Schouten, "everyone in the Miller system is on the same page to ensure that the best sets are executed flawlessly."

CHAPTER
20

Hewlett-Packard—Taking Category Management beyond Traditional CPG

Category management is relatively new to Hewlett-Packard (HP), but the company is nonetheless blazing a trail in the information technology (IT) industry in Europe and elsewhere. Few competitors are deploying this process.

In Europe, HP has started its category management effort in the supplies category which consists of inkjet print cartridges, laserjet print cartridges, and paper. This is the category that most resembles businesses in the fast-moving consumer goods (FMCG) industry. Products have an affordable purchase price and relatively high rotation, as well as a longer shelf presence for the SKU reference. The main differences with traditional FMCG products are that the products in the supplies category have a higher average purchase price, are very much dependant on the sales of hardware (printers), and are not usually impulse buys, but planned purchases.

In many ways, the time is right for category management. Both the category and HP's sales have increased significantly in recent years. The growth has drawn attention to the retail shelf and the need for space management, and with the business dynamics changing as the category becomes more mature, the need for more efficient management of the shelf space is becoming more crucial.

Such innovation is nothing new for the $83-billion parent company founded in 1939 by Bill Hewlett and Dave Packard in Palo Alto, California. Today, HP provides products, services, technologies, and solutions to consumers, businesses, and governments in the United States and around the world. The offerings include home computing, printing, and imaging, as well as IT infrastructure and global services.

HP's work in category management in Europe provides a rare glimpse into how to introduce new concepts and processes in emerging categories in retail trade channels that are unfamiliar with them.

"Category management has clearly helped our business," reports Vadim Surgunovi, who is responsible for HP's category management efforts throughout Europe, the Middle East, and Africa. "It has influenced the way we approach our category and our accounts. We've been able to make major inroads on a qualitative, as well as on a quantitative level, increasing consumer satisfaction and sales performance: we are now managing our shelf space."

HP has taken the decision to address its retail partners' specific needs in terms of shelf management by providing them with different levels of category management. All of them aim to achieve tactical excellence in terms of assortment and merchandising for an optimal selection experience.

"We want to offer a practical and easy-to-implement solution which is less time consuming for both the retailer and the manufacturer and directly tackles the in-store environment optimization process" explains Surgunovi.

Start with the Basics

According to Surgunovi, retailers in the IT industry have not yet been ready for the complete category management process, but they are searching for the category captain's advice (HP) on how to increase shelf efficiency.

Most retailers are familiar with planograming, but not always with the process of category management. So reactions can be different when addressing the topic: some are excited, while others more hesitant.

"Category management sounds very complex and time consuming at first. They sometimes also wonder whom the process will benefit more: the category or the manufacturer," says Surgunovi.

"The way we have positioned category management and the fact that we keep the process simple and straightforward helps to reassure them. And by bringing in a third party, we ensure objectivity," he goes on to say. "We also reinforce the fact that retailers always have the final call about the category's destiny. We are in a partnership, we listen to each other, but at the end they are the final decision makers and we will work along an agreed consensus."

Another challenge HP faces in practicing category management has to do with the kind of data available. In most of the FMCG channels, sales data and market overview information are available and/or can be purchased. Manufacturers can therefore take the initiative of working with this information and developing a proposal themselves.

"In our industry, there is limited syndicated category data available on the market. We need to rely on various sources of data, both external and internal, as well as on retailers' own POS data." says Surgunovi.

Because HP wants to keep its category management efforts simple, data exchanges mainly use Excel spreadsheets and occasionally EDI (electronic data interchange).

Since HP started implementing category management in 1998, it has been managing numerous projects across all major European countries. The projects are coordinated by the account managers on a country level together with third-party agencies. They report to Surgunovi for category management matters.

"I define the strategies and objectives of our program, design the processes, optimize the infrastructure, and work with the account managers and agencies on getting the agreements with retailers," he explains. "We have achieved excellent results so far and are continuously reviewing how we do category management, adapting processes and infrastructure in order to offer a better service to our retail partners."

Step by Step

HP is familiar with the traditional eight-step category management process, and has deliberately chosen to adapt the process into an "HP way" of running category management. One aspect of this is to keep the process more accessible to retailers by simplifying the first five steps: category definition, role, assessment, scorecard, and strategies.

"The first five steps still are extremely important to us," he explains. "They are fully integrated into the process, but with less complexity than in the FMCG industry. They allow us to address the retailer at a more strategic level, which is also one of the purposes of category management, and help us define in what direction the project should evolve in order to maximize the category's objectives"

So the core importance for HP and its retailers today in the category management process, has been the last three steps of the original process: tactics, implementation, and review.

"Our main focus has always been to optimize our in-store environment in order to get the right assortment of products on the shelf, increase the selection on the shelf, and to address the retailer's specific consumer profile. This will contribute to maximize sales opportunities, improve the total customer experience and therefore drive sales," he says.

Reviewing and implementing are key for ensuring the objectives are met and the success of the projects secured in the long run.

Looking Forward

Surgunovi is optimistic about the future. The market is warming to the notion of category management and HP is prepared to work with progressive retailers who are receptive to new concepts.

"Our way of doing category management and our infrastructure will evolve with the market," he predicts. "But the real action for HP's category management efforts will remain at the shelf. Delivering a great purchasing experience on the shelf to our consumers by providing them with the right products, in the right channel, and in an optimized in-store environment, will support sales growth for both manufacturer and retailer."

THE WAY FORWARD

Category management will evolve as retailers and manufactures refine the process in an attempt to serve consumers better, and as technology continues to improve. The customization of category management comes down to several key steps that every practitioner follows regardless of how elaborate or bare bones the individual process becomes. It is all part of the way forward.

Lessons Learned from the Real World

The companies presented in the portfolio of case studies in Part III are among the best practitioners of category management in the industry. The ways they handled challenges may be familiar to any executive whose work involves this process, or they may be new methods that can be adopted. Either way, a comparative look at their stories reveals that these companies have much in common.

Objectives

In practical terms, category management is a process that involves managing product categories as individual business units. Retailers want to increase category sales in the store. Manufacturers and their sales agencies share this goal, but they would like to see sales of their brands increase as the category grows.

Retailers have a more ambitious objective in mind these days. "Our strategic vision was to gain a competitive advantage in the market through the use of category management," recalls Mark Rice, manager of space management and category development at Big Y supermarkets. "We wanted to be perceived by consumers as the premier supermarket in the area. We wanted to meet their needs better than the competition. We wanted to be the preferred one-stop variety shopping experience where consumers get superior value."

The focus on satisfying the needs of demanding consumers has become more important to retailers over the years. Even their trading partners now share this objective.

"The core of our category management program revolves around our ability to understand how the shopper buys the category," explains Al Fan, director of category management for refrigerated and frozen categories at General Mills. Such knowledge will enable the company to advise retailers on which products to stock for the shoppers in their stores.

Starting Point

The starting point for the process of category management is the traditional eight steps. That doesn't mean retailers and the manufacturers that advise them actually conduct eight distinct steps today. Some do and some don't. Many have streamlined and customized the process, but the spirit of the original remains and serves as a guiding light.

Another starting point today is the consumer; that is, accumulating and analyzing consumer data such as household panel data, demographic data, and sometimes data from a retail loyalty card program. Trading partners didn't start with these resources years ago; most were not available then.

"Looking at numbers is fine, but I need to have a better understanding of consumer insights and what's going on with the competition to make decisions that are actionable rather than doing a huge amount of deep-dive analysis just involving numbers," says Michael Terpokosh, who heads up the category management program for SUPERVALU.

For Chiquita, the focus is on what drives purchase and consumption, satisfaction and dissatisfaction, habits and practices. What are the key satisfaction gaps and wishes for the future? "We started with the consumer for a couple of reasons," explains Sherrie Terry, vice president of category development. "At the end of the day, we sell a commodity. The only thing that really differentiates us is the power of our brand and understanding what consumers think about our brand."

Process

Many companies have customized the traditional eight steps to suit their needs. In general, they share a common overall process, but with variations in execution. The macro steps are data gathering, assessment, decision making, and implementation.

SUPERVALU has five steps, while Miller Brewing promotes four. Big Y still follows the original eight, but spends more time on certain steps such as strategy, tactics, and implementation.

At the Hershey Company, the traditional eight-step program remains the cornerstone of training, but the company adapts its process to align with the needs and capabilities of its customers.

"We've become flexible in working with accounts based on their needs, whether a retailer rigorously follows the entire eight-step process or works with a modified version. Once you have the 'basic training' in the fundamental business drivers, you can adapt to any process," explains Michelle Gloeckler, vice president of customer marketing at Hershey.

Sales agencies have to be the most flexible with the category management process because they represent so many different manufacturers. At CROSSMARK, account executives don't try to redefine the process, but work within the retailer's process instead. Over the years, they've worked closely with retailers as they reduced the steps in category management from the traditional eight to six or five.

"For the most part, we work with what they have established, take the manufacturer's approach, and customize it with what the retailer does," explains Joe Crafton, president of strategic alliances. "We also incorporate a lot of consumer insights into the template. Retailers are looking for manufacturers to bring in new learning such as consumer and shopping behavior."

Much the same is true at Acosta Sales and Marketing Company. Because category management is retailer driven, the agency aims for whatever the customer knows and is comfortable with. Sometimes that means taking a lead role and other times it doesn't.

"We fall in line with their templates and comply with their process," says Michael Bernatchez, senior vice president of corporate marketing. "No matter what the approach, however, the category management process basically tries to look at the consumer purchase dynamics and financial implications of merchandising, assortment, pricing, and shelving (MAPS) decisions at both the category and brand level."

Closing Thoughts

May the novices in category management be inspired by the stories of these manufacturers, distributors, and sales agencies. May the experienced practitioners add to their knowledge of the process. May even the grizzled veterans take away at least one or two new ideas. Collectively, may the lessons learned move the art and science of category management forward.

The process that began in the early 1990s with a focus on product categories has evolved. Whether they use four steps, eight steps, or some number in between, today's leading category management practitioners make sure that consumer understanding is at the heart of the process.

Proactive Category Management

SHAN KUMAR

In the mid-1980s, Dr. Brian Harris developed a formal process for managing product categories as business units. Today, some retailers embrace category management as the only way to get things done. It is their Holy Grail. Meanwhile, others claim that the process is simply additional unproductive work. It is a ploy by consultants to make money.

Shan Kumar is the chief financial officer and vice president of marketing for Altierre Corporation, an RFID start-up in Silicon Valley. He has worked at Safeway, the U.S. grocery retailer, in various positions in strategic planning, marketing systems, corporate brands, and corporate marketing. While there, he helped to develop a category business planning process called SCOP (Safeway Category Optimization Program). In 2002, he joined another U.S. grocery chain, Albertson's, as vice president of category marketing. He established their approach to category business planning called Accelerated Category Business Planning (ACBP). Both SCOP and ACBP are still in place.

In reality, most retailers practice some form of category management. It is the only way they can manage their enormous workload. A typical supermarket retailer carries some 40,000 stock keeping units (SKUs), and a typical category manager handles an average of 3,500 SKUs. Since it is almost impossible to manage such variety, supermarket retailers follow the 80/20 rule; that is, they manage the 20 percent of items that drive the best results for the category and depend on lead vendors for expertise. The real issue is not about whether to adopt category management; it is whether to practice it reactively or proactively. The latter is the right choice.

For those retailers who are able to dedicate resources to tap into customer segmentation expertise (loyalty card or panel based), the paradigm is getting shifted toward optimizing customer segment "fair share gaps" as opposed to market share-based fair share gaps. This is not the demise of category management, it is simply the next logical step making the retailer focus on its customer base as opposed to all consumers. Again, unless the retailer has made the commitment to build the execution platform that can move from "mass" marketing to "segmented marketing," this will simply be "nice to know."

Operating supermarkets in today's competitive environment requires a differentiated consumer value proposition. And differentiation calls for a proactive top-down retailer agenda; that is, a game plan that connects the dots across all categories consistently. Each category plays a role in the offense and the defense. Retailers cannot continue with business as usual and simply react to vendor programs and allowances. It is not enough to execute a vendor's recommendations to make shopping easier in the baby and hair care aisles. The vendor is presenting the same program to every retailer. It is not going to lead to the differentiation of the total store.

The next question is whether a category manager can focus on the strategic and tactical aspects of proactive category management at his or her desk. Remember: Retail is detail. There is a lot of busy work involved in managing "desks." There is no time to manage categories strategically. Mangers can barely get the weekly ads done with the typical workload, let alone spend any dedicated time on individual categories. Furthermore, a retailer will never gain consistency across desks given the turnover and lack of comprehensive category management tools. Most category managers use a multitude of spreadsheets to manage their desks. A separate planning process is the only way to dedicate the right resources to look at the categories strategically, gain consistency in strategies across categories, deploy best practices, and leverage vendor expertise.

In the past, most retailers and vendors have fallen into the trap of "template overload" and "analysis paralysis." They lost sight of the underlying principles of the best practices recommended by the Food Marketing Institute (FMI). Most retailers simply asked vendors to fill out templates and never took ownership for the plan with accountability for execution and results. They failed to recognize it as a business strategy, failed to recognize the need for organizational commitment, failed to align the scorecard, and failed to establish a proactive formal business process with accountability. Although competitive dynamics are changing rapidly, there are quite a few retailers out there living in the old paradigm of making money by "buying." Their profit and loss (P&L) accountability is not aligned with making money by "selling."

Most vendors would probably say that category management will not succeed until slotting and coop allowances go away. They certainly act as blinders, but they are not roadblocks. A committed retailer can make allowances work to drive consumer-focused growth.

The irony is that the same vendors are concerned about eliminating slotting and coop allowances until a retailer has a formalized pro-active consumer-focused planning processes that give their products a fair chance at distribution, space, and promotions. It is a cultural change and has to be driven from the top on both sides of the table.

Another blinder that often detours category management efforts is P&L accountability. Until category managers can be true business managers with P&L accountability instead of being second guessed, they will not be able to maximize results. This is a competitive ne-cessity in today's marketplace. Successful retailers like Jewel, Costco, Target, and Wal-Mart have long recognized this issue. When their category managers make a commitment, it is a done deal.

Winning the battle for share-of-wallet in today's competitive en-vironment requires traditional supermarket retailers to go beyond operating a location-driven business. They need to clearly define their proposition in terms of offerings, shopping experience, and value. Since they carry 200-plus categories that all compete for scarce resources, they need to have a process in place to balance the right trade-off in resource allocation that will reinforce the total store value proposition.

To balance the top-down needs and bottom-up category require-ments, retailers have to evolve to a closed loop, integrated strategic planning process to manage the business proactively, execute with excellence, and deliver financial results. Being proactive enables the retailer to bring all categories together and deliver a consistent "total store brand proposition." The process needs to connect the dots with top-down and bottom-up planning. The strategic frame-work needs to be built on an integrated platform of the four Cs (consumer, customer, competition, and company) and the four Ps (people, processes, partner alliances, and P&L accountability).

Retailers need to establish this process with the following clear objectives:

- Define banner positioning in terms of target customer segments and competition.
- Establish top-down growth and go-to-market differentiation strategies by banner.
- Get multiple silos (merchandising, operations, vendors) on the same page in a proactive manner with defined accountability for execution.
- Seamlessly integrate the multitude of marketing-merchandising planning processes.
- Develop category marketing plans that differentiate the retailer.
- Leverage CPG expertise and resources at brand, category, and total store levels.
- Execute with excellence and deliver results.

In Figure 22.1, the processes on the left (vendor business planning, category business planning, and store execution planning) require collaboration with vendors to leverage their category and consumer expertise. The remaining processes are internal to the retailers but must be connected to the collaboration processes to close the loop on execution. Lack of integration can lead to sub-optimizing the results.

The focus of the efforts should be to deliver the differentiated banner proposition of the retailer. The implications then for current practices are:

Assortment/shelf plans   →   Category marketing plans
Average customer   →   Segmented customers

FIGURE 22.1   Integrated Marketing/Merchandising Planning

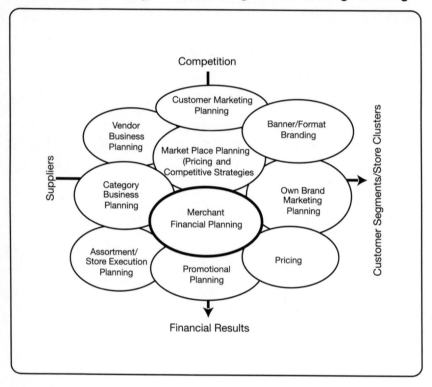

Average market/store	→	Competitive clusters/formats
Independent category plans	→	Integrated marketing plans
Fair share gaps by retailer geography	→	Share-of-wallet by competitive clusters
Single category captain	→	Lead and validate category captains

This paradigm shift has significant implications for data requirements. The consumer and competitive dimensions, in addition to the traditional retailer-defined category definitions, have to become part of the syndicated data. Retailers need to define their own three Cs to deliver a differentiated proposition. If not, they fall into the trap of market averages. That has been the drawback of traditional category management.

Many executives will be shaking their head at this level of complexity. Syndicated data providers will say, "Here he goes again!" When Safeway decided to have syndicated data providers customize its databases with consumer decision tree-based definitions, there was major pushback from the trade as well as the data providers. In fact, there was an effort by some in the industry toward standardizing the category definitions. It turned out that the success of SCOP in delivering more than committed results was mainly due to the adoption of the consumer decision tree as the foundation of Safeway's go-to-market strategies. It forced category managers to think in terms of consumer requirements.

Similarly, today's environment calls for category managers to think in different terms. Whose wallet are they competing for? Who are they competing with? Their category strategies must be congruent with banner competitive strategies, which may spell out where they are going to play the defensive game and the offensive game. One-size-fits-all mass marketing is no longer a viable option for traditional supermarket operators since they no longer have the low-price advantage in the marketplace. Their only option is to adapt segmented marketing or mass customization by customer/competitive segments. With retail consolidation, their tasks have become more complex as they now need to manage multiple banners, multiple channels, and multiple marketplaces. They need to balance leveraging scale for cost advantage without compromising banner relevancy in individual marketplaces.

Tesco, in England, is a great example of how a traditional retailer can win the battle against the might of a Wal-Mart. They have segmented their stores into convenience, metro, core, and extra. They also have segmented their customers and tailored their marketing programs accordingly. Although Tesco has been successful by just using its loyalty card data, that approach will not be sufficient in the United States. Given the fragmentation of shopping trips in the United States, most retailers cannot depend entirely on their loyalty card data. Customer loyalty to any given chain has significantly eroded in the past five years. They will need syndicated panel data that has the total household expenditure across all retailers and have the breadth and depth to provide detailed share-of-wallet information by household and store clusters.

I clearly see panel data becoming the foundation for category-customer management. With the expansion of number of households, ACNielsen panel data has become rich enough to provide the customer and competitive insights at competitive cluster/category/brand levels. This must be reinforced by attitudinal surveys linked to actual behavior in the panel. Just imagine if you can have the panel data insights provide the ability to drill down customer "disconnects" from total store all the way to category/brand level. You could actually define your gaps in terms of customer acquisition, conversion, and retention by competitive store clusters. The attitudinal data can provide insights into the "disconnects" on trip drivers to the retailer or to an aisle within the store.

If this can be linked to a retailers' point-of-sale (POS) and loyalty card data, you will no longer be dealing with averages that cannot be drilled down to determine the actual causal factors by store. You could now link it to an actual store where the actual gap is and have operations involved in addressing it.

This no doubt increases the level of complexity for both retailers and vendors. A new planning and execution technology platform is going to be critical to address this issue. A comprehensive work flow-based "category manager work bench" interface will be absolutely critical to manage the complexities of balancing neighborhood relevance, segmented marketing, and work simplification.

As retail consolidation continues, supermarket operators will be able to dedicate high-powered leadership and supporting organization structure to address these complexities better. It is now typical for vendor teams to have representatives from finance, promotion management, supply chain, process management, and marketing management on their teams. You are now going to see retailers mirror this kind of cross-functional team within each product group. The biggest change is likely to be a customer marketing manager residing within each product group. Managing the customer portfolio through acquisition, conversion, and retention of right customer segments is going to be a key pillar for profitable growth.

Retailers are going to raise the bar on the quality of their category management groups as well as their technology infrastructure. Given the growth of private labels and their importance on banner differentiation, retailers will soon begin to take more of the strategic category management in-house with the vendors playing an advisory role. Also, the role of allowances will diminish as segmented marketing forces retailers to pay more attention to managing the right customer mix rather than collecting allowances. Differentiation and managing the customer mix are going to be the biggest drivers of profitable sales growth for retailers. This is another step in the evolution of retailers from traditional "pile high, sell low" merchandisers to true marketers.

Linking Category Management and Loyalty Marketing

GLENN HAUSFATER

T here's no question that linking category management and loyalty marketing has been—and remains—a hot topic in the supermarket industry. For over a decade, supermarket executives have identified this linkage as one of the top opportunity

Glenn Hausfater, managing director of Partners in Loyalty Marketing (PILM), relies on his 20 years of experience in loyalty marketing, customer segmentation, and targeting to advise a blue-chip client list of consumer packaged goods manufacturers and retailers. Before starting Chicago-based PILM, he was director of database marketing at Kraft Foods and vice president at Spectra/Market Metrics. Glenn is a recognized authority on relationship marketing, especially for consumer products. He speaks frequently at industry conferences and contributes articles and opinion columns to trade journals. He teaches loyalty marketing workshops for the Food Marketing Institute (FMI) and the Grocery Manufacturers Association (GMA).

areas they see for their companies. The reason for this is clear: The number one challenge for the supermarket industry is to sharpen its focus on serving its customers.

Let's start this discussion of "linkage" with some definitions:

> *Category management* (CM) is the discipline of managing product categories as business units. Strategies focus on category role, among other issues, and tactics focus on variety management, pricing, promotion, and so on. The goal of the process is maximizing profitable sales for the category.

> *Loyalty marketing* (LM) is the supermarket industry's version of customer relationship management (CRM). CRM uses data to understand the current and potential value of customers to the company. Its focus is on using a combination of promotions and nonmonetary incentives to retain and sell more to existing customers. The goal of these efforts is maximizing profitable sales to groups of like-valued customers.

While CM and LM seem pretty different, there's an important commonality. Ask yourself: "How does one maximize profitable category volume?" The 32,000 ft.-high consultant's answer is: "Meet your customers' needs better than the competition."

It just makes plain sense that the kind of customer-specific information found in LM databases should be a key enabler of successful CM. This commentary will cover the state of linkage today, and discuss some insights that point to the path forward.

Why Linkage Has Been So Hard

The difficulty of linking CM and LM reflects both issues related uniquely to these processes and broader issues affecting the entire supermarket industry. Although CM and LM share common goals, they have a separate focus from each other. The primary focus of CM is increasing category performance. For LM, the emphasis is building and holding the business of your best customers.

Sometimes the two processes are well aligned; other times they aren't. For example:

- Promoting the larger sizes of items, or store brand items, to heavy buyers of a category is typically good for the category and enhances the store's price reputation with these valuable customers.

- Conversely, category managers will often run a "blow out" sale on an item not particularly favored by heavy buyers, but on which the manager got a hot deal from the supplier. This may be good for category profitability, but has little impact on sales. It often encourages cherry-picking by low-loyalty shoppers.

The issues related to industry-wide trends can best be illustrated with an example from my home base of Chicago. There's an auto dealer that advertises on morning drive-time radio with the jingle: ". . . big enough to save you money, small enough to serve you well." This phrase nicely captures the ongoing challenge for the supermarket industry (as well as this auto dealer).

On the one hand, chains are increasingly competing with the low-price leader, and CM, coupled with supply chain initiatives, is the process they're using to achieve that status.

On the other hand, shopper loyalty depends on being the store that has "exactly what I'm looking for," meaning customer-driven variety and service. This often requires a "suboptimal" item mix compared to the CM-driven variety management, and added supply chain cost.

Many supermarkets are trying to reconcile these competing orientations (value-driven versus customer-focused) by using LM to achieve customer focus and CM to achieve a value positioning. So far, this reconciliation strategy doesn't seem to be working well, but there are a few bright spots on the horizon that we'll discuss next.

Loyalty Marketing—A Brief History

Loyalty marketing in the supermarket industry is synonymous with the plastic cards that shoppers almost universally carry in their wallets or on their key chains. The first supermarket card program was launched in 1985 at Ukrop's in Richmond, Virginia, as part of the Citicorp point-of-sale (POS) initiative. While the Citicorp experiment ultimately came to an end, Ukrop's saw the potential in identifying their customers by name and especially of understanding the purchasing behavior of its best shoppers.

Ukrop's continued the program on its own. Throughout the 1990s, card programs increased in number driven largely by independents instead of national chains. The objective of these programs was almost universally stated by independents as "to get a lock on my best customers." Hence, "shopper cards" quickly became "loyalty cards."

National chains watched LM spread among independents and heard at conferences how effectively card data could be used to reduce costs, improve assortment, and create new forms of product promotion. Gradually, card programs spread to chains as well, driven by a combination of marketing utility and by the falling cost of the computer hardware required for a program. Also important was the formation of RMS, a company founded by former Citicorp POS employees, which brought to market relatively inexpensive and effective software for managing loyalty card programs and data.

Today, all national supermarket chains have card programs. So do most regional players and many independents. Just as 10 years ago, the independents saw card-based loyalty programs as their "Secret

Weapon" against the national chains; today the nationals see their loyalty programs as a not-so-secret weapon they can use to counter Wal-Mart's expansion into groceries.

At last count by ACNielsen and TDLinx, almost 14,000 supermarkets (40 percent of all U.S. grocery stores) were covered by card programs representing 48 percent of all-commodity volume (ACV). Both numbers have continued to increase year-over-year for the past decade. In most major markets, over 85 percent of all shoppers carry supermarket loyalty cards. Shoppers generally see their loyalty cards as time-savers—"Don't need to clip coupons to get the best deals"—and a money saver. Yet, the sad truth is that most customers—especially a store's best customers—say that loyalty programs don't make them feel in anyway "special" or like a "preferred shopper."

Loyalty Marketing—Key Insights

Supermarket operators were quite surprised by what their LM data showed them. First and foremost, it showed them that a minority of shoppers actually drove their business:

- The top 30 percent of shoppers ranked on total spend—either for a store or a chain—generally account for 65 percent of total sales.
- The top 10 percent alone account for over 40 percent of total sales.

This same 30 percent/65 percent dynamic held for the chain as a whole, for individual stores, and for virtually each and every category.

Conversely, this 30 percent/65 percent rule meant that fully 70 percent of a chain's shoppers drove less than one-third of sales. Most of these shoppers make only one trip (or less) per month to the chain. Often, retailers find that these lower tier shoppers are not profitable.

The next shock came when LM managers looked at the loyalty level of the top 30 percent of shoppers. For most chains, these "high value" shoppers give the chain less than half of their total (all-outlet) grocery spending. Net, the first thing that LM data demonstrated was that operators had a big customer loyalty problem on their hands. The bulk of their shoppers were occasional ones, and even their weekly shoppers were spending substantial amounts with their competition.

Defining the Opportunity

LM managers had strong motivation to close the "loyalty gap" that their chains faced, and senior management was obviously supportive of these efforts. The challenging aspect of closing the loyalty gap is that it doesn't involve just a single category. In fact, the mix of categories involved differs for each and every shopper. Hence, closing the loyalty gap requires *customer-specific* marketing. However, supermarkets—thanks to category management—are set up predominantly to do *category-specific* marketing.

So, here's the issue: In today's supermarket industry, nobody owns the customer!

While there's no disputing that CM has had an enormous positive impact on the supermarket industry, it's also one of the main impediments to using LM data to meet customer needs better than the competition.

Approaches to Linkage: Give the Customer a Seat at the Table

At some chains (mostly independents), the position of loyalty marketing manager has been eliminated and replaced with a "customer category manager." What this change does is make sure that during development of ads, discussions of change of operations, and other changes the impact on customer loyalty is considered just as strongly as the impact on, say, dairy case profitability. Big Y in Springfield, Massachusetts, was the first company to make this change and it's been effective at helping it to grow in a very competitive region. I expect to see more retailers do likewise. Its primary benefit is that it makes clear who in management *does* "own the customer."

Approaches to Linkage: LM as a Category Tactic

Much more commonly, we see chains viewing LM as a set of tactics that fall under the promotion tab in the category planning process. This is by far still the prevailing way in which LM and CM coexist and cooperate in most chains, but it doesn't always work effectively. Here's a scenario that continues to play out daily in supermarket LM departments:

- The LM manager gets together with vendor and designs a mail program to Top Shoppers who are also Top Buyers of the supplier's brand.
- The LM manager goes to the category manager to proudly present the program. The reaction is: "You're going to do *what* with my money?"
- Recall that in most supermarket chains, dollars are provided by suppliers to category managers.
- No money is earmarked specifically for the top shopper. For most chains, their top shoppers are on their own—an unfunded entity.

Don't get me wrong; in many chains category managers were quite supportive of LM. But category managers are no fools; they know that the bigger the program, the better. So, the push was always to mail as deeply among category buyers as possible. Since most suppliers have a burning desire to target competitive buyers, they'd be willing to fund the program expansion.

But what happened from the customer standpoint?

- First, the expansion to lower tier category buyers meant that offers went to lower frequency shoppers and that drove down both response rate and ROI. Suppliers and category managers ultimately concluded that LM mailers were much less effective than a simple circular ad.

- Second, because it was a brand/category offer, mailers provided little opportunity for the supermarket to communicate with shoppers about anything other than the product attributes.

- Third, because of the supplier's desire to target competitive buyers, customers complained, "You only send me offers for brands that I don't buy."

Conclusion: Treating LM as a tactic subsumed by CM does not strike the right balance between the two processes—generally customer loyalty loses out.

The most common promotional vehicle today that uses LM data is the mailer. Mail programs have become a staple of the supermarket industry, but they're rarely retailer driven. Suppliers fund most of the mailers and, especially for smaller, low penetration brands, mail is an effective marketing tactic. Other programs are funded as part of a *brand-specific* relationship marketing program. These mailers are "co-branded," but the content is primarily the brand's, not the retailer's.

Looking forward, we're seeing an interesting and exciting change in the way mail programs are created and structured in supermarkets. A few retailers such as Kroger and Stop & Shop have recently launched their own mail programs aimed at building their relationship with top shoppers. Using a model first developed and used very successfully by Tesco in the United Kingdom:

- The content and featured brands in these mailers will be chosen by the retailer with the aim of achieving retailer objectives.
- The mailers are versioned relative to shopper segments identified by the retailer. The big change here is that the segments are defined by shopper needs (gourmet cooks, convenience oriented, etc.) versus exclusively in terms of heaviness of category usage (heavy cheese buyers, etc.).
- The mailers will go out according to an explicit seasonal circulation plan, versus only when there's a supplier willing to fund one.

Since these programs are still in their early stages, we'll need to wait to evaluate their success. In the interim, it will be particularly important to watch whether they stay faithful to LM principles or become just another vehicle with space "rented" to whatever vendor has funding.

Approaches to Linkage: Share-of-Wallet

We noted earlier that one of the key insights coming out of LM data was that shoppers—even top shoppers—were not very loyal to any given supermarket chain. Several different companies developed ways to estimate each customer's share of total grocery spending captured by a retailer. This is a truly exciting concept. LM databases tell retailers everything their customers buy in store, but almost nothing about what those customers are buying from the competition.

In general, these approaches use a combination of LM data and data from an all-outlet household panel like ACNielsen's Homescan. They estimate share of wallet either for individual customers or for customer segments. The tools gave retailers a list of customers showing how much of that customer's total spending on groceries they are capturing. Some also allow retailers to drill down and see how much of each customer's spending they are capturing by category.

Using our version of this tool, we found that roughly a third of most retailers' top shoppers gave the retailer virtually *all* of their grocery spending. Effectively, there was no sales growth potential relative to this segment of top shoppers, but substantial downside to losing one of them. The other two-thirds of top shoppers gave the retailer only half of their total household grocery budget. For this segment, there was both a sales growth upside and the downside risk of loss.

True database marketers like catalogers would know exactly what to do with this kind of insight into shopper behavior. Supermarket retailers struggled with it:

- First, while they appreciated the downside risk of losing a top shopper, it wasn't clear what action they could take to mitigate the risk or who would pay for it.
- Second, it was hard to make the trade-off between spending to hold on to a valuable customer versus spending to acquire a new one or up-sell a mid-tier one.
- Third, even given information on category share of spending, it was hard to know which category manager should take the lead in retaining at-risk top shoppers.

A relatively new tool called Category ShareCast is being offered by Spectra (a unit of VNU). The unique aspect of this tool is that it not only allows segmenting of shoppers (and stores) based on "share of wallet," but provides a full suite of tools via Spectra's other products for understanding them and reaching them effectively. Again, this is somewhat of an early stage development and we look forward to seeing case studies of how retailers have used Category ShareCast to truly move their business.

Approaches to Linkage: Top Shopper Index

While LM as a promotional tactic receives the bulk of attention, many retailers have sought ways to use LM data to fine-tune other CM tactics: price, assortment, and shelving.

The most common approach has been to use the LM data as an override of decisions reached through the normal category planning process. For example:

- Before delisting an item, several retailers look to see what percent of that item's volume is driven by top shoppers.
- By comparing the percent of item volume driven by top shoppers to the percent of category volume they drive, retailers can assess whether, *within the category,* the particular item is a favorite of top shoppers. This is sometimes called the Top Shopper Index (TSI).
- If the TSI is high, it means that top shoppers disproportionately buy the item. Then, it makes sense for the retailer to override its normal velocity hurdle and keep the item on the shelf.

The core idea is to use LM data to fine-tune product assortment to better align with the item preference of top shoppers. In our experience, the TSI is quick to calculate and easy to implement with the existing category management process.

The counterweight to the TSI approach is that traditional grocery retailers—in competing with Wal-Mart—are increasingly focused on efficiency. Hence, it's difficult to override velocity thresholds when your main competitor is rigorous in trimming slow-moving items. There's another issue with the TSI type approach: it's by and large redundant. Since top shoppers account for nearly 70 percent of all sales, item-level movement analyses are essentially skewed in their favor by the inherent volumetric importance of top shoppers.

So far, the TSI approach has proved most useful at identifying situations where the retailer's own merchandising tactics have encouraged cherry-picking by low-tier shoppers. Going forward, we expect to see a modified version of the TSI developed and lead to a series of simple, easy-to-implement applications that can improve assortment, set, and merchandising overall.

Approaches to Linkage: Loyalty Strategy

All of the approaches reviewed here essentially treat LM as a tool at the disposal of category managers. We see a very different approach being taken by many small operators, and a few regional operators.

- The secret of success in these situations is that "build customer loyalty" and "retain top shoppers" are core business strategies.
- Hence, rather than subsuming LM as a tactic under CM, these operators essentially subsume CM as a tactic under their broader strategy of customer loyalty.

- The question they asked across the board when it comes to cate-gory strategies and tactics is: "What's the impact of this decision on my top shoppers and their loyalty?"

We think this approach is going to spread among regional chains and smaller ones. It's already being practiced with great success at Ukrop's and Wegman's, two chains in which the shop-ping experience has been totally transformed relative to traditional supermarkets.

The transformation reflects that these chains have committed themselves 100 percent to "customer-focused variety and service." They haven't stopped competing with Wal-Mart; rather they've successfully changed the rules of the game. Going forward, we ex-pect national chains primarily to focus on playing the current game, and for regional chains to continue to both redefine the game and to win at it.

The Path Forward: Shopper Upgrade

As the previous comments indicate, it's not very likely that na-tional chains are going to abandon the discipline of CM and focus with laser precision on customer loyalty the way regionals are. However, there is an approach that links LM and CM in a way that's different from simply viewing LM as a CM tactic. This alter-native approach is grounded in the key retailing insight that "full-line" shoppers always drive more sales than customers who shop just a few categories.

The central idea behind this approach is to create a "top shop-per category profile" by looking at top shoppers in terms of the percentage distribution of their spending at a retailer that goes to each category:

- This provides a benchmark against which the distributions of each and every other shopper can then be compared.
- We've found that the closer a mid-tier shopper's profile matches that of a top shopper, the more likely it is to be upgradeable.
- We think this is because the overall category profile measures the extent to which a mid-tier shopper is truly relying on that retailer as a key source of groceries.

This approach facilitates the LM-CM linkage because once the upgradeable shoppers are identified, you can return to their profile and select underperforming and overperforming categories relative to the top shopper profile. What we've seen using our own version of this approach (PILM *Shopper Upgrade Model*) is that for most chains, the underperforming categories for upgradeable shoppers are paper products and nonedibles. In contrast, there's typically a longer list of overperforming categories, reflecting the uniqueness of each shopper's household.

Several retailers have had good success upgrading shoppers by sending them paired offers: one for an overperforming category and one for an underperforming one. For most chains, we find that the vast majority of upgradeable households are subsumed by around 5 underperforming categories and 10 overperforming ones. This results in at most 50 different offer combinations and that's a manageable number for most retailers. Going forward, we expect to see other approaches brought to market that use LM data to develop promotion plans that span categories in a similar way.

The Path Forward: Top Shopper Insight

For both smaller operators and national chains, the other key use of LM data to improve CM is in the area of shopper insights. By and large, retailers don't sponsor much research on their own, so they're dependent on suppliers for shopper insights. These insights are almost always either category- or channel-specific. That means most retailers don't really know very much about their shoppers, especially the incredibly important top shoppers.

When we've interviewed top shoppers for major chains, the insights are rich and substantive. For example:

- At most chains, top shoppers will tell you that they are very value oriented.
- However, when you ask them how they shop for values, they tell you it's by comparing shelf tags in-store and looking at end-caps.
- For top shoppers, their drive for value is played out almost exclusively *inside* the store, not by comparing one retailer's circular items to another's.

We all know that end-caps drive sales. Top shopper research explains why that's so and how retailers can plus-up their price reputation even more so.

Likewise, even among top shoppers there's still substantial resistance to store brand items. However, time and again top shoppers say that they were able to clear the hurdle when they tasted the product and realized it matched national brand quality. The implications for merchandising and promoting private label products are clear. Going forward, we expect to see the LM database become a central focus of retail research, especially research aimed at understanding the needs of top shoppers.

Conclusion

Traditional supermarkets are working hard to find the right balance of being value driven versus reflecting customer-driven variety and service. The linkage of category management and loyalty marketing is still viewed as an important way to reconcile these two competing orientations. As these examples show, some linkage approaches work better for retailers leaning toward a value orientation. Others work better for retailers aiming to drive up their customer focus. There's no one right answer or one right approach.

24

The New Category
Management Emerges

DIRK SEIFERT, PhD

T he key to sales and profits in the packaged goods industry is the consumer who resides between the manufacturer and the retailer. To develop and optimize the relationship with consumers, trading partners have to leverage consumer touch points. Some of them relate to the manufacturer (television, radio, and the

Dirk Seifert, PhD, is chief operations officer of an international retail company and former head of a category management research group at Harvard Business School. He has also held senior management positions at Procter & Gamble and Metro Group. He is the coauthor of *Collaborative Customer Relationship Management.* His work has focused on collaborative planning, forecasting, and replenishment (CPFR); efficient consumer response (ECR); customer relationship management (CRM); and strategic marketing.

Internet), while others relate to the retailer (point-of-sale data and customer service). All of them relate to an improved ability to understand, serve, and reach consumers.

In the past, there has been little harmony between trading partners, and information was not exchanged. But in the future, they will clearly define the touch points together and will harmonize the customer relationship marketing effort. That is when collaborative customer relationship management (CCRM) will blossom and connect with the process of category management. CCRM is an integrative concept, which manages the customer touch points of retailers and suppliers to the consumer. It represents a further development of category management and the demand side of efficient consumer response (ECR).

CCRM is the area where one deploys new technologies. Retailers and suppliers use state-of-the-art technology like mass customization and online guerilla marketing to reach the customer in an integrative approach.

For example, major manufacturers are gathering huge amounts of data on consumers via the Internet. Sharing this information with retailers would be a step forward. This information could be integrated into the category management process in terms of learning more about the customer, defining the category role, and so on.

Shift in Power

In the past, the marketplace was characterized by a push-and-pull effect. Procter & Gamble (P&G) advertised a new product on TV (push), prompting the retailer to stock the product (pull). Today, media is so diverse that the push-pull technique doesn't work so well anymore. That's because retailers have become the gatekeepers of the shelf. If Wal-Mart does not list a new product from a company like P&G, that manufacturer will be in big trouble by missing key distribution. That's one factor in the relational shift that has taken place between retailers and manufactures, with retailers now holding more power.

Another factor has to do with the fact that retailers are accumulating more consumer insights through their POS data, while at the same time hiring better people to build their competence in category management. Some retailers are wondering whether they even need manufacturer data anymore.

A third factor centers on private labels. Retailers are producing better private label products and, thereby, strengthening their bond with the consumer. Tesco is a strong retail brand in the United Kingdom. Trader Joe's is a unique retail brand in the United States. Aldi's private label brand is more popular than many national brands in Germany. Aldi uses a hybrid marketing strategy that consists of being the cost and price leader while having the highest quality. Such a competitive position is invincible in the marketplace.

As a result of this power shift, private labels will be a growing threat to manufacturers in the future because they challenge their national brands. Manufacturers must do a better job of sharing their expertise with retailers. They have to redefine the relationship and work closely with retailers in areas like product introductions. Ultimately, manufacturers need to help retailers target consumers, because that is what category management is all about.

It is very important for manufacturers to understand the retail strategy and to align their category management efforts accordingly. Most projects fail because the strategies of the trading partners don't work together. For example, a manufacturer might have a completely different strategy than Wal-Mart. The latter offers

everyday low prices, and that's how it wants to sell. Some manufacturers don't like this approach, but they realize it far too late. The
result is more mistrust than before.

But if the two strategies are lined up, it is a great source of
strength. Manufacturers need to help retailers by understanding
their goals and competitive challenges. This will be even more important in the future.

With retailers and manufacturers working more closely, sharing
more insights, and focusing on consumer touch points, several steps
in the category management process would be improved.

Category Strategy

Strategy is a difficult step in category management. Manufacturers
need to develop a marketing and procurement strategy in order to
meet performance measures. To do that, they have to align departments in their company. Sometimes those departments haven't
worked together before.

In the proper organization approach, category managers must
have expanded capabilities. To develop category strategy, they must
have the power to align marketing, procurement, and supply chain
management.

Category Roles

Determining category roles is the best approach for differentiating
a store from the competition. Let's look at strategic planning and
micromarketing in a trading area where a lot of elderly people live.
What should the destination categories be? Many older people have
pets, so pet food could be a destination category. This decision has
consequences on the allocation of resources. How much space and

manpower should be given to pet food? The role of the category determines the result and priority among other categories. Retail chains that want to improve their competitive position must hone their understanding of this step in category management.

Category Tactics

Category tactics are the steps taken to implement category strategy. Proper execution of tactics is very important to be successful in category management. In the past, retailers jumped too fast into category tactics without doing strategy, definition, and role beforehand. But if these steps are done first, it is clear what has to be done and what tactics are needed.

Let's look at strategic assortment planning (SAP) as a way to differentiate stores. For advanced retailers, it is a key tool. In category management, the tactic of efficient assortment is related to SAP. For example, 7-Eleven in Tokyo changes its assortments three or more times a day. Why?

To satisfy consumer needs. In the morning, the stores serve breakfast to people on the way to the office. In the afternoon, they promote lunch, snacks, and drinks. In the evening, they cater to people who either stay in the office late or people on their way home who use the two hours in the train to eat and drink.

So, the assortments change several times a day as a way for the retailer to differentiate against competitors. If the assortments stayed the same all day, the store would be unattractive for certain customer target groups all day.

This tactic will be coming to Europe very soon. 7-Eleven is already successfully using SAP in Scandinavia and you will see them bring it to Germany. The process makes customers more loyal to stores because they know the assortments change during the day based on their needs.

Efficient assortment will be a key factor going forward. Retailers know they need to use techniques like micromarketing to define strategic assortments. The old-fashioned way of marketing the same way across a country misses the opportunity to create value for customers. Catering to everyone the same way is not differentiating the store.

Tactics are related to efficient product introduction (EPI), which is an advanced technique used by very sophisticated retailers and manufacturers. EPI means sharing knowledge and giving some retailers a certain product before others. It requires trust between trading partners.

This technique, which is not widespread, is all about customer touch points. The retailer has a customer touch point with the POS data and gets positive and negative feedback that way. If the chain shares this information in a structured way with the manufacturer, the latter should give the retailer special treatment. I work with manufacturers that don't invest in marketing but invest in state-of-the-art manufacturing and research instead. I tell them what my customers need.

Category Evaluation

There is not enough effort spent on evaluation in today's category management process. Analysts often don't have the time. Sometimes there are simply no people to do the work. But this is a very important part of the process because you learn a great deal.

A very important part of this step is to work on the category management forecast that must be defined early. Sometimes it is defined in the first step with strategy analysis. This is where top management agrees on a scorecard that is used later on in several reporting periods to measure key performance indicators and to enable comparison analysis.

In the past, category management was developed separately in the sales department of the manufacturer and in the purchasing department of the retailer. But there now needs to be a collaborative spirit and a cross-functional effort involving other departments. The retailer must provide data needed for the scorecards and to harmonize category management targets with corporate targets of the manufacturer.

In the end, it is clear that the future of category management will be very different than its past. Trading partners sharing information to target the consumer together is the key. Those companies that leverage collaborative CRM will be the leaders of category management and, therefore, the leaders in the marketplace.

ACKNOWLEDGMENTS

Writers

John Karolefski is a veteran business writer and editor of *CPGmatters.com*, an e-zine covering in-store marketing and category management. John writes about consumer packaged goods marketing and technology for several trade publications. He is the coauthor of two books: *TARGET 2000: The Rising Tide of TechnoMarketing* and *All About Sampling*. He was formerly the editor-in-chief of *Brand Marketing* magazine and senior editor of *Supermarket News*. John speaks at various industry conferences and has appeared on CNN and CBS Radio to discuss marketing issues.

Al Heller, president of Distinct Communications, LLC, is an award-winning writer and was formerly editor-in-chief of *Nonfoods Merchandising* and *Supermarket HQ Quarterly* magazines and executive editor of *Drug Store News* and *Drug Store News for the Pharmacist*. He is the author of three books, including *Category Management in the Mass Market: Best Practices* and *Selling into Home Depot*. He has authored major studies on shoppers, information technology, customer loyalty, and brands, and coauthored others on trip management and consumables merchandising. Al writes extensively on health care and pharmacy.

VNU associates who contributed to this book include:

Project Manager: Matt Bell

Editorial Leadership Team: Maggie Arguelles, Dan Brown, James Dodge, Paul Lainis, and Johnny Moore.

Content/Expertise/Design/Technical Contributors: Randy Armstrong, Mirza Baig, Barbara Benington, Doug Bennett, Samir Bhaloo, Jill Blanchard, Jeanette Borchardt, Joe Bucherer, Mark Chesney, Rob Clark, Peter Conti, Jan Crawford, Gary Crisafulli, Jim Dippold, Ingrid Dreimann, Tom Duffy, Susan Dunn, Maura Ehlebracht, Dennis Eidson, Anne Fenton, Bob Ferraro, Karen Fichuk, Ted Fichuk, Rodrigo García Escudero, Stafano Giusti, Jeff Glauber, Todd Hale, Diane High, Carol Hill, Steve Kent, Doug Kimball, Pam Leibfried, Janice Linnane, Tom Markert, Emil Martinez, Art Massa, Mike Noonan, Martin Nadel, Jens Ohlig, Renee O'Malley, Michalis Pantavos, John Porter, Marina Quaranta, Laurie Rains, Gary Ritzert, Crystal Rollins, Mary Ellen Ryan, Danny Sacco, Ed Sachs, Daniel Sampietro, Aaron Simmons, Stuart Taylor, Rose Temple, Andrea Toro, Jean-Jacques Vandenheede, Mathijs van der Zwet, Peter van der Meer, Jeff Weghorst, Allison Welch, Peg Wendell, Gail Zielinski, and Kathy Zonyk.

Special Thanks to: The Center for Retailing Excellence and Dr. Julie J. Gentry, both of the Sam M. Walton College of Business and the University of Arkansas, Dr. Brian Harris of The Partnering Group, Dr. Robert Blattberg of the Kellogg School of Management at Northwestern University, Al Fan and Chana Weaver of General Mills, Mark Rice and David Foley of Big Y, Michael Terpkosh of

SUPERVALU, Gary Bernius and Joe Crafton of CROSSMARK, Michael Bernatchez and Paul Mulvaney of Acosta Sales and Marketing Company, Sherrie Terry of Chiquita, Michelle Gloeckler of the Hershey Company, Vadim Surgunovi of Hewlett-Packard, Jeff Schouten of Miller Brewing Company, Shan Kumar of Altierre Corporation, Glenn Hausfater of Partners in Loyalty Marketing, and Dr. Dirk Seifert formerly of Metro Group.

INDEX